The United Nations

The Internationalist Conspiracy
to Rule the World

The United Nations

The Internationalist Conspiracy
to Rule the World

William F. Jasper

THE JOHN BIRCH SOCIETY
Appleton, Wisconsin

First Printing . . . . April 2001
Second Printing . . . . . August 2001
Third Printing . . . . . . October 2001

Published by
The John Birch Society
Post Office Box 8040
Appleton, Wisconsin 54912
(920) 749-3780

Printed in the United States of America
LC Control Number
2001 135039
ISBN: 1-881 919-04-8

To the memory of my father, with whom so much of this book, and my life, are intertwined. A man of faith, love, courage and dedication — always my *beau ideal* of manhood — he died on the feast day of his patron, St. Joseph, as the final two chapters were being typed at his bedside. And to my mother, his loving and constant companion of fifty-four years, who, with him, raised eleven children, teaching them devotion to God, family, and country.

Contents

Introduction

In his famous "Give Me Liberty or Give Me Death" oration at St. John's Church on March 23, 1775, Patrick Henry said: "For my part, whatever anguish of spirit it may cost, I am willing to know the whole truth; to know the worst and provide for it." At that time, Americans stood at a crossroads, facing great danger. Today, Americans face a different but in many ways even greater danger — in large part because too few of us understand the threat. This book is intended for those who want to know the worst and by knowing the worst will want to take responsible steps to see that the worst does not happen.

Another great statesman, the Englishman Edmund Burke, wisely observed: "The people never give up their liberties but under some delusion." As William F. Jasper establishes in this book, the American people are the target of an incredibly well organized campaign of deception. That deception is designed to rob each of us of our heritage of freedom and build what would inevitably become an Orwellian global tyranny.

Determined to contribute what he could to prevent that from happening, Mr. Jasper has tapped his more than 25 years of experience studying the United Nations and subversive organizations to provide us an incredible tool. Not since Gary Allen's *None Dare Call It Conspiracy* (1972) has one book provided so much documented perspective to help Americans grapple with dangerous and cleverly orchestrated misconceptions.

As Mr. Jasper clearly demonstrates, the danger we are speaking of does not spring from the United Nations itself. For the moment, at least, the UN is still largely a paper tiger. Instead, the danger comes from the very serious plans and actions of powerful elites, particularly American elites.

These internationalists see the UN as their primary vehicle for gaining unrestrained power. Below the surface of public attention, they have been working for decades to disarm America and build the United Nations into an all-powerful world government. We are now facing the culmination of their subversive schemes.

In this carefully documented study, Mr. Jasper shows that with the United Nations the American people are being offered what amounts to poison disguised as candy. From all directions we are being propagandized that "global problems require global solutions." And we are told this means that we have to give more power to the UN. Mr. Jasper exposes that power grab — one of the greatest "trust me" schemes in all of history — as totally corrupt.

Terrorists R Us
In *The United Nations Exposed*, William Jasper helps us all confront fundamental facts so we can step back and question the received wisdom. For example, why should we expect that justice can be served by giving supreme power to an organization that warmly embraces the most murderous regimes in all history?

The men who gave us our Constitution had a profound understanding of history and a resulting deep distrust of human nature. They designed a system of government that was based not on confidence in men but on a recognition that not even the best of men, let alone the worst, could be "trusted" with power. They designed a system of checks and balances to impede the improper ambitions of men to seek and abuse power over others.

The United Nations embodies few of those checks and balances. It recognizes no authority greater than itself and what serves the purportedly noble purposes of the UN, *as interpreted by the UN*. Has human nature changed since our nation was founded? Has experience in the recent, deadly 20th century given us reason to now have confidence that smiling, well-spoken leaders can be trusted with enormous power? Of course not! In this book, Mr. Jasper gives us plenty of reasons not just for caution but for outright alarm at the "trust me" schemes proposed.

At UN conferences, as Mr. Jasper has observed firsthand, the atmosphere is decidedly anti-American. Fidel Castro regularly receives enthusiastic ovations at UN functions, as do other similarly oppressive dictators. As another indication of the anti-freedom mind-set at the UN, consider that Sam Nujoma, the former terrorist leader of SWAPO, who is now the UN-installed president of Namibia, was selected to be honorary co-chair for the UN Millennium Summit of World Leaders in New York.

Expecting an empowered UN to dispense global justice is like inviting the criminals to join the police force, the prosecution, and the judiciary in order to stamp out crime. Mr. Jasper shows us that behind the humanitarian rhetoric, a much more sinister agenda is at work, the agenda of a highly organized cabal that every responsible American needs to understand. In *The United Nations Exposed*, William Jasper shines a powerful spotlight on that agenda.

After years of reporting and research on this topic, Mr. Jasper is uniquely qualified to write this book (see "About the Author," page 353). He shows indisputably, in the UN proponents' own words, that their real agenda is world government, whether they deceptively call it world governance (same definition), or the international rule of law.

Mr. Jasper also shows that those who are working to empower the UN fully realize that they cannot sell their desired "revolution in political arrangements" on its merits. They have to deceive and are quite willing to do so to obtain the power they seek. The evidence of such arrogant duplicity alone should inspire any prudent American to withdraw all trust and seek different leadership.

The subversive drive to empower the UN is succeeding primarily because most Americans neither perceive the danger nor the direction from which the threat is coming — we are being betrayed from within our own camp.

The tough reality, one that most otherwise informed Americans have yet to recognize, is that many of our top leaders, despite their smiles and nice-sounding words, are up to their eyeballs in advancing this subversive revolution. The main threat does not come from the plans of petty bureaucrats or wide-eyed radicals or even as a Communist plot from abroad. It comes from within. And that circumstance makes the threat much more dangerous and difficult to combat.

Fortunately, Mr. Jasper doesn't just leave us with a horrible problem. In the last chapter of *The United Nations Exposed*, the author explains what responsible, freedom-loving Americans can and must do to escape a looming tyranny.

Unique Contribution

In this major exposé, William Jasper has accomplished something truly unique and important. Throughout his book, he demonstrates that it is American elitists — in particular members of the New York-based Council on Foreign Relations — who are pulling the strings and orchestrating the "consensus" for empowering the United Nations. In that work, they are amply supported by associated think tanks and foundations.

If one understands that the United Nations was designed and brought to life by the Council on Foreign Relations, then the parent's continued interest in and domination of its offspring should not be surprising. However, the Council has gone to great lengths to hide its domination and to create the illusion that the United Nations truly represents the interests of a community of independent member nations. William Jasper has performed a great service in exposing that deception so credibly.

Another stellar accomplishment of *The United Nations Exposed* is the clear explanation of the strategies and tactics being employed today to deceive Congress and the American people into allowing a steady transfer of power to the United Nations.

Certainly one of the greatest deceptions is the appearance of nearly universal support for the UN agenda. Mr. Jasper documents, better than anyone else has yet done, how this orchestrated "consensus" is accomplished. Even veteran critics of the UN will learn much from Mr. Jasper's work.

Organization and Approach

The principal focus of *The United Nations Exposed* is the underlying game plan of UN proponents as opposed to their smokescreen of pretexts. Mr. Jasper's approach is to explain how key UN initiatives advance the subversive goal of building an unchallengeable UN superstate. But in order to expose such plans credibly, Mr. Jasper first lays a brilliant foundation (Part I) to clearly establish the globalists' true intentions.

The extreme utopian pronouncements of UN supporters cited in the Prologue should be enough to convince most Americans that we should stay clear of the UN. But once the real agenda behind the United Nations described in Part I is clearly understood, no citizen or statesman should have to spend a minute deciding whether to seriously consider committing this nation to a UN convention or treaty. Any more than one would have trouble deciding whether to accept candy from a known drug dealer.

The heart of the book — Part II, "Stealth Strategies for Building the Superstate" — provides the most important new insights. In this series of chapters, Mr. Jasper shows how, through breathtaking pretexts and deceptions and elaborate networks, the globalist architects are building their house of world order. Creating much wider understanding of these deceptions is the key to countering the attempted public manipulation.

Part III, "Bringing It Home," shows what the dishonest drive for world government will mean to the individual and his family. Chapter 12, "The UN's One-World Religion," exposes the efforts to undermine Christianity and other traditional faith-based religions. The goal is to replace them with a strange new mix that is more compatible with universal worship of the Almighty State as the object deserving our supreme loyalty. Chapter 13, "The UN Declares Total War on the Family," lays bare the Orwellian dimension of the drive to empower the UN.

The last chapter, one of the best in the book, examines not only the necessity for action, but also the principles of effective action.

A Realistic Solution

It is our hope that after reading this book you will want to help stop the drive to destroy American freedom and independence that Mr. Jasper describes. There are a number of steps we recommend.

The first is to take the time to understand the message in this book and convince yourself of its accuracy. Check out the references. Visit the websites cited herein for more information. Order additional literature. Talk to members and staff of The John Birch Society. Satisfy yourself that our information is reliable and that our long-range goal — "less government, more responsibility, and, with God's help, a better world" — is something you too can recommend with pride.

And then act! Self-education without action merely breeds frustration. As the saying goes, no one should want to be the best informed inmate of a concentration camp.

But action must follow an appropriate, realistic plan. As Mr. Jasper points out, effective action must spring from a clear understanding of the threat, as well as a solid understanding of the strengths remaining in our culture and in the American system of government we have inherited. Otherwise, action will be ineffective, quite possibly even counterproductive. Rereading the last chapter in this book is a good starting point.

As another step, we strongly encourage you to share copies of this book with family, friends, and associates. And finally, contact us for more information on our organized, concerted-action program.

A very common mistake is to underestimate the problem and look for the quick fix or the political leader to support who will fix our problems for us. But the threat Mr. Jasper describes is the result of decades of work by determined enemies of freedom who have organized and labored to achieve great influence. There is no quick fix. They most certainly will not be stopped by an *uninformed* public electing a man on a white horse to the presidency.

The challenge we face is nothing less than to change the course of history. The John Birch Society has much more than a dream. We have a plan, but we need your help. We hope to hear from you!

Tom Gow
Vice President, The John Birch Society
April 7, 2001

Prologue

For I dipt into the future, far as human eye could see,
Saw the Vision of the world, and all the wonder that would
  be ...
Heard the heavens fill with shouting, and there rain'd a
  ghastly dew
From the nations' airy navies grappling in the central blue ...
Till the war-drum throbb'd no longer, and the battle-flags
  were furl'd
In the Parliament of man, the Federation of the world.
There the common sense of most shall hold a fretful realm in
  awe,
And the kindly earth shall slumber, lapt in universal law. [1]
  — Alfred Lord Tennyson, "Locksley Hall," 1842

World peace through world government and world law. It is an ancient idea that has fastened itself mightily on the minds of men in many ages. "The abolition of war and the establishment of a world government are the two main themes of contemporary utopianism," notes philosopher Thomas Molnar in *Utopia: The Perennial Heresy.* "These objectives are as old as utopian thought itself." [2] Never before, however, has our human race been so close to inaugurating this utopian "ideal" — to establishing and empowering government on a planetary scale. Global "crises" — environmental decay, poverty, overpopulation, economic and political instability — and the still-present threat of war and nuclear holocaust demand "global solutions." Transnational problems and growing interdependence defy our antiquated "world order" of nation states. So say a growing chorus of media-designated "experts."

But our planet and our age have had more than passing

1

acquaintance with utopias empowered. And without exception, the promises of the utopian dream have yielded to dystopian nightmares. The tens of millions of victims of Lenin, Stalin, Hitler, Mao, Ho, Kim, Fidel, Pol Pot, Amin, Lumumba, Qaddafi, Khomeini, and dozens of other murderous despots cry out to us. They warn us against the utopian siren call. They warn us of the fundamental truth embodied in George Washington's definition of government:

> Government is not reason; it is not eloquence; it is force! Like fire, it is a dangerous servant and a fearful master.[3]

World government, of course, would necessitate worldwide force — unprecedented power on a global scale. Make no mistake about it, that is what the advocates of "an empowered United Nations" are really after. And what is most disturbing is that they have very nearly succeeded in grasping hold of this power, without most inhabitants of this planet having the slightest idea of the "happiness" being planned for them.

A chilling insight into the kind of future we might expect under the global regime of an omnipotent, omni-benevolent United Nations is provided in a presentation on "world order" given by a high UN official to the American Association of Systems Analysts. The official, Robert Muller, held many top UN posts over a 35-year career at the UN, including that of Secretary of the UN's Economic and Social Council (ECOSOC). In his book *New Genesis: Shaping a Global Spirituality*, Muller recounts how he explained to the systems analysts the myriad activities in which the UN was even at that time (the 1970s) deeply involved:

> Yes, the UN is concerned with our globe's climate....
>
> Yes, the UN is concerned with the total biosphere through project Earthwatch, the Global Environment Program of UNEP and UNESCO's program, "Man and the Biosphere."

Yes, the UN is dealing with our planet's seas and oceans....

Yes, the UN is dealing with the world's deserts....

Yes, the UN is dealing with the human person, that alpha and omega of our efforts.... The person's basic rights, justice, health, progress and peace are being dealt with from the fetus to the time of death.

Yes, the UN is dealing with the atom in the International Atomic Energy Agency....

Yes, the UN is dealing with art, folklore, nature, the preservation of species, germ banks, labor, handicrafts, literature, industry, trade, tourism, energy, finance, birth defects, sicknesses, pollution, politics, the prevention of accidents, of war and conflicts, the building of peace, the eradication of armaments, atomic radiation, the settlement of disputes, the development of worldwide cooperation, the aspirations of East and West, North and South, black and white, rich and poor, etc. [4]

Muller then records: *"I went on like this for more than an hour. When I finished, I still had a bagful to say, but I was exhausted by my exaltation at the vastness of the cooperation I had seen develop.... Something gigantic was going on, a real turning point in evolution* ... glorious and beautiful like Aphrodite emerging from the sea. This was the beginning of a new age.... The great hour of truth had arrived for the human race."[5] (Emphasis added.)

The epiphany appears to have nearly overwhelmed him. Later upon reflection, however, Muller found to his dismay that there were vital spheres of human and planetary concern not yet brought within the UN's superintending care. "I had found several gaps," he records. Gaps? What possible "gaps" could there be? A great many, it seems. For "there was no worldwide cooperation for the globe's cold zones, the mountains, our topsoil, standardization, world safety ... *the family, morality, spirituality, world psychology and sociology, the world of senses, the inner realm of the individual, his needs, values, perceptions, love and happiness* ... on consumer protection ... on the world's elderly, on world law, *on the ultimate meaning of human life and its objectives.*"[6] (Emphasis added.)

Muller fumed that "political men were still dragging their feet in antiquated, obsolete quarrels which prevented them from seeing the vast new universal scheme of evolution which was dawning upon the world."[7] Indeed. Parochial politicians were stifling the messianic mission of Mr. Muller and his fellow UN savants, whose only desire is to "transform" the world.

Much has been done to alleviate those hindrances and deficiencies, however. New United Nations treaties and conventions are rushing to fill in the "gaps" Muller was so worried about. The colossal UN bureaucracy Muller outlined in his book has been greatly augmented. One UN program alone, the massive Agenda 21, "proposes an array of actions which are intended to be implemented by every person on Earth."[8] (See Chapter 6.) And the UN's newly created International Criminal Court (see Chapter 8) poses the very real prospect of American citizens being delivered up for trial before international tribunals, without any of the protections guaranteed in our Constitution.

Although his name is not universally known, Mr. Muller is not some inconsequential UN bureaucrat whose utopian rantings can be lightly dismissed. He is author of the "World Core Curriculum," now used in many schools worldwide, and is chancellor of the UN's University for Peace in Costa Rica. Muller, who is a self-professed disciple of the theosophist/satanist Alice Bailey, is revered in globalist circles and is one of the most frequently quoted "sages" and architects of the UN's new world religion.*

In his book *My Testament to the UN*, Muller pays tribute to the UN's New Age spiritual guru, Sri Chinmoy, and approvingly quotes Chinmoy's "prophecy" regarding the UN's ultimate destiny:

No human force will ever be able to destroy the United Nations, for the United Nations is not a mere building or a mere idea; it is not a man-made creation. The United Nations is the vision-light of the Absolute Supreme, which is slowly, steadily and unerringly illumining the ignorance, the night of our human life. The divine success and supreme progress of the United Nations is bound to become a reality. At his choice hour, the Absolute Supreme will ring His own victory-bell here on Earth through the loving and serving heart of the United Nations. [9]

Yes, for Muller and his fellow votaries of one-world paganism, who populate the higher echelons of the UN and the globalist movement, the United Nations is *divine* and is leading us to, as Muller says, "the apotheosis [deification] of human life on earth." [10] Human life, that is, personified by Muller and the UN's spiritual elites, who, naturally, will lead and rule in this new world order.

Professor Molnar dissects this idolatry and monumental conceit with piercing precision: "At utopia's roots there is defiance of God, pride unlimited, a yearning for enormous power and the assumption of divine attributes with a view to manipulating and shaping man's fate." [11]

Where does this supreme arrogance invariably lead? The record of history is pitiless. Dr. Molnar continues: "In a raving moment, the story goes, Caligula wished that mankind had only one head so that he might chop it off with one blow. So, too, the utopian: he wants to deal with one entity so as to simplify his own task of transforming indomitable human nature into a slave." [12]

---

* At the beginning of his World Core Curriculum Muller states that his underlying philosophy "is based on the teachings set forth in the books of Alice A. Bailey by the Tibetan teacher Djwhal Khul and the teachings of M. Morya." This is quite an admission considering that Mrs. Bailey's exalted position in the occult Theosophical firmament is second only to that of Theosophy founder and high priestess Madame Blavatsky. Bailey, who alleged that Khul and Morya communicated with her telepathically, was a rabid Luciferian and founded the Lucifer Publishing Company and the Theosophical journal *Lucifer*.

Procrustes, according to Greek legend, was a demented high-wayman who "fit" his victims to his guest bed either by stretch-ing them, if they were too short, or chopping off their feet, if they were too tall. Likewise, the utopian: When the "humanity" he "serves" fails to fit his Procrustean bed, he lops off not only the feet but the head too.

Renewed Revolution
The UN's Robert Muller fully recognizes the revolutionary nature of his mission. "As on the eve of the French Revolution," he exclaims, "... we must outgrow the increasingly erroneous notion of good and bad as seen by a particular group ... and define new concepts of what is good or bad for the entire human family. This is absolutely essential." [13] Muller and other enthusi-asts for a "new world order" under UN hegemonic rule invariably share this sympathetic fascination and fixation with the abomi-nations and terror of the French Revolution.

So, too, have the greatest mass murderers of this century. One of the most notorious is Cambodia's Communist butcher Pol Pot, who was steeped in the French Revolution while a student in Paris. He was inspired, no doubt, by Jean-Baptiste Carrier, the French Revolution's bloodthirsty beast of the Committee of Public Safety, who pledged: "We shall turn France into a ceme-tery rather than fail in her regeneration." [14] In his powerful 1994 study *Death by Government*, Professor R. J. Rummel writes that "no other megamurderer comes even close to the lethality of the Communist Khmer Rouge in Cambodia during their 1975 through 1978 rule." [15] As advocated by Muller, Pol Pot and his Angka Loeu comrades "defined new concepts of what is good or bad." And, notes Rummel, "in less than four years of governing they exterminated over 31 percent of their men, women, and children...." [16] Over two million souls — slaughtered in the most inhuman ways imaginable.

John Barron and Anthony Paul, in their book *Murder of a Gentle Land*, record the UN's response to the Cambodian bloodbath:

After the desolation of the cities, the early massacres, and in the midst of the first famine, one of the Angka Loeu leaders, Ieng Sary, in his incarnation as foreign minister, flew to a special session of the United Nations General Assembly. Upon landing in New York, he boasted, "We have cleansed the cities," and when he appeared at the United Nations, the delegates from around the world warmly applauded.[17]

And why not applaud? They were merely welcoming one of their own. Butchers, terrorists, and dictators have always received favored treatment at the UN: Khrushchev, Brezhnev, Gorbachev, Fidel Castro, Idi Amin, Yasir Arafat, Colonel Qaddafi, Teng Hsiao-ping, Jiang Zemin, Hafez al-Assad, Nelson Mandela, Sam Nujoma, and dozens of other murderous thugs — all have received rapturous greetings, *as well as concrete political and economic support*, at and from the United Nations. The hard facts are that many of the "honored" members of the United Nations are themselves practitioners of what Professor Rummel calls democide, the intentional murder, by government, of noncombatants — by the millions. Just the top 15 democide regimes, he notes, "have wiped out over 151 million people, almost four times the almost 38,500,000 battle dead from all this century's international and civil wars up to 1987."[18]

"Democide is committed by absolute Power; its agency is government," notes Rummel.[19] And limiting that agency's power for democide is a prime civic duty. This is a "fact of life" (and death) which we cannot afford to ignore. Here are two more from the professor: "A preeminent fact about government is that some of them murder millions in cold blood. This is where absolute Power reigns. A second fact is that some, usually the same that murder millions, also murder tens of thousands more through foreign aggression."[20]

Appeals to "empower" the United Nations are worse than foolish; they are evil and must be opposed by all honorable people. History more than amply vindicates Lord Acton's axiom that

"power tends to corrupt and absolute power corrupts absolutely." [21] This has proven true even when rulers have started out as
relatively virtuous; even more so when already-corrupt men
grasp hold of absolute power.

A Grim Reality

As this study will demonstrate, the primary movers in the ongoing drive to "transform" the United Nations, and to transfer the
powers of sovereign governments to this global monstrosity, are
not misguided, well-intentioned utopians. We will not dissuade
them with facts, arguments, and debates pointing out the errors
and dangers inherent in their tyrannical proposals. They are not
interested in facts, arguments, and debates — except as it serves
as a cover for their totalitarian agenda. We are dealing with a
self-perpetuating conspiracy of immensely wealthy, utterly
wicked, power-mad megalomaniacs who want to rule the world.
It is that simple.

During the course of the past century, this cabal of one-world
Insiders has gradually gained control of the levers of power in the
federal government, the Democrat and Republican Parties, and
many major corporations, universities, think tanks, media, and
tax-exempt foundations. Operating through respectable-appear-
ing front groups — principally the Council on Foreign Relations
(CFR), the Trilateral Commission (TC), the Bilderberg Group
(BG), and the Committee for Economic Development (CED) —
these one-worlders have hijacked our country. While systematically destroying our constitutional republic and gradually converting it into a socialist dictatorship, they also have been busily
fomenting wars and revolutions, toppling free governments that
were friendly to America, and repeatedly aiding ruthless
Communist dictators and Third World thugs who are America's
enemies. The blood of millions of victims is on their hands.

Now they are pressing forward with ever-increasing audacity,
demanding the power to refashion the world according to their
Procrustean logic. If we do not stop their megalomaniacal

scheme, they will, in the words of the French Revolutionist Carrier, turn the world "into a cemetery rather than fail in her regeneration."

Yes, these are very serious charges, but they reflect a very grim reality. They are, unfortunately, more than sustained by mountains of evidence. We have attempted here to clear away some of the haze that has long hidden these mountains, so that you, the reader, may make some very serious decisions based upon historical facts, perspective, and truth that previously have been denied to you. History is a very bloody and unforgiving crucible that we ignore at our own great peril. However, history need not fatalistically repeat itself. Informed, courageous, responsible individuals can and do change the course of history. We pray that you, dear reader, and many others like you, will rise to the challenge in this hour of deadly peril.

Part I
Foundations

Chapter 1

The Threat

*America is surrendering its sovereignty to a world govern-
ment. Hooray.... World government is coming. Deal with it.*[1]
— *The New Republic* magazine, cover story headlines for
January 17, 2000

*We need a system of enforceable world law — a democrat-
ic federal world government — to deal with world problems.*[2]
— Walter Cronkite, 1999

*We must do everything we can to abolish the United
States.*[3]
— Professor Mortimer J. Adler of the University of
Chicago and the Aspen Institute, editor of *Great Books of
the Western World*, 1945

As the year 2000 approached, prophecies of doom proliferated
everywhere — in the major media, the Internet, talk radio,
financial newsletters — offering dire predictions of massive computer failures, electrical grid blackouts, global technological
meltdowns and "the end of the world as we know it." The dread
Y2K forecasts were, of course, as everyone now knows, wildly
exaggerated; the specter of global industrial collapse turned out
to be a colossal bogeyman.*

---

*The New American magazine, of which this author is a senior editor, can claim
the stellar, if not singular, distinction of having called the shots correctly on Y2K.
In two major articles by Dennis Behreandt — "Millennium Mayhem" (September
14, 1998), and "Y2K Is Here!" (April 26, 1999) — and in smaller articles, *TNA*
repeatedly challenged, with calm reason and careful research, the widespread
doomsday scenarios and "head for the hills" alarms that were leading many otherwise responsible citizens to give up the battle against collectivism and
immorality. See www.thenewamerican.com/Y2K.

However, while fears of the Y2K phantom menace seized the minds of billions of people worldwide, a very real global peril went largely unnoticed. That global danger is with us still. And it truly threatens to bring about "the end of the world as we know it." The world as we know it is being radically "transformed." We are not referring here to the usual apocalyptic alarms about "global warming" and other eco-doom scenarios, economic "globalization," the mind-numbing pace of technological innovation, or the specters of biological and nuclear warfare.

We are talking about a revolutionary transformation that has been gathering steam since World War II and is now entering its final stages. It is a revolution that, if completed, will mean the end of the United States of America — as well as the abolition of every other sovereign, independent nation. This radical revolution is simultaneously overturning the nation-state system that has been the foundation for governance on this planet for the past several hundred years, and forging a world government with unprecedented powers.

This is the most profound and far-reaching revolution ever to hit our planet. If allowed to proceed to completion, it will usher in an Orwellian global tyranny under the United Nations. We know that to many people this is an astounding statement. You, dear reader, may be among those who find such a claim to be "ridiculous," "absurd," "nutty." After all, you reason, the United States is the most powerful nation on earth, "the last superpower" — and the UN is a paper tiger, a joke, a bunch of global bureaucrats belching platitudes about peace and brotherhood and proposing grandiose schemes. Sure, it may waste some of our money, but it is no *threat* to the U.S. The UN has no military of its own to impose global laws or regulations upon unwilling Americans. In fact, the UN must come hat in hand to the U.S. every time it determines to send peacekeepers into some new area torn by conflict. And hasn't the UN been complaining for years about U.S. refusals to pay dues? The UN looks like a pretty helpless, toothless "threat," you say.

And you would be right — except for one very important thing:

You would have completely misunderstood the nature of the danger and direction from which the threat is coming. Observers who have carefully followed and analyzed international developments and the policies and institutions of the UN have never worried that UN Secretary-General Kofi Annan — or one of his predecessors or successors — would impose a UN dictatorship upon a strong and resistant United States. That is not going to happen. We are not worried that an imminent UN tyranny is about to be militarily imposed upon Americans against the wishes of our own government. Or that, like the Y2K computer bug, some midnight soon the UN will strike, overwhelm the U.S. military, and we will wake up in the morning with blue-helmeted policemen on every street corner.

The danger is very real, nonetheless, but it emanates not so much from Kofi Annan, the UN itself, or any foreign, external source as it does from those within our own government who seek to impose a "new world order" upon us. As one of our more famous former U.S. presidents accurately noted:

> Shall we expect some transatlantic military giant, to step the ocean, and crush us at a blow? Never!
>
> All the armies of Europe, Asia and Africa combined ... could not by force, take a drink from the Ohio, or make a track on the Blue Ridge, in a trial of a thousand years.
>
> At what point, then, is the approach of danger to be expected? I answer, if it ever reach us, it must spring up amongst us. It cannot come from abroad. If destruction be our lot, we must ourselves be its author and finisher. As a nation of freemen, we must live through all time, or die by suicide. [4] [Abraham Lincoln, 1838]

The Danger Springs From Within

The danger has indeed sprung up amongst us. There are many who go by the name "American" who prefer to think of themselves as "global citizens" or "citizens of the world" and who consciously are leading us to national suicide. An alarming number of American citizens who hold high elective and appointive office, and who have taken oaths to defend our nation, our Constitution, and our laws, are now committed to a "new world order" which does not allow for a free, independent, sovereign United States of America. They are joined by prominent individuals holding influential positions of trust in many of our private institutions. In the new "*inter*dependent" world order they envision, a U.S.A. with continuing superpower status is viewed as a "threat" to global peace and security.

Let us be completely blunt: These globalists are after power — raw, absolute, global power, unimpeded by constitutional restraints, the rule of law, and the natural checks and balances against worldwide power provided by sovereign nation-states. We all ought to be familiar with this dangerous lust for power. The 20th century, which we so recently left, was washed in the blood of millions of victims sacrificed on the altars of powerlust. The leaders of totalitarian socialism — of both the Communist and Fascist varieties — trod the same paths to power that are now taken by our globalist would-be rulers. Lenin, Hitler, Mao, Fidel, Pol Pot, and innumerable lesser thugs all came to power invoking virtue and noble ideals. They appealed to fears about supposed emergencies and crises. They incited and mobilized resentment and hatred of one group or class for another, and made scapegoats of their opponents. They gradually centralized and consolidated power and eliminated all legal and structural restraints on their exercise of it.

In every case, a small circle of power-lusting conspirators used large movements of idealists and dupes to accomplish their schemes. In every instance, the danger signs were there for those who were willing to see. The opportunities were there for those with courage to stop the madness by exposing and opposing the criminals before they could seize total political power. Alas, in each case, too few citizens were willing to see and to act courageously. For this they paid a horrendous price. The signs are here for us to see today; we will have no excuse if we fail to act with responsibility and courage. Our price for failing to do so will be far more terrible than anything this planet has yet seen.

Millennium Meetings

In September 2000, some 150 presidents, premiers, dictators, and potentates converged on New York City for the UN Millennium Summit, the most spectacular UN gathering ever. Serving as co-chairman of the week-long political gala was Sam Nujoma, the Communist terrorist who was installed as "President" of Namibia in 1990 by the United Nations, the Soviet Union, and the U.S. State Department. The Summit attendees all received a copy of *We the Peoples: The Role of the United Nations in the 21st Century*, a report "authored" by Kofi Annan to guide the UN's "reform agenda" at the event.

Annan's *We the Peoples* proposed nothing less than a global, socialist superstate dressed in New Deal verbiage. The Annan plan even adopted Franklin Delano Roosevelt's Brain Trust rhetoric of "Freedom from Fear" and "Freedom from Want" as titles for the report's sub-themes. It called for, among other things:

- a global war on poverty (imagine a planetary version of our costly federal Department of Health and Human Services!);
- ending "gender discrimination" (i.e. mandated gender quotas) "in wages, property rights, and access to education";
- government-provided education, school lunches, and health care for all;
- a global youth employment initiative, under the direction of the International Labor Organization and the World Bank;
- creation of an International Criminal Court; and
- adoption of the Kyoto Protocol, which mandates drastic reductions in so-called "greenhouse gases." [5]

We the Peoples also proposed "new forms of global governance," "global norms," "global rules" — all of which infer a role for the UN as global legislator. None of this surprises us, of course; UN poohbahs like Annan are well known for their self-aggrandizing pontifications and appeals for new global powers. However, this was not a typical, run-of-the-mill summit; something new and more sinister was at work here. The Millennium

Summit showcased a frightening new level of capability for sophisticated orchestration of an intensive, worldwide, multi-pronged, multi-level propaganda campaign. This astonishing process is capable of mobilizing and coordinating the activities of an impressive number of politicians, UN officials, corporate leaders, major organs of the media, academic institutions, think tanks and innumerable private, special-interest groups. Thus a relatively small but noisy, lavishly funded, and incredibly well organized minority has shown that it can generate tremendous, synchronized pressure completely out of proportion to its real size. This pressure is generated by deception, by falsely presenting the appearance of irresistible, universal support for UN proposals.

The concentrated pressure is aimed at intimidating, silencing, and neutralizing all active and potential opposition, among both elected officials and private citizens. And it works with frightening effect. The element of surprise, together with concerted force, overwhelms the opposition.

Virtually all of the Heads of State attending the Summit took their turns at the UN General Assembly rostrum and echoed Kofi Annan's appeals for global governance, some adding even stronger appeals for global taxation, a permanent UN military, a global environmental police force, etc. Meanwhile, outside the UN, crowds composed of members of various non-governmental organizations (NGOs) clamored for the creation of a Global Peoples Assembly, a sort of UN Congress to enact global legislation. A few blocks away another global confab was underway promoting the same one-world agenda. The State of the World Forum 2000, sponsored by the Gorbachev Foundation, featured a week-long series of symposia with prominent participants from the worlds of international business and finance, labor, academe, philanthropy, religion, environmental activism, government, intergovernmental organizations, and non-governmental organizations — all beating the drums for world government under an empowered and greatly expanded UN.

However, all of these meetings, symposia, demonstrations and speeches might be dismissed as bluster, globaloney, rant and cant — except for several important facts:

- They were preceded and accompanied by similar one-world endorsements from some of America's top officials and political and intellectual leaders;
- They were preceded and accompanied by *concrete actions* and proposals by leading U.S. political and intellectual leaders to implement these proposals;
- Very wealthy and powerful U.S. individuals, companies, and institutions have committed massive financial support to establishing "global governance";
- The UN system has been expanding dramatically in size and scope and now constitutes a huge planetary bureaucracy;
- Equally important (and dangerous) as the expanding super-structure of the UN itself is the proliferation of the UN's sub-ordinate international organizations and institutions, such as NATO, the Organization of American States (OAS), the International Monetary Fund (IMF), the Organization for Economic Cooperation and Development (OECD), the World Trade Organization (WTO), etc.;
- A huge network of radical NGOs, financed by governments and tax-exempt foundations, and masquerading as authentic representatives of "global civil society," can now assemble mobs at will to "lobby" for the cause *du jour*;
- This drive for an empowered UN is the culmination of plans set in motion decades earlier by a power-seeking cabal (see Chapter 3).

Top Leaders Advocate World Government
On February 18, 2000, the World Federalist Association (WFA), one of the largest and most ardent organizations promoting world government, took out a full-page advertisement in the *New York Times* to proclaim triumphantly that "Cronkite and Clinton make a strong case for recasting the United Nations as a world federation."[6]

The Clinton referred to was, of course, then-President Bill Clinton, while the other name referred to famed television newsman Walter Cronkite. The World Federalist Association ad noted: "Last October, President Clinton applauded federalism — the basis for the U.S. Constitution — as 'the arrangement of government most likely to give us the best of all worlds — the integrity we need, the self government we need, the self-advancement we need — without pretending that we can cut all cords that bind us to the rest of humanity....' The President claimed that '... we become more of a federalist world when the United Nations takes a more active role in stopping genocide ... and we recognize mutual responsibilities to contribute and pay for those things.'"

President Clinton's speech was delivered at the Forum of Global Federation Conference in Mont-Tremblant, Canada. Both the group he addressed and the WFA, which placed his words in their newspaper ad, recognized the importance and true meaning of his speech when he predicted that there will be "more federalism rather than less in the years ahead."

What kind of "federalism" was Mr. Clinton predicting and endorsing? He cited "as Exhibit A the European Union," or EU, which is rapidly subsuming its member countries in a colossal, socialist, and increasingly tyrannical superstate.

The WFA's *New York Times* ad noted that in the same month that Clinton was making his above-mentioned federalism speech, former CBS anchorman Walter Cronkite received the WFA's "Norman Cousins Global Governance Award for his promotion of world government in his autobiography *A Reporter's Life*." In accepting the award, Cronkite said: "Those of us who are living today can influence the future of civilization. We can influence whether our planet will drift into chaos and violence, or whether through monumental educational and political effort we will achieve a world of peace under a system of law where individual violators of that law are brought to justice.... We need a system of enforceable world law — a democratic federal world government — to deal with world problems."[7]

At the World Federalist tribute to Cronkite, First Lady Hillary Rodham Clinton — now a U.S. senator — offered her congratulations via closed-circuit TV. She said, "For more than a generation in America, it wasn't the news, until Walter Cronkite told us it was the news." Hillary continued, "For decades you told us, 'the way it is.' But tonight we honor you for fighting for 'the way it could be.' ... [T]hank you, Walter, thank you for inspiring all of us to build a more peaceful and just world."

Please keep in mind the significance of such a statement. The cause for which Cronkite was being honored was the cause of world government, and world government would mean the end of U.S. sovereignty, the end of our country, the end of our Constitution — the document to which her husband had sworn allegiance (and to which she also has sworn allegiance in her Senate oath).

However, Bill Clinton himself had already praised an earlier recipient of the Norman Cousins Global Governance Award: his old Oxford University roommate, Strobe Talbott, whom he had appointed U.S. Ambassador at Large. That praise came in the form of a letter dated June 22, 1993, which was read at the WFA awards ceremony two days later. Mr. Clinton's letter praised WFA founder Norman Cousins' lifetime effort "for world peace and world government" and noted that Talbott's "lifetime achievements as a voice for global harmony have earned him this recognition." [8]

Specifically, the World Federalists were honoring Talbott for a pro-world government essay he had written for *Time* magazine entitled "The Birth of the Global Nation" (July 20, 1992 issue). Therein Talbott approvingly forecast that in the future "nationhood as we know it will be obsolete; all states will recognize a single, global authority." "[I]t has taken the events in our own wondrous and terrible century to clinch the case for world government," he said. [9]

Talbott's advocacy of world government did not prevent President Clinton from appointing him Deputy Secretary of State. That should not surprise anyone. Clinton, like Talbott, is a member of the world-government-promoting Council on Foreign Relations (CFR), as were over 400 other members of his administration. In addition, both are also "members in public service" of the Trilateral Commission (TC), an even more exclusive establishmentarian club greasing the skids for global governance.

Greasing the Skids
These groups have orchestrated an outpouring of symphonic appeals for world government and have been preparing the American psyche for a major globalist push to provide the United Nations, the WTO, and other international institutions with legislative, executive, and judicial powers. This is a small sampling of that orchestrated outpouring:

- Richard Falk (CFR), Professor of International Law at Princeton University, an influential legal scholar, wrote "On the Creation of a Global Peoples Assembly" for the Summer 2000 *Stanford Journal of International Law*, with Professor Andrew Strauss. Said Falk and Strauss: "At this historical juncture we believe that the time for the establishment of a global assembly is ripening. We believe that our circumstances and values are raising a crucial new question: If democracy is so appropriate in the nation-state setting, why should not democratic procedures and institutions be extended to the global setting?... The existence and empowerment of a Global Peoples Assembly (GPA) would, at the most general level, challenge the traditional claim of states that each has a sovereign right to act autonomously...." [10] Falk and Strauss subsequently penned a similar appeal, "Toward Global Parliament," for the January/February 2001 issue of the CFR journal, *Foreign Affairs*. [11]

- The headline on the cover of *The New Republic* for the liberal-left journal's January 17, 2000 issue proclaimed, "America is surrendering its sovereignty to a world government. Hooray."

Inside, teaser copy above a less descriptive title ("Continental Drift") declared: "World government is coming. Deal with it." The author of the piece, senior editor Robert Wright, noted: "Much power now vested in the nation-state is indeed starting to migrate to international institutions," and "world government … is probably in the cards.... And, what's more, it's a good idea." [12]

- Writing in *Foreign Affairs*, the highly influential quarterly of the Council on Foreign Relations (CFR), Representative Jim Leach (R-Iowa) declared: "Since one of the most effective antidotes to the irrationality of ancient enmity is the swift justice of the law, a turn (or in the case of the United States, return) to the compulsory jurisdiction of the World Court would appear to be one of the most appropriate and achievable objectives of the decades ahead." [13]

- Henry Grunwald (CFR), a former editor in chief of Time Inc. and former U.S. ambassador to Austria, authored a January 1, 1999 *Wall Street Journal* op-ed article entitled "A World Without a Country?" and subtitled "Not right away. But the idea of the nation-state is in for some profound changes." In his *Journal* article, Grunwald predicts that the "nation-state will undergo sharp limitations of its sovereignty" and that, "just as the old, petty principalities had to dissolve into the wider nation-state, the nation-state will have to dissolve into wider structures." Moreover, "it will be increasingly difficult for the future nation-state to argue that its treatments of its own citizens is a purely internal matter." [14]

- On October 14, 1999, the *Wall Street Journal's* lead editorial praised the Royal Swedish Academy of Sciences for awarding Robert Mundell the Nobel Prize for Economics. The *Journal* noted that Mundell "was the chief intellectual proponent of the euro" and acclaimed him for championing the "common currency" for Europe. [15] The *Journal* then devoted nearly one-third of a page to reprinting a 1990 essay by Mundell advocating a world central bank, including this large blow-up quote: "We have a better opportunity to create a world central bank with a stable international currency than at any previous time in history." [16] A world central bank would globalize the centralization already being wrought by the European Central Bank, which is bringing the countries of the EU under the control of one-world Eurocrats in Brussels and Frankfurt. The end result of the Mundell-*Journal* vision is a world economic cartel leading to world political control under the United Nations.

- Dr. Rashmi Mayur is Director of the International Institute for a Sustainable Future, editor of *The War & Peace Digest,* and a regular speaker at UN and other globalist programs. In an essay entitled "World Government," in the March/April 2000 issue of the *Digest*, he states: "The world is not working, and each day we are getting closer to an unprecedented catastrophe, possibly bringing an end to human civilization and earth's ecological system on which life's survival depends.... If the human civilization is to survive in the next millennium, there must be world rule of law, in which laws apply equally to all human beings and all societies.... Such a rule of law can only be implemented by an institution which has legitimacy and power on a global scale, that is, World Government.... [I]ts responsibility would be total and global." Dr. Mayur continues, "Our children have dreams.... Humanity has no future until we realize their dreams: *World Government Now*." [17] (Emphasis in the original.)

- On May 15, 2000 Representative James McGovern (D-Mass.) introduced a resolution (H. R. 4453) calling for the creation of a standing 6,000-man UN Rapid Deployment Police and Security Force that could quickly be deployed to conflict situations worldwide. According to McGovern, "a lot of lives could have been saved" in East Timor if the UN had been equipped with such a force. "This force will allow the Security Council ...

to deploy well-trained peacekeepers within 15 days of a resolution," McGovern said. [18]

• In 1998, while the United Nations was holding a summit in Rome to establish an International Criminal Court, three U.S. Supreme Court Justices traveled to Europe to visit the European Court of Justice (ECJ), which is now running roughshod over the national governments of the EU. In several frightening admissions, these justices (Ruth Bader Ginsburg, Sandra Day O'Connor, and Stephen Breyer — all CFR members) expressed their admiration for the ECJ and stated that they anticipate using and citing judgments from the ECJ and other jurisdictions in the future. [19]

• In 1999 the International Academy of Humanism published the *Humanist Manifesto 2000*, signed by an impressive lineup of educators, authors, scientists, diplomats, philosophers, and political figures, including 10 Nobel Laureates. It includes this appeal: "We believe that there is a need to develop new global institutions.... These include the call for a bicameral legislature in the United Nations, with a World Parliament elected by the people, an income tax to help the underdeveloped countries, the end of the veto in the Security Council, an environmental agency, and a World Court with powers of enforcement." [20]

These are but a few of the numerous examples in an accelerating campaign of elite opinion molders and government officials who favor this new world order. The mere fact that so many prominent citizens are promoting such an obviously subversive and harmful agenda should be alarming in and of itself, even if they were taking no concrete actions to implement it.

But they have gone far beyond mere advocacy to actually ensnare us in international treaties, conventions, and programs that are bit by bit destroying U.S. sovereignty and independence and subjecting us to rule by unaccountable international bureaucrats and institutions. The vast majority of Americans have no idea that a huge array of UN schemes — some of which we have already become officially a party to, and others which are awaiting action by the U.S. government — pose very real threats to their freedom. These include:

The World Trade Organization
The massive environmental manifesto, Agenda 21
The Biodiversity Treaty
The Global Warming Convention
Programs for national and personal disarmament
The Tobin Tax and global income tax
The vast expansion of UN military operations
Proposals for a standing UN military force
The UN's new International Criminal Court
The Convention on the Rights of the Child
The UN's global Education for All program

In the chapters that follow, we will be closely examining these schemes, as well as the forces promoting them and the pretexts under which they are being promoted.

Chapter 2

Disarmament and Submission

A world effectively controlled by the United Nations is one in which "world government" would come about through the establishment of supranational institutions.... [T]he present UN Charter could theoretically be revised in order to erect such an organization equal to the task envisaged, thereby codifying a radical rearrangement of power in the world. [1]

* * *

National disarmament is a condition sine qua non for effective UN control.... The overwhelming central fact would still be the loss of control of their military power by individual nations. [2]

— Lincoln P. Bloomfield (CFR), 1962 U.S. Department of State *Study Memorandum No. 7, A World Effectively Controlled By the United Nations.*

In Stage III progressive controlled disarmament ... would proceed to a point where no state would have the military power to challenge the progressively strengthened U.N. Peace Force. [3]

— U.S. Department of State document, *Freedom From War: The United States Program for General and Complete Disarmament in a Peaceful World,* 1961

The fact is, I see no compelling reason why we should not unilaterally get rid of our nuclear weapons. [4]

— Paul H. Nitze (CFR), former U.S. arms control negotiator in 1999 *New York Times* op-ed

Following World War I, a powerful cabal of one-world internationalists offered humanity a "solution" to the horrible ravages of war: world government. The League of Nations was their instrument of salvation and U.S. President Woodrow Wilson was their prophet. (These individuals and groups will be examined further in the next chapter.)

"The dream of a world united against the awful wastes of war is ... deeply imbedded in the hearts of men everywhere," Wilson proclaimed. Wilson believed that "all nations must be absorbed into some great association of nations...." [5] The new League he proposed would provide "collective security," i.e., it would use collective force against designated "aggressors," through some undefined instrumentality.

The U.S. Senate, however, refused to ratify the League of Nations Covenant. Americans were suspicious of entanglements with the constantly warring European powers and wanted no part of submersion in a world super-state. They saw through the sophistry and the seductive "peace" appeals. Any League strong enough to "enforce peace" globally would also possess the power to impose tyranny worldwide. There would be no way to limit its power.

Without U.S. membership, the League of Nations was doomed. However, in the wake of the even more massive death and destruction wrought by World War II, the organized one-world forces succeeded in pulling the United States into the League's successor, the United Nations. In the decades since, these advocates of a "new world order" have been working assiduously to invest the United Nations gradually with legislative, executive, and judicial powers that will transform it into a global government.

From the viewpoint of these "Insiders," who plan to be the rulers of this new world government, providing the UN with unchallengeable *military* power is a paramount objective. Tragically, very few Americans realize that the post-World War II "arms control" process and the various "arms control" treaties to which we are party have been designed to achieve precisely that objective. And this incredible scheme is far closer to final fruition than most Americans would ever imagine.

A Damning Piece of Evidence

Professor Lincoln P. Bloomfield of the Massachusetts Institute of Technology is very important to our consideration here for his revelations about this conspiracy for world conquest. Unintended revelations, we hasten to add. Dr. Bloomfield is the author of one of the most critical and damning pieces of evidence to fall into our hands concerning the conspiracy by Insiders in our own government to destroy the United States and subject the American people, along with the people of all the world, to an all-powerful United Nations.

What is so astounding is that even four decades after this scheme was discovered and exposed, Dr. Bloomfield and his co-conspirators are not only still free (in fact they have never even been officially investigated) but are actively pursuing the same criminal scheme. Even more extraordinary still, as the reader will soon see, the treasonous scheme Bloomfield devised is quite obviously still serving as a guiding light to official U.S. policies.

We are referring to the secret 1962 study Dr. Bloomfield authored for the Kennedy State Department entitled *Study Memorandum No. 7, A World Effectively Controlled By the United Nations*. The title itself is startling, but the contents are absolutely shocking for their audacity and treachery.

In the study's opening summary, Professor Bloomfield writes:

> A world effectively controlled by the United Nations is one in which *"world government" would come about through the establishment of supranational institutions*, characterized by mandatory universal membership and some ability to employ physical force. Effective control would thus entail a preponderance of political power in the hands of a supranational organization.... [T]he present UN Charter could theoretically be revised in order to erect such an organization equal to the task envisaged, *thereby codifying a radical rearrangement of power in the world.*[6] [Emphasis added.]

Dr. Bloomfield continued:

> The principal features of a model system would include the following: (1) powers sufficient to monitor and enforce disarmament, settle disputes, and keep the peace — *including taxing powers ...* ; (2) an international force, balanced appropriately among ground, sea, air, and space elements, consisting of 500,000 men, recruited individually, wearing a UN uniform, and controlling a nuclear force composed of 50-100 mixed land-based mobile and undersea-based missiles, averaging one megaton per weapon; (3) governmental powers distributed among three branches...; (4) compulsory jurisdiction of the International Court....[7] [Emphasis added.]

In this blueprint for global tyranny financed by the U.S. government, Bloomfield repeatedly stated a key point, that "it is world government we are discussing here — inescapable."[8] And he leaves no doubt that the scheme would mean subjecting the U.S. to this omnipotent "contemplated regime" (his words).[9] He emphasizes, for instance, that:

> National disarmament is a condition sine qua non for effective UN control....
>
> The essential point is the transfer of the most vital element of sovereign power from the states to a supranational government....
>
> The overwhelming central fact would still be the loss of control of their military power by individual nations.[10]

Dr. Bloomfield lamented that it would be extremely difficult to sell this program for world government to the American people. However, it would be possible, he wrote, if our national leaders utilized "a grave crisis or war to bring about a sudden transformation in national attitudes sufficient for the purpose." The MIT professor went on to suggest that "the order we examine may be brought into existence as a result of a series of sudden, nasty, and traumatic shocks."[11]

The Bloomfield scheme is as old as tyranny itself: Create a crisis and then offer a solution. That solution always entails, of course, "temporary" seizure of total power.

Official "Disarmament" Plans

Dr. Bloomfield's study was not just a professorial pipe dream destined to be unread and forgotten in some musty, dusty archive.*
It describes what has become the operational policy of the U.S.
government. Bloomfield, we should point out, was, and is, a
member of the Council on Foreign Relations, and it was his fellow CFR members in President Kennedy's CFR-dominated State
Department who initiated the official implementation of this
scheme.

In 1961, the Kennedy administration promulgated the now-infamous disarmament plan entitled *Freedom From War: The
United States Program for General and Complete Disarmament
in a Peaceful World.* Also known as Department of State
Publication 7277, this plan, which is very similar to the
Bloomfield study, presented a three-stage program for the transfer of U.S. arms to the United Nations.

During Stage II (the stage we are currently in), the document
mandates: "The U.N. Peace Force shall be established and progressively strengthened." [12] This will be accomplished "to the end
that the United Nations can effectively in Stage III deter or suppress any threat or use of force in violation of the purposes and
principles of the United Nations." [13] This incredible, treasonous
policy — which has been actively but quietly brought along
toward completion during successive administrations — concludes as follows:

> In Stage III progressive controlled disarmament ... would proceed to a point where *no state would have the military power to
> challenge the progressively strengthened U.N. Peace Force.*[14]
> [Emphasis added.]

---

*The full text of the Bloomfield study is available electronically from our *Get US
out!* of the United Nations website: www.getusout.org.

Pause and reflect for a moment on the enormity of the audacity and treason involved in such an incredible plot. It says that under the system it envisions, "no state" (meaning no country, including the United States) would be able to challenge the UN's power. This means that the U.S., like every other nation, would become a vassal of an omnipotent UN.

Who would actually be in control of this power? Thomas Jefferson wisely admonished: "In questions of power let no more be heard of confidence in man, but bind him down from mischief by the chains of the constitution." [15] *No* human being or group of human beings should be entrusted with the kind of power contemplated here. Are we to believe that perhaps the UN is populated with *angelic* beings? Anything but! The tower on New York's East River is better known as Terrorists, Tyrants, and Thugs "R" Us. This "House of Peace," remember, regularly erupts in obscene exaltation for Fidel Castro, "Butcher of Tiananmen Square" Li Peng, and other leaders of the most brutal regimes in history.

The disarmament scheme's leading proponents in the U.S. government have publicly sworn oaths to uphold *our* constitutional form of government and to defend it against all enemies foreign and domestic. These same individuals straight-facedly pretend to be doing exactly that, and the vast majority of Americans innocently take them at their word. After all, these are "respected statesmen" whose names and faces have become familiar and who have been anointed by the Establishment media and political powers. *Surely* they would not betray us. Yet, that is precisely what they have done and are doing.

We do not use the terms treason lightly or loosely; we mean it in the precise and literal sense intended by the Founding Fathers. According to our Constitution: "Treason against the United States shall consist only in levying war against them, or in adhering to their enemies, giving them aid and comfort." [16] The *Freedom From War* plan manifestly fits this definition. It would render all Americans subject to a foreign power (the UN) controlled by one-world internationalists who have made no secret of their hostility toward our system of government, and by totalitarian regimes that clearly mean us harm.

Freedom From War was amplified in April 1962 by another disarmament document entitled *Blueprint for the Peace Race: Outline of Basic Provisions of a Treaty on General and Complete Disarmament in a Peaceful World*. As before, its third stage calls for the strengthening of the UN Peace Force "until it had sufficient armed forces and armaments so that no state could challenge it." [17]

That is where the current CFR leadership in the Bush administration, working together with the heirs of Gorbachev and Yeltsin in Moscow, are planning to take us with the current round of disarmament talks and the ongoing push to arm the United Nations with a standing army. Their true intent is not the *elimination* of weapons, but the *transfer* of weapons and military forces from nation-states to the UN, creating a monopoly of power that will enable them to enforce their envisioned new world order.

A Strange Alliance

On October 19, 1994, former Soviet dictator Mikhail Gorbachev released the *Final Report of the Global Security Project* at the CFR's Pratt House headquarters in New York City. [18] The Global Security Project (GSP) is a *joint* effort of the Gorbachev Foundation and the CFR. Besides our same Dr. Bloomfield, other CFR "security experts" on the project include Richard Falk, Saul Mendlovitz, Jonathan Dean, Jeremy J. Stone, and the arch-subversive Daniel Ellsberg (of the Pentagon Papers infamy). They were joined by the late Senator Alan Cranston, a longtime pro-Communist, [19] a past president of the World Federalists, and a member of the Trilateral Commission.

The Gorbachev/CFR GSP *Final Report* calls for the creation of a UN "readiness force" provided by UN member states. It proposes "drastic cuts by nuclear weapons states to the level of 100 nuclear warheads, to be achieved within ten years, by 2005 A.D." [20] These reductions would be made "irreversible" by the transfer of all weapons-grade "fissile material" to the UN's International Atomic Energy Agency (IAEA). It also recommends that the UN Security Council press all other nations likewise to place their nuclear facilities under UN control — or face "joint punitive action." [21] In line with the Bloomfield study and *Freedom From War*, the GSP calls for the worldwide abolition of conventional armed forces by nation-states. [22]

For those who still can't recognize the obvious, James Garrison, co-founder and president of the Gorbachev Foundation/USA, candidly admitted the game plan in a 1995 newspaper interview. "Over the next 20 to 30 years, we are going to end up with world government," he said. "It's inevitable," Garrison continued, "... through this turbulence is the recognition that we have to empower the United Nations and that we have to govern and regulate human interaction...." [23]

An "Independent" Commission?

In the spring of 1995, shortly after the release of the GSP *Final Report*, another one-world volley pushing the same global disarmament program came in the form of *Our Global Neighborhood,* the report of the "independent" Commission on Global Governance (CGG). The CGG includes among its august membership former presidents and prime ministers, many of whom are also leaders of the Socialist International, the principal global organization of Marxist parties promoting world government and East-West convergence. [24] *Our Global Neighborhood* was released on the eve of the United Nations Social Summit in Copenhagen, Denmark. The influential CGG report insists that the UN and other international institutions must be vested with ever greater legislative, executive, and judicial powers — including new regulatory, taxing, police, and military capabilities including a standing UN "peace force."

Interestingly, one of the CGG's key consultants/advisors for this report was again our same Dr. Bloomfield. In the years between his 1961 study and his efforts for the GSP and CGG reports, Bloomfield continued to serve the world government cause: teaching at MIT, serving as director of global issues for the National Security Council, sitting on international panels, and authoring additional pleas to empower the UN. He is like hundreds of other CFR members who rotate in and out of "government service" to prestigious (and profitable) positions in finance and consulting (for instance, Goldman Sachs, Chase Manhattan, the Blackstone Group, or Kissinger Associates), academe (Harvard, Yale, Princeton, Columbia, Stanford, MIT, Johns Hopkins, etc.), think tanks (CFR, the Brookings Institution, the Institute for International Economics, Rand Corporation, the Woodrow Wilson Institute, etc.) or the corporate world, which includes many top Fortune 500 companies whose boards of directors and top officer slots have become heavy with CFR members.

Harlan Cleveland

Also serving with Bloomfield as consultants to the CGG were CFR members Michael Clough, Peter Haas, and Harlan Cleveland,[25] a notorious pro-Communist security risk in the Kennedy administration who helped draft the *Freedom From War* program for U.S. disarmament.[26] Mr. Cleveland was one of the early UN "founders" at the 1945 San Francisco Conference. In the student yearbook at Princeton University, he listed himself as a "Socialist."[27] Later, he wrote articles for *Pacific Affairs*, the journal of the Institute of Pacific Relations (IPR), an infamous Soviet espionage operation that played a critical role in delivering China to the Communist forces of Mao Tse-tung. The IPR was described by the Senate Judiciary Committee as "an instrument of Communist policy, propaganda and military intelligence."[28]

While Cleveland was deputy chief of the United Nations Relief and Rehabilitation Administration (UNRRA) mission in Italy, that organization helped implement "Operation Keelhaul," the treasonous and brutal betrayal that delivered nearly five million Europeans to Stalin's death squads and concentration camps. Cleveland's boss at UNRRA was Soviet agent Harold Glasser.[29] Cleveland was later appointed U.S. ambassador to NATO. As we will see in ensuing chapters, he is typical of the one-world subversives who have penetrated and infested the top levels of the federal government for several decades.

Mr. Cleveland has kept active writing and speaking on behalf of the UN, international socialism, and world government over the past half century. In 1976, he authored *The Third Try at World Order: U.S. Policy for an Interdependent World,* published by the World Affairs Council of Philadelphia and the Aspen Institute, both of which are longtime advocacy centers for world government, intimately linked with the CFR.

In that book, Cleveland laments that the first try at "world order" collapsed with the failure to secure U.S. entry into the League of Nations and that the second failure resulted from a United Nations that was not invested with sufficient authority and power to enact and enforce world law.[30] According to Cleveland, the third try, now underway, is an attempt to arrive at world governance piecemeal, by strengthening the UN to deal with various global crises involving, for instance, the global environment, food reserve[s], energy supplies, fertility rates, military stalemate, and conflict in a world of proliferating weapons.[31]

Power of the Purse Supports the Sword

Planners such as Cleveland recognize that transferring arms alone is not enough to establish a standing UN army. That and other UN schemes require a steady revenue stream that is not beholden to the nation states that the UN seeks to dominate.

Since 1991, Cleveland has served as president of the World Academy of Art and Science. In 1995, besides contributing to the CGG's *Global Neighborhood* report for the UN Social Summit in Copenhagen, Cleveland also headed up an international cast of scholars to produce a special UN anniversary issue of *Futures,* the prestigious journal of forecasting. Entitled "The United Nations at Fifty: Policy and Financing Alternatives," the report proposed a number of schemes for global taxation.

In his lead-off essay, Cleveland asserted that "we will be relying more and more [on the UN] for peacekeeping and peaceful settlement, for the promotion of fairness in the human family, and for fostering human development.... Financing the UN is no longer an issue to be ignored, bypassed, or swept aside.... It is high time we looked hard at how best to finance a widening range of international functions that grows more obviously necessary with every passing year."[32]

Rather than relying on "the worn-out policy of year-to-year decisions by individual governments" on how much of their citizens' money to give to the UN, said Cleveland, "what's needed is a flow of funds for development which are generated automatically under international control."[33] He suggests, for instance, UN taxes on passports, on international travel, on ships (for the use of international waters), on international financial transactions, and on emissions of CFCs, CO_2, methane and other gases.[34] When it comes to the potential sources of global taxation, said Cleveland, "the list is limited only by the human imagination."[35]

That naked admission should strike terror into the heart of every taxpayer familiar with the imaginative capabilities of one-world socialists like Cleveland. In typical socialist fashion, these globalists see every productive human effort as a taxable activity, a potential "revenue stream" for the UN.

The global tax proposal that has won the most support is the so-called Tobin Tax (after Nobel Laureate economist and CFR member James Tobin), which would raise hundreds of billions of dollars annually by taxing international financial transactions. The Tobin Tax and other proposed global taxes would radically rearrange the entire international system, transferring one of the most important elements of national sovereignty to global institutions and providing the UN with independent and unaccountable revenue sources that would enable its constant expansion.

In the past decade, these proposals have gone from the purely theoretical to near practical reality. Yet most Americans have no idea that such schemes are even in the offing. How can it be that something so imminent and monumentally important could be so completely unknown? Harlan Cleveland explains it this way: "Over the years, a good deal of thinking has been done, mostly *below the surface of public attention*, on this whole subject."[36] (Emphasis added.)

You see, in the elite circles of power in which Cleveland and his CFR associates operate, the internationalists have been discussing and refining these one-world schemes for many years. They do not spring it on the general public, though, until they have lined up winning support for it. It's called getting your ducks in a row.

New World Army

Besides conspiring to deliver our nuclear arsenal to the UN, one-world architects like Cleveland, Bloomfield, et al., also have been pushing full tilt to build a globe-straddling UN conventional army. Everyone who wasn't hibernating for the past 10 years or stranded on a desert isle has heard of Operation Desert Storm, the massive, U.S.-led, UN-sanctioned 1991 invasion of Iraq, which President George Bush (CFR) declared was necessary to liberate Kuwait, stop the "naked aggression" of Saddam Hussein, and promote "a new world order."[37]

But how many people have heard of, or remember, Operations Desert Spring, Laser Strike, Northern Watch, Southern Watch, Eagle Eye, Joint Falcon, Joint Forge, Deliberate Forge, or Determined Forge? Probably not very many. And yet these are all ongoing multinational military operations — in Iraq, Kosovo, Bosnia-Herzegovina — involving large numbers of U.S. military personnel and assets.

And how many people have heard of, or remember, Operations Shining Hope, Noble Anvil, Desert Fox, Desert Thunder, Bevel Edge, Noble Obelisk, Joint Endeavor, Deliberate Guard, Determined Guard, Decisive Enhancement, Decisive Edge, Desert Strike, Desert Focus, or any of the dozens of other UN, NATO, and other multilateral deployments of U.S. armed forces throughout the world over the past decade?

A May 2000 report prepared for the Joint Chiefs of Staff notes:

"Since 1990, the United States military has participated in more than 90 'named' operations around the world." "Of these," it states, "more than 55 involved the deployment of a substantial number of forces to combat operations, peacekeeping missions or humanitarian endeavors."[38] Such missions have been costly. According to the General Accounting Office, these missions, which it calls "Operations Other Than War" (OOTW), will cost taxpayers $4.7 billion for Fiscal Year 2000. These wars that are no longer called wars have cost $21.3 billion since 1991.[39]

These costly "operations" rob dollars from our defense budget, which should be reserved for protecting *America's* national interests. In fact, there is no constitutional authority for our military to be used for any other purpose than national defense. Besides consuming scarce defense dollars, the UN OOTW capers have greatly strained our weapons and personnel resources. In July 1999, Congressman Floyd Spence, chairman of the House Armed Services Committee, warned:

> Over the last nine months, the Joint Chiefs of Staff have concluded that the ability of the U.S. armed forces to meet the requirements of the National Military Strategy entails "moderate to high risk." This disturbing assessment was made even before Operation Allied Force commenced in the Balkans. As a "major theater war," Operation Allied Force overextended the U.S. Air Force, placing heavy demands on aerial refueling, reconnaissance and electronic warfare units.... This "high-risk" strategy is unacceptable.... Unless our nation fields the forces and provides the resources necessary to execute the National Military Strategy, we will surely inherit a more dangerous world in which America's credibility and resolve are put to the test with alarming frequency.[40]

"An Air Force that is today forty percent smaller than it was in 1990," noted Chairman Spence, "committed over 40% of its assets to Operation Allied Force, a higher percentage than was committed during Operation Desert Storm."[41] Rep. Spence quoted General Michael Hawley, who was Commander of the Air

Combat Command during Operation Allied Force. "We cannot continue to accumulate contingencies," warned General Hawley. "At some point, you've got to figure out how to get out of something." [42]

But more "hot-spots" keep cropping up. Coups, revolutions, wars, and conflicts — in Fiji, Sri Lanka, Indonesia, Congo, Sierra Leone, Sudan, Nigeria, Rwanda, Kosovo, Bosnia, Cyprus, Lebanon — guarantee opportunities galore for the global interventionists running U.S. foreign and military policy. Not surprisingly, these "opportunities" are being cited by one-world advocates as proof of the need for a standing UN Army.

On May 15, 2000 Representative James McGovern (D-Mass.) introduced a resolution calling for the establishment of a 6,000-strong UN force that could quickly be deployed to conflict situations worldwide. According to McGovern, "a lot of lives could have been saved" in East Timor if the UN had been equipped with such a force. [43] "This force will allow the Security Council, subject to a US veto, to deploy well-trained peacekeepers within 15 days of a resolution," McGovern said. [44] His proposed UN Rapid Deployment Police and Security Force would only be for short-term deployment ("a few months," he says) while more permanent coalition forces are assembled. [45]

As we will see in future chapters, this effort to create a permanent UN army is gathering steam, with all the usual CFR puppeteers orchestrating a global "consensus." Tragedy and tumult provide pretexts galore for intervention. Often these conflicts have been fomented in the first place by Communist-trained guerrillas who have strong UN support. And, as we shall see in Chapter 9, United Nations intervention frequently adds to these tragedies by helping the worst tyrants crush their opposition and solidify their power.

Chapter 3

The Secret Network of Power

We are at present working discreetly with all our might to wrest this mysterious force called sovereignty out of the clutches of the local nation states of the world. [1]
— Arnold Toynbee,
Royal Institute of International Affairs, 1931

We shall have world government, whether or not we like it. The question is only whether world government will be achieved by consent or by conquest. [2]
— James P. Warburg (CFR), testimony before the Senate
Foreign Relations Subcommittee, 1950

I know of the operations of this network [the international Round Table groups, including the Council on Foreign Relations] because I have studied it for twenty years and was permitted for two years, in the early 1960's, to examine its papers and secret records. [3]
— Professor Carroll Quigley of Georgetown University,
"mentor" to Bill Clinton, 1966

Over the next 20 to 30 years, we are going to end up with world government. It's inevitable.... [W]e have to empower the United Nations and ... we have to govern and regulate human interaction. [4]

— Jim Garrison,
President of the Gorbachev Foundation/USA, 1995

In Jonathan Swift's adventure parable, the giant Gulliver is bound by the tiny Lilliputians in a single night. Their ropes were mere threads to him, and he could have easily snapped them individually or in small numbers. Yet, once those threads had multiplied to thousands, he would be rendered completely helpless. It was thus absolutely essential, from the standpoint of his little captors, that they complete their project before he awakened. So too, with our situation today. The American giant is fast asleep, completely unaware of the growing danger. In this case, however, the Lilliputians have inside help. They have traitors inside our camp who are slipping the American Gulliver sedatives and tranquilizers.

The strands that are multiplying about the American people and gradually being forged into steel manacles are the work not of a single night but of decades. The network of individuals and organizations leading this effort for global conquest has worked patiently and assiduously to build a worldwide "movement" which, on the surface, appears to be a completely absurd mixture of incongruous and opposing parts. It is a fusion of radical socialists, feminists, pacifists, environmentalists, and communists together with international bankers, industrialists, and corporate CEOs, including some of the world's wealthiest capitalists. Yet the disparate members of this odd alliance chant the one-world mantra in unison: "Global problems require global solutions." And global solutions, they assure us, can only be provided by a world government — one with ever-increasing powers.

In this chapter, we are going to briefly examine some of the main groups and individuals in the 20th century who forged the conspiratorial drive for world government. This includes the venerated founders of the United Nations and many well-known and respected leaders in the fields of politics, business, finance, and academia.

UN: Creature of the CFR

The United Nations, we learn as schoolchildren, represents mankind's highest aspirations and ideals. According to textbook lore and steady propaganda in the major media, the UN is the world's "last best hope for peace." Following World War II, we are told, the heroic and visionary UN founders came together to save humanity from the certain annihilation that would result if a nuclear war were allowed to occur.

That is a myth, a lie. The UN, as we will show, is completely a creature of the Council on Foreign Relations (CFR), and was created for purposes entirely different from the noble ones usually cited. It was created to accumulate and usurp power so that eventually it could become a vehicle for imposing totalitarian control over our entire planet.

The plans for the United Nations were drafted in 1943 by the Informal Agenda Group (IAG), a secret steering committee set up by FDR's Secretary of State Cordell Hull. Besides Hull himself, the IAG was composed of Leo Pasvolsky, Isaiah Bowman, Sumner Welles, Norman Davis, and Morton Taylor. As Professors Lawrence Shoup and William Mintner point out in their critical study of the CFR, with the exception of Hull, all of the secret IAG participants were CFR members. "They saw Hull regularly to plan, select, and guide the labors of the [State] Department's Advisory Committee. It [the CFR] was, in effect, the coordinating agency for all the State Department postwar planning."[5]

At the UN's founding San Francisco Conference, 43 of the U.S. delegates — virtually our entire contingent — were, or would later become, members of the CFR, including: Hamilton Fish Armstrong, Ralph Bunche, John J. McCloy, Leo Pasvolsky, Nelson Rockefeller, Harold Stassen, Adlai Stevenson, Isaiah Bowman, and John Foster Dulles (the last two being founding members of the CFR).[6] Of course, the top man at that conference, serving as acting Secretary-General, was Soviet agent Alger Hiss, also a CFR member. Hiss not only ran the UN show at San Francisco and appointed many of the delegates and UN officers, but he also played a key role in drafting the UN Charter.[7]

Secret Shadow Government

From FDR's administration to the present, the CFR's pernicious influence in American society and government has grown dramatically. The CFR has become in effect the secret shadow government of the United States; its members have dominated every administration since World War II. Presidents Eisenhower, Nixon, Ford, Carter, Bush, and Clinton were members, as were hundreds of their appointments. (President George W. Bush is not a member, but his vice president, Dick Cheney, is, as are many of the top Bush cabinet picks. See Chapter 9.) No other organization even comes close to exercising this kind of political power in the United States.

Author/journalist Richard Rovere (CFR) has described the Council as "a sort of Presidium for that part of the Establishment that guides our destiny as a nation."[8] Historian Arthur M. Schlesinger Jr. (CFR) has termed it a "front organization [for] the heart of the American Establishment."[9] *Newsweek* has referred to the Pratt House* one-world coterie as "the foreign policy establishment of the U.S."[10] Professors Lawrence Shoup and William Mintner have dubbed the organization "the Imperial Brain Trust."[11] Author and hard-core radical activist Richard Barnet (CFR) wrote, as far back as 1972, that "failure to be asked to be a member of the Council has been regarded for a generation as a presumption of unsuitability for high office in the national security bureaucracy."[12]

In his 1979 memoir *With No Apologies*, Senator Barry Goldwater noted that despite the heated rhetoric and change in party label from one administration to the next, the same internationalist policies continue unabated:

> When a new President comes on board, there is a great turnover in personnel but no change in policy. Example: During the Nixon years Henry Kissinger, CFR member and Nelson Rockefeller's protégé, was in charge of foreign policy. When Jimmy Carter was elected, Kissinger was replaced by Zbigniew Brzezinski, CFR member and David Rockefeller's protégé.[13]

---

*The Harold Pratt House in New York City is the headquarters for the Council on Foreign Relations.

On October 30, 1993, the *Washington Post* printed one of the most candid (and rare) admissions against interest by the Establishment: a column by *Post* writer Richard Harwood, entitled "Ruling Class Journalists." Mr. Harwood openly conceded that the CFR's "members are the nearest thing we have to a ruling establishment in the United States." [14]

To illustrate his claim, Harwood pointed to the Clinton administration. "The president is a member," Harwood noted. "So is his secretary of state, the deputy secretary of state, all five of the undersecretaries...." [15] And on and on he went, through a litany of the CFR membership roster in the Clinton regime.

How can it be that an organization that has gained such incredible influence and power, that has virtually hijacked the American government, is so little known to the American public? The *Post's* Mr. Harwood provides the answer:

> The editorial page editor, deputy editorial page editor, executive editor, managing editor, foreign editor, national affairs editor, business and financial editor and various writers as well as Katharine Graham, the paper's principal owner, represent *The Washington Post* in the council's membership.[16]

Ditto for the other media giants: the *New York Times*, *Wall Street Journal*, *Los Angeles Times*, *Newsweek*, *Time*, *US News & World Report*, NBC, CBS, ABC, et al. CFR members Tom Brokaw, Dan Rather, Ted Koppel, Diane Sawyer, James Lehrer, Bernard Kalb, Irving R. Levine, David Brinkley, Barbara Walters, and Morton Kondracke, along with hundreds of other influential "journalists" and media executives, serve as propagandists for the Pratt House thought cartel.* In the words of Harlan Cleveland, they make sure the CFR's subversive operations stay "mostly below the surface of public attention."

Bilderberg Group: Power-mad Elitists

David Rockefeller gratefully acknowledged this indispensable "cloaking" service provided by the CFR/TC-dominated media at a meeting of the secretive Bilderberg Group (BG). Gathering at Sand, Germany in June 1991, this coterie of elite one-worlders had important global intrigues to plan and coordinate for the final decade of the millennium. Many top media Insiders were in attendance, but as in years past, they would reveal not a word of what they had heard at the confab to their readers or viewers.

Despite the Bilderbergers' elaborate security precautions, however, the word did leak out in two French publications, *Minute* and *Lectures Francaises*. [17] Hilaire du Berrier, publisher of the authoritative, Monte Carlo-based *HduB Reports*, was the first to inform Americans of goings-on at the BG conference at Sand. Du Berrier, who has been closely following and chronicling the activities of the New World Order operatives for more than four decades, reported on the conference in his *HduB Reports* for September 1991. [18] His Bilderberg revelations then reached a much larger audience in *The New American* magazine, where he is a contributor. [19]

What did David Rockefeller, then the chairman emeritus of the American Establishment, have to say to the assembled aristocracy of the U.S. media? An amazing, stunning mouthful, that's what. We'll let you judge for yourself. This is part of Rockefeller's greeting to his Bilderberg boon companions:

> We are grateful to the *Washington Post*, the *New York Times*, *Time* magazine, and other great publications whose directors have attended our meetings and respected their promises of discretion for almost forty years. It would have been impossible for us to develop our plan for the world if we had been subject to the bright

---

*The CFR's *2000 Annual Report* states that 386 of its members are "Journalists, Correspondents, and Communications Executives." As in past *Annual Reports*, it also notes, under the heading, "Rules, Guidelines, and Practices": "Full freedom of expression is encouraged at Council meetings. Participants are assured that they may speak openly, as it is the tradition of the Council that others will not attribute or characterize their statements in public media or forums or knowingly transmit them to persons who will. All participants are expected to honor that commitment." This is the Pratt House equivalent of *Omerta*, the Mafia "oath of silence."

lights of publicity during these years. But the world is now more sophisticated and prepared to march towards a world government which will never again know war but only peace and prosperity for the whole of humanity. The supranational sovereignty of an intellectual elite and world bankers is surely preferable to the national autodetermination practiced in the past centuries. It is also our duty to inform the press of our convictions as to the historic future of the century. [20]

Incredible, no? Well, what else would you expect from a cabal of power-mad elitists who consider the whole world to be their own private oyster? These "enlightened ones," these illuminati, have been busily redesigning, reshaping, and "transforming" the world according to their own desires throughout the past century. They intend to be the planetary overlords in the new world order. As Mr. Rockefeller said, it would have been "impossible" for them to have come so far with their super-subversive plot except that their co-conspirators in the media kept "the bright lights of publicity" off their dark schemes.

The *Post's* Richard Harwood noted concerning the CFR media oligarchy: "They do not merely analyze and interpret foreign policy for the United States; *they help make it.*" [21] (Emphasis added.) He might also have said that they smother, suppress, censor, quash, and kill much of the real news (and grossly distort the rest) in order to help make "policy." While endlessly, piously prattling about their sacred role as "watchdogs," and "the public's right to know," these criminal hypocrites have been engaged in the biggest cover-up in history.

How did the CFR claque come to acquire so much power? In this compressed study, we can only briefly attempt to answer that question.*

CFR Historian Speaks Out
One of the most informative and penetrating revelations concerning the CFR power network came in 1966 with publication of

Tragedy and Hope: A History of the World in Our Time by Professor Carroll Quigley of Georgetown University. A celebrated historian who was sympathetic to the CFR's globalist agenda, Quigley wrote:

> I know of the operations of this network [the international Round Table groups, including the Council on Foreign Relations] because I have studied it for twenty years and was permitted for two years, in the early 1960's, to examine its papers and secret records. I have no aversion to it or to most of its aims and have, for much of my life, been close to it and to many of its instruments.... In general, my chief difference of opinion is that it wishes to remain unknown. [22]

And what are the "aims" of this network? According to Dr. Quigley: "[N]othing less than to create a world system of financial control in private hands able to dominate the political system of each country and the economy of the world as a whole." [23]

The network to which Quigley referred had provided the "brain trust" and the financial impetus behind the drive for the League of Nations, the effort Mr. Cleveland referred to as the "First Try" at world order. Leading that drive for the network was Col. Edward Mandell House, the key advisor and "alter ego" of President Woodrow Wilson. When the League of Nations was thwarted by the U.S. Senate, Col. House and his colleagues determined to continue their struggle by other means. House was part of a cabal called "The Inquiry," a group of 100 "forward-looking" social engineers who created the Versailles Peace Treaty at the close of World War I. [24] This group formed the American nucleus

---

*The development of this conspiratorial power network has been extensively examined in such studies as: *The Shadows of Power: The Council on Foreign Relations and The American Decline* by James Perloff (Western Islands, 1988); *Global Tyranny ... Step By Step* by William F. Jasper (Western Islands, 1992); *None Dare Call It Conspiracy* by Gary Allen (Concord Press, 1971); *The Insiders,* 4th Edition, by John F. McManus (The John Birch Society, 1995); *The Wise Men* by Walter Isaacson and Evan Thomas (Simon & Schuster, 1986); among others.

of what was to become the Council on Foreign Relations. The Inquiry's British counterparts created a companion organization — the Royal Institute of International Affairs (RIIA). [25]

These groups were the product of an earlier secret society formed in February 1891 by Cecil Rhodes, the legendary "diamond king" and "colossus" of Africa, with British journalist William Stead. Rhodes, although famous as "the richest man in the world," was an ardent disciple of socialist Professor John Ruskin, under whom he had studied at Oxford. Dr. Quigley explains: "In this secret society Rhodes was to be leader; Stead, Brett (Lord Esher), and Milner were to form an executive committee; Arthur (Lord) Balfour, (Sir) Harry Johnston, Lord Rothschild, Albert (Lord) Grey, and others were listed as potential members of a 'Circle of Initiates'; while there was to be an outer circle known as the 'Association of Helpers' (later organized by Milner as the Round Table organization).... Thus the central part of the secret society was established by March 1891." [26]

The plan developed by Rhodes and his small circle of co-conspirators was one in which "a world system of financial control in private hands" would be used to bring about world government.

"This system," notes Quigley, "was to be controlled in a feudalist fashion by the central banks of the world acting in concert, by secret agreements arrived at in frequent private meetings and conferences." [27] Professor Quigley explained further:

> The apex of the system was the Bank for International Settlements in Basle, Switzerland, a private bank owned and controlled by the worlds' central banks which were themselves private corporations. Each central bank, in the hands of men like Montagu Norman of the Bank of England, Benjamin Strong of the New York Federal Reserve Bank, Charles Rist of the Bank of France, and Hjalmar Schacht of the Reichsbank, sought to dominate its government by its ability to control Treasury loans, to manipulate foreign exchanges, to influence the level of economic activity in the country, and to influence cooperative politicians by subsequent economic rewards in the business world. [28]

In January 1924, Reginald McKenna, who was then chairman of the board of the Midland Bank (and had been Britain's Chancellor of the Exchequer in 1915-16), confirmed that the British system was completely dominated by the conspiratorial monied aristocracy. "I am afraid the ordinary citizen will not like to be told that the banks can, and do, create money," said McKenna. "And they who control the credit of the nation direct the policy of Governments and hold in the hollow of their hands the destiny of the people." [29]

On November 11, 1927, the *Wall Street Journal* called Montagu Norman, governor of the Bank of England, "the currency dictator of Europe." Norman, a strange, furtive intriguer given to wearing disguises, using assumed names, and incessantly flitting about the world on mysterious missions, confirmed the *Journal*'s assertion before the Macmillan Committee on March 26, 1930. [30]

A Higher Power

But as Professor Quigley points out, Norman answered to powers who stood in the shadows. "It must not be felt that these heads of the world's chief central banks were themselves substantive powers in world finance," writes Quigley. "They were not. Rather, they were the technicians and agents of the dominant investment bankers of their own countries, who had raised them up and were perfectly capable of throwing them down." [31] Those bankers to whom Quigley refers were members of the Rhodes-Milner network. Their immense power and influence were exercised through the Royal Institute of International Affairs, the CFR, and their many other levers of control in the government, the major political parties, academe, business, and the media.

As Rhodes biographer Sarah Millin put it: "The government of the world was Rhodes' simple desire." [32] The Rhodes Scholarships, like the Round Table groups, were integral to this global scheme. Part of Rhodes' plan was to bring bright, ambitious young men to Oxford University for indoctrination and recruitment into his grand conspiracy. Co-conspirator William Stead said that Rhodes' own words were that after 30 years there would be "between two and three thousand men [mathematically selected] in the prime of life scattered all over the world, each one of whom will have had impressed upon his mind in the most susceptible period of his life the dream of the Founder [Rhodes]." [33]

What were the qualities looked for in these specially selected "scholars"? According to Rhodes himself: "smugness, brutality, unctuous rectitude, and tact." [34] Which pluperfectly described the ruthless Cecil Rhodes. And just as aptly fit his most famous Rhodes Scholar and one-world acolyte: Bill Clinton. [35]*

Over the years, Round Table-style groups parallel to the CFR have been established in France, Germany, Italy, Belgium, Norway, Sweden, India, Canada, Japan and dozens of other countries. Rhodes' disciples have thus built a global network of unprecedented power, capable of influencing, manipulating, sabotaging, and controlling political and economic events on a scale previously unimaginable.

"When the influence which the [Royal] Institute wields is combined with that controlled by the Milner Group in other fields — in education, in administration, in newspapers and periodicals — a really terrifying picture begins to emerge," wrote Quigley in *The Anglo-American Establishment*,[36] which was published posthumously in 1981. He explained:

> The picture is terrifying because such power, whatever the goals
> at which it may be directed, is too much to be entrusted safely to
> any group.... No country that values its safety should allow what

---

*Other American "Rhodies" who have been boosted to pinnacles of power in the fields of politics, business, media, and academia include Harlan Cleveland, George Stephanopolous, Strobe Talbott, Ira Magaziner, Robert Reich, Nicholas Katzenbach, Lloyd Cutler, Erwin Canham, Dean Rusk, Richard N. Gardner, James Hester, Representative Carl Albert, Senator J. William Fulbright, Senator Richard Lugar, Senator Bill Bradley, Senator David L. Boren, Justice Byron White, Justice David Souter, Hedley Donovan, Howard K. Smith, Walt Rostow, Stringfellow Barr, General Bernard Rogers, Admiral Stansfield Turner, James Woolsey, and Joseph Nye.

the Milner Group accomplished in Britain — that is, that a small number of men should be able to wield such power in administration and politics, should be given almost complete control over the publication of the documents relating to their actions, should be able to exercise such influence over the avenues of information that create public opinion, and should be able to monopolize so completely the writing and the teaching of the history of their own period. [37]

Admiral Chester Ward, who was himself a member of the CFR for 16 years, saw that "terrifying picture" up close. Admiral Ward, who resigned in disgust, was not exaggerating when he charged that the CFR agenda is to promote "disarmament and submergence of U.S. sovereignty and national independence into an all-powerful one-world government." [38] The leadership of the group, he wrote, "is composed of the one-world-global-government ideologists — more respectfully referred to as the organized internationalists." Moreover, he charged, the "lust to surrender the sovereignty and independence of the United States is pervasive throughout most of the membership.... The majority visualize the utopian submergence of the United States as a subsidiary administrative unit of a global government...." [39]

Admiral Ward's shocking charge is more than substantiated by innumerable writings, speeches and actions of CFR members both in and out of government. Even more astounding than this incredible treachery by American leaders to subvert and destroy our liberty is the extensive record of treason showing that these same one-world advocates have been pursuing their evil purpose in concert with the most brutal and murderous totalitarian dictators in the history of our planet. That is the subject of our next chapter.

Chapter 4

"Capitalists" and the Communist Dimension

[T]he American Communists worked energetically and tirelessly to lay the foundations for the United Nations which we were sure would come into existence. [1]
— Earl Browder, General Secretary of the Communist Party USA

This task is the task of the world proletarian revolution, the task of the creation of the world Soviet republic. [2]
— V.I. Lenin,
1920 Congress of the Communist International

[A] World Union of Soviet Socialist Republics uniting the whole of mankind under the hegemony of the international proletariat organized as a state. [3]
— "Program of the Communist International," 1928

The ultimate object of the parties of the Socialist International is nothing less than world government. As a first step towards it, they seek to strengthen the United Nations.... [4]
— Declaration of the Socialist International
1962 Conference, Oslo, Norway

[T]he conflict between the two great superpowers ... will be replaced by the USDR (a union of socialist democratic republics). This will be a penultimate stage of progress toward a truly global world federal union...." [5]
— Professor Mortimer Adler, socialist, author, 1991

We saw in the last chapter that, like the Communists (see above quotes), the American one-world Insiders, operating primarily through their CFR front, "worked energetically and tirelessly to lay the foundations for the United Nations." [6] We saw also that from start to finish the UN has been wholly a CFR-conceived and driven operation. This is a fact that the historical record overwhelmingly and indisputably proves.* The historical record also proves with super-abundant documentation that these globalist architects intended that the United Nations and its related international institutions would be gradually enlarged and strengthened until, ultimately, it would subsume all nations under an all-powerful, one-world government. [7]

It is also beyond dispute that the leaders of the world Communist conspiracy were solidly behind the formation of the UN and have supported every effort to enlarge, strengthen, and empower it over the past half century. This is plainly evident from the official speeches, writings, and actions of top Soviet leaders and Communist leaders worldwide, as well as from official documents of the Communist Party of the Soviet Union (CPSU). We have also very extensive testimony to this effect from numerous top Soviet defectors and former American Communist officials.

That the Communists would support an institution for world government is no mystery; the essence and substance of the whole Communist program has been the pursuit of that very object. As long ago as 1915, before the Bolshevik Revolution, Vladimir Lenin himself proposed a "United States of the World." [9] Soviet dictator and mass murderer Joseph Stalin, as far back as 1922, stated: "Let us hope that by forming our confederate republic we shall be creating a reliable bulwark against international capitalism and that the new confederate state will

---

*Robert W. Lee writes in his 1981 exposé, *The United Nations Conspiracy*, "When the San Francisco Conference convened on April 25 of that year [1945] to finalize and approve the UN Charter, more than forty members of the United States delegation had been, were, or would later become members of the CFR." [8] Mr. Lee lists the CFR founding fathers of the UN in Appendix C to his book. (Or see: www.getusout.org.)

be another step towards the amalgamation of the toilers of the whole world into a single World Socialist Soviet Republic." [10]*

Earl Browder, general secretary of the CPUSA, stated in his book *Victory and After* that "the American Communists worked energetically and tirelessly to lay the foundations for the United Nations which we were sure would come into existence." [11] Moreover, this leader of the American Reds declared:

> It can be said, without exaggeration, that ever closer relations between our nation and the Soviet Union are an unconditional requirement for the United Nations as a world coalition....
>
> The United Nations is the instrument for victory. Victory is required for the survival of our nation. The Soviet Union is an essential part of the United Nations. Mutual confidence between our country and the Soviet Union and joint work in the leadership of the United Nations are absolutely necessary. [12]

Clearly, Communist leaders have always advocated, supported, and promoted the goal of world government generally, and the United Nations particularly, in word and deed. Dr. Bella Dodd, a former top CPUSA official, told of her role in the Communist campaign for the UN: "When the Yalta conference had ended, the Communists prepared to support the United Nations Charter which was to be adopted at the San Francisco conference to be held in May and June, 1945. For this I organ-

---

*In his 1932 book *Toward Soviet America*, William Z. Foster, national chairman of the Communist Party USA (CPUSA), wrote: "The American Soviet government will join with the other Soviet governments in a world Soviet Union.... A Communist world will be a unified, organized world. The economic system will be one great organization, based upon the principle of planning now dawning in the U.S.S.R. The American Soviet government will be an important section in this world organization." [13]

In 1936, the official program of the Communist International proclaimed: "Dictatorship can be established only by a victory of socialism in different countries or groups of countries, after which the proletariat republics would unite on federal lines with those already in existence, and this system of federal unions would expand ... at length forming the World Union of Socialist Soviet Republics." [14]

ized a corps of speakers and we took to the street corners and held open-air meetings in the millinery and clothing sections of New York where thousands of people congregate at the lunch hour. We spoke of the need for world unity and in support of the Yalta decisions." [15]

Shortly after the founding of the UN, in March of 1946, Stalin declared: "I attribute great importance to U.N.O. [United Nations Organization, as it was then commonly called] since it is a serious instrument for preservation of peace and international security." [16] On one level, Stalin's expressed desire for "peace" and "security" is an obviously disingenuous propaganda ploy devoid of any meaning, in the sense that most people ascribe to those words. However, in the Communist sense, where "peace" and "security" are defined as an absence of resistance to Communism, Stalin's endorsement of the UN is perfectly understandable. He knew that the UN's very nature and structure would contribute to Communist advantage, since his agents had helped design it. And he knew that the UN was permeated with Communist agents who would assure that it remained a Communist instrument.

For these same reasons, *The Constitution of the Communist Party of the United States of America* (1957 version) states that "the true national interest of our country and the cause of peace and progress require the solidarity of all freedom-loving peoples, peaceful coexistence of all nations, and the strengthening of the United Nations as a universal instrument of peace." [17]

Reds Among the Founders

Of course, the Communists were not only working *outside* the UN to stir up support for the new global organization, they were also running things on the *inside* — in concert with their like-minded, one-world CFR cohorts. Keep in mind that it was Soviet agent Alger Hiss (CFR), acting director of the State Department's Office of Special Political Affairs, who served as executive secretary of the critically important 1944 Dumbarton Oaks Conference, where the UN Charter was drafted. [18] In that "noble" endeavor, Stalin's secret agent Hiss and Stalin's open agent V. M. Molotov were the two prime players. The Communists couldn't lose: "our guy" and "their guy" were both "Stalin's guys," two hands on the same hairy body.

But it was much worse than that; Hiss was far from the only Communist agent in (not under) the UN bed. The July 1944 Bretton Woods Conference was as important for the about-to-be-born UN as was the Dumbarton Oaks Conference. Bretton Woods established the post-World War II global economic policies and architecture, including the International Monetary Fund (IMF) and World Bank group of institutions. Bretton Woods was planned and initiated by the Economic and Finance Group of the Council on Foreign Relations. The leader of the conference and the head of the U.S. delegation was Assistant Secretary of the Treasury Harry Dexter White, a secret member of a Soviet espionage ring. [19] Assisting White as technical secretary of the conference was another Soviet agent at the Treasury Department, Virginius Frank Coe.

In his important book on the UN, *The Fearful Master*, author G. Edward Griffin wrote:

> In 1950 the State Department issued a document entitled *Postwar Foreign Policy Preparation, 1939-45*.... This and similar official records reveal that the following men were key government figures in UN planning within the U.S. State Department and Treasury Department: Alger Hiss, Harry Dexter White, Virginius Frank Coe, Dean Acheson, Noel Field, Lawrence Duggan, Henry Julian Wadleigh, John Carter Vincent, David Weintraub, Nathan Gregory Silvermaster, Harold Glasser, Victor Perlo, Irving Kaplan, Solomon Adler, Abraham George Silverman, William L. Ullman and William H. Taylor. With the single exception of Dean Acheson, *all of these men have since been identified in sworn testimony as secret Communist agents!* [20] [Emphasis in original.]

UN Charter: A Marxist-Leninist Blueprint
With the pedigrees of these designers in mind, it should come as

no surprise that the great UN Charter, so reverentially extolled by all internationalists, is a purely Marxist-Leninist blueprint. But you needn't take our word for it; that's the assessment of former top Communist Party member Joseph Z. Kornfeder. In his sworn testimony before Congress in 1955, 10 years after the founding of the UN, Mr. Kornfeder stated:

> I need not be a member of the United Nations Secretariat to know that the UN "blueprint" is a Communist one. I was at the Moscow headquarters of the world Communist party for nearly three years and was acquainted with most of the top leaders.... I went to their colleges; I learned their pattern of operations, and if I see that pattern in effect anywhere, I can recognize it....
>
> From the point of view of its master designers meeting at Dumbarton Oaks and Bretton Woods, and which included such masterful agents as Alger Hiss, Harry Dexter White, Lauchlin Currie, and others, the UN was, and is, *not* a failure. They and the Kremlin masterminds behind them never intended the UN as a peace-keeping organization. What they had in mind was a fancy and colossal Trojan horse.... Its [the UN's] internal setup, Communist designed, is a pattern for sociological conquest; a pattern aimed to serve the purpose of Communist penetration of the West. It is ingenious and deceptive. [21]

Kornfeder's evaluation of the UN is backed up by no less an authority than former UN Secretary-General U Thant. Mr. Thant was a Marxist, winner of the Soviet Union's Lenin Peace Prize. "Lenin was a man with a mind of great clarity and incisiveness," Thant said, "and his ideas have had a profound influence on the course of contemporary history." The Burmese Marxist continued: "[Lenin's] ideals of peace and peaceful coexistence among states have won widespread international acceptance and they are in line with the aims of the U.N. Charter." [22]

There you have it, and from an unimpeachable source: The aims of the UN Charter are "in line" with the "ideals of peace" of Lenin, the Communist dictator and butcher. On this one point, at least, we can find no cause for disagreement with Mr. Thant. Of course, it is of utmost importance that one keep in mind that "peace," in Marxist-Leninist terms, does not mean an absence of war, but an absence of resistance to Communism.

Serving Red Imperialism

The Kremlin's agents wasted no time in using the newly created UN machinery to advance global Communist imperialism. Innumerable examples have been documented of UN agencies providing concrete, material aid to Communist regimes and revolutionary efforts, and, conversely, opposing, thwarting, and destroying non-Communist and anti-Communist governments and movements. [23]

A condensed survey of the United Nations Relief and Rehabilitation Administration (UNRRA), which was established by the CFR Insiders in our government even *before* the founding of the UN, provides a tragic look at what was to follow. Under the direction of Herbert H. Lehman (CFR), the UNRRA staff was turned into an international cabal of Communists from various countries who applied the billions of dollars of UNRRA's "humanitarian aid" (taken from U.S. taxpayers) to Communist revolutionary purposes.

The U.S. Ambassador to Poland, Arthur Bliss Lane, told what he had witnessed of UNRRA's pro-Communist actions at the end of World War II. "Over my personal protest," said Ambassador Lane, "Lehman had appointed as director of the first UNRRA mission to Poland the Soviet member of the UNRRA council, Mr. Menshikov, whose first duty would be ... distribution of UNRRA supplies." As a result, supplies could be obtained "only by those persons holding a specified type of ration card issued solely to government employees or to members of the Workers and Socialist parties." [24] Which greatly assisted the Red takeover of Poland.

Likewise, Colonel Jan Bukar, in his testimony before Congress, described a similar experience in Czechoslovakia: "In the distribution of the goods through UNRRA, the people who got any portion of the goods had to be enrolled as members of the Communist Party ... [and] I want again to state that through UNRRA the Communist Party gained many members."[25]

"With a total disregard of our national interests," wrote author and investigative reporter Eugene W. Castle, "UNRRA money was unreservedly given to the Communist-ruled nations behind the Iron Curtain. It fed discontented peoples and strengthened the Red grip on their governments."[26]

In China, millions of dollars in UNRRA funds and supplies were going to Communist Madame Sun Yat-sen and Mao Tse-tung for their ultimate triumph over General Chiang Kai-shek.[27] This same pattern would appear again and again over the following decades through such UN institutions as UNICEF, UNESCO, WHO, UNHCR, FAO, UNFPA, IMF, the World Bank, etc.

Red Trojan Horse

Millions of lives could have been saved and untold misery, murder, terror, and destruction averted, if U.S. officials had been forced by an informed American public to heed the warnings of credible witnesses and an incredible trail of evidence. The tragic history that has unfolded since the testimonies of Dr. Bella Dodd, Col. Bukar, Mr. Kornfeder, and others has more than vindicated their most frightening alarms. The UN has indeed proven to be a gigantic and deadly Trojan horse. The following are but a few of the many advantages that the Communists expected to realize from the creation of the UN:

- Economic assistance through the vast array of UN agencies.
- Enormous potential for expansion of espionage, subversion, and terrorism through the diplomatic immunity offered UN officials.
- Use of the UN podium for Communist propaganda purposes.
- Use of UN diplomatic and propaganda machinery to attack and undermine anti-Communist countries and to support pro-Communist regimes and organizations.

- Transfer of tremendous sums of money from the American producers to corrupt, collectivist projects and potentates throughout the world.
- Steady erosion of U.S. sovereignty through a myriad of UN treaties and agreements.
- Depletion and weakening of U.S. military resources in UN operations worldwide.
- Gradual subordination of U.S. military command to international authority (UN, NATO, SEATO, CENTO, OAS, etc.).

Unfortunately, the UN has delivered for the Reds beyond their wildest dreams. In the field of espionage and subversion alone, it has been a huge bonanza. During U.S. Senate hearings in 1952, Senator James O. Eastland stated:

> I am appalled at the extensive evidence indicating that there is today in the United Nations among the American employees there the greatest concentration of Communists that this committee has ever encountered.... [A]lmost all of these people have in the past been employees of the United States Government in high and sensitive positions. [28]*

By the mid 1960s, frustrated Americans were angrily (and accurately) charging that the United Nations "was conceived by Communists, founded by Communists, has always been controlled by Communists, and has been used increasingly — and ever more brazenly — to carry out Communist purposes."

---

*Over the ensuing years, numerous investigations and reports have exposed the subversion, terrorism, and espionage activities of many foreign nationals operating through the UN as well, especially those from Russia, China, Cuba, and the Soviet bloc states. "Oh, but that is ancient history and no longer a concern, now that the Cold War is over," warble the UN's defenders. Not true; the UN continued to be a nest of spies. On October 24, 1991, the *Wall Street Journal's* deputy features editor Amity Shlaes (CFR) commented on evidence indicating that the UN Secretariat headquartered in New York City was still under the domination of old-line Communists, noting that following the supposed collapse of the Soviet Union, "Westerners who worked at the U.N. ... found themselves surrounded by what many have called a communist mafia." [29]

Who Is Really in Charge?

However, this characterization of the UN was not *completely* accurate. As we have demonstrated in bare outline, Communists played key, central roles at all levels in planning, promoting, establishing, and manning the UN, and they have used it to great effect for their evil objectives ever since. Nevertheless, it is far too simplistic to view the UN and its operations purely as a "Communist plot."

As our preceding chapters demonstrate, there was another force at work on this grandiose and malevolent project as well — represented by the "one-world-global-government ideologists" described by Admiral Ward. Many of these individuals obviously were not Communists; in fact they were arch-capitalists, titans of Wall Street, with names like Rockefeller, Morgan, Carnegie, Lamont, Warburg, and Schiff. And yet, they did indeed work hand in hand with the masters of the Kremlin to establish a system that they intended would supplant our own constitutional system of government and grow into a global leviathan state. And their successors have continued this subversive cooperation with both overt Communist leaders (as in China) and "ex-Communist" leaders (as in Russia), who now claim to be "democratic reformers."

Professor Carroll Quigley, the Insider historian we met in the previous chapter, conceded that anti-Communists who had pointed to this strange and diabolic Communist-capitalist symbiosis were not hallucinating:

> There does exist, and has existed for a generation, an international Anglophile network which operates, to some extent, in the way the radical Right believes the Communists act. In fact, this network, which we may identify as the Round Table Groups, has no aversion to cooperating with the Communists, or any other groups, and frequently does so. [30]

"It was this group of people," said Quigley, "whose wealth and influence ... provided much of the framework of influence which the Communist sympathizers and fellow travelers took over in the United States in the 1930s. It must be recognized that *the power that these energetic Left-wingers exercised was never their own power or Communist power* but was ultimately the power of the international financial coterie...."[31] (Emphasis added.) Regarding that secretive coterie, he described the "relationship between the financial circles of London and those of the eastern United States which reflects one of the most powerful influences in twentieth-century American and world history. The two ends of this English-speaking axis have sometimes been called, perhaps facetiously, the English and American Establishments. There is, however, a considerable degree of truth behind the joke, a truth which reflects a very real power structure. It is this power structure which the Radical Right in the United States has been attacking for years in the belief that they are attacking the Communists."[32]

Congressional Investigations

The treasonous workings of this elite were partially revealed, the professor noted, by congressional investigators in the 1950s who, "following backward to their source the threads which led from admitted Communists like Whittaker Chambers, through Alger Hiss and the Carnegie Endowment to Thomas Lamont and the Morgan Bank, fell into the whole complicated network of the interlocking tax-exempt foundations."[33]

"It soon became clear," Quigley observed, "that people of immense wealth would be unhappy if the investigation went too far and that the 'most respected' newspapers in the country, closely allied with these men of wealth, would not get excited enough about any revelations to make the publicity worth while...."[34] Here the professor sins by gross understatement and distortion. These "people of immense wealth" and their "closely allied" media did indeed get "excited," so much so that they went to incredible lengths to sabotage and stop the investigation, smear its principal players, and smother the facts it had uncovered.

Thus, it is not surprising that the Reece Committee, established by Congress in 1953 to investigate the tax-exempt foundations, fell far short of fully exposing the mounting peril. Nevertheless, the committee's report did sound a serious alarm, warning that the major foundations (Carnegie, Ford, Rockefeller) and interlocking organizations like the CFR "have exercised a strong effect upon our foreign policy and upon public education in things international." [35]

The committee stated: "The net result of these combined efforts has been to promote 'internationalism' in a particular sense — a form directed toward 'world government' and derogation of American 'nationalism.'" [36]

The Reece Committee also charged that these foundations (which were invariably directed by CFR members) "have actively supported attacks upon our social and government system and financed the promotion of socialism and collectivist ideas." [37] It declared, moreover, that the CFR had become "in essence an agency of the United States Government" and that its "productions [books, periodicals, study guides, reports, etc.] are not objective but are directed overwhelmingly at promoting the globalist concept." [38]

A far more important revelation disclosed by the committee's chief investigator never made it into congressional testimony or the committee's published report. Investigator Norman Dodd recounted that during his visit to the Ford Foundation, the institution's president, Rowan Gaither (CFR), unexpectedly admitted that he and his colleagues were operating under directives "to the effect that we should make every effort to so alter life in the United States as to make possible a comfortable merger with the Soviet Union." [39] This of course fit perfectly with the pattern that Dodd and the committee members had observed in the subversive projects and organizations funded by the foundation, but the admission flabbergasted them nonetheless.

Common Ground: Power

At this point a great many readers undoubtedly are scratching their heads in bewilderment. "I don't get it," they say. "Why would wealthy capitalists conspire with Communists and promote Communism? Don't they stand to lose the most if Communism were to triumph?"

If you are among the bewildered head scratchers, don't feel bad. The confusion is understandable; the idea of wealthy capitalists scheming with bloody Bolsheviks does challenge some long-accepted and basic assumptions and definitions most of us hold concerning socio-economic-political relationships and the way the world works. We agree that all capitalists *should* oppose collectivism in all its forms (i.e., communism, socialism, fascism), but it is a fact that many do not. Many "capitalists," while paying lip service to "free enterprise" and "market economics," actually abhor the competition of the marketplace. They would much rather use government force (laws and regulations) to beat their competition than try to produce better widgets more efficiently and constantly have to come up with improvements, innovations, and better management, marketing, and production.

They realize that communism, socialism, and fascism are never the "share the wealth" schemes they pretend to be; they are inevitably and invariably "control the wealth" schemes, in which an elite oligarchy employs political power (backed up by military and police force) to control all the wealth. They realize that step one in any "share the wealth" program is to "collect the wealth" (or "collectivization," as the Communists call it). And they realize that once "step one" is completed no collectivist regime ever proceeds to "step two": share the wealth. The collectivized wealth remains in the hands of the ruling elite and their managerial class underlings (the privileged *nomenklatura* in the Soviet Union) while the toiling masses remain mired in grinding poverty, unable to escape by any amount of honest effort.

It is a well documented fact that some of the best-known "malefactors of great wealth" in this past century (and currently) have indeed conspired and collaborated with the most murderous dictators in history (Lenin, Stalin, Tito, Mao, Ceausescu, et al.) in the quest to establish their criminal scheme of totalitarian world government. [40]

The vast majority of these wealthy Insiders were not (and are not) themselves Communists — although some definitely were (and are). Armand Hammer (CFR), Frederick Vanderbilt Field (CFR), and Corliss Lamont, for instance, were all immensely rich Communists. The non-Communist Insiders see the Communists (and their various Marxist brethren) as indispensable "partners" in the pursuit of "world order." The Communists are brutally blunt instruments, but adequately efficient, for destroying the old order and constructing the new. The Insiders, of course, periodically condemn their Communist partners and have frequently initiated massive military and intelligence operations ostensibly to oppose Communism. In fact, they repeatedly sold the United Nations and many of its programs to the American public as a means of opposing and/or taming the Communist threat.

However, the one-world Insiders were faced with a dilemma: how to modify the image of the brutal Communist menace to enable an eventual merger of the West with the U.S.S.R. without simultaneously undermining the impetus for collective global security and world government that the Communist threat provides.

"If the communist dynamic were greatly abated," wrote Professor Bloomfield in the previously mentioned study (see Chapter 2), "the West might well lose whatever incentive it has for world government.... [I]f there were no communist menace, would anyone be worrying about the need for such a revolution in international political arrangements?" [41] According to Bloomfield, "if the communists would agree, the West would favor a world effectively controlled by the United Nations." [42] Thus the concealed objective of U.S. policy, as Bloomfield acknowledged, was not to defeat Communism, but rather "to transform and tame the forces of communism ... to the point where the present international system might be radically reshaped." [43]

Perhaps the reader has already perceived that since the rise of Mikhail Gorbachev and "perestroika," and the subsequent "collapse" of Communism, we have been traveling the CFR-laid course "to transform and tame communism." And the world is indeed being "radically reshaped." A very important part of that reshaping process involves finding, or rather, manufacturing, credible menaces to substitute for Communism as "incentives for world government." In the following chapters, we will witness — again and again — the Insider-Communist conspiracy at work synthesizing these substitute menaces, and, in Bloomfield's words, "a series of sudden, nasty, and traumatic shocks"[44] to bring about "the order" they desire. We will also see the incredible global activist networks they have established and the elaborate processes they have set up to propagandize and organize on behalf of their criminal "new world order."

Part II
Stealth Strategies for Building the Superstate

Chapter 5

Orchestrating the Globalist Concert

More and more, NGOs [Non-Governmental Organizations] are helping to set public policy agendas.... It is this movement ... that has such significance for governance.... What is generally proposed is the initial setting up of an assembly of parliamentarians ... and the subsequent establishment of a world assembly through direct election by the people. [1]
— Commission on Global Governance, *Our Global Neighborhood*, 1995

National governments are not simply losing autonomy in a globalizing economy. They are sharing powers — including political, social, and security roles at the core of sovereignty — with businesses, with international organizations, and with a multitude of citizen groups, known as nongovernmental organizations (NGOs).... Increasingly, NGOs are able to push around even the largest governments. [2]
— Jessica T. Mathews (CFR, TC), *Foreign Affairs*, January/February, 1997

Establishing the dialogue with NGOs that have issues relevant to your company is a bottom line issue for Wall Street. [3]
— Robert Hormats (CFR Director), vice-chairman, Goldman Sachs

You will become the new superpower.
— Kofi Annan, UN Secretary-General, addressing the NGO Millennium Forum, May 2000 [4]

*Especially significant, of course, is the development of an
NGO network worldwide and its increasing role in the development of a culture of democracy throughout the world....
Civil society, in order to be an effective partner with government and business in providing global governance in the 21st
century, must develop a clear vision of basic values and a better future.* [5]

— Steven C. Rockefeller, Chairman of the Earth Charter
Drafting Committee and Chairman of the Rockefeller
Brothers Fund, addressing the UN Millennium Forum,
May 2000

During World War II, a Soviet spy network in Nazi-occupied
Europe kept Stalin supplied with first-rate intelligence on
German military plans and political developments. It came to be
known as the Red Orchestra (Rote Kapelle). The network sent its
information to its Moscow superiors via secret radio transmitters
that operated only for short bursts and moved constantly to
avoid detection by the Gestapo. Nazi intelligence referred to the
transmitters as "music boxes" and assigned the names of musi-
cal instruments to the distinctive, but elusive, operators.

The elaborate Red Orchestra espionage operation was set up
several years before the start of the war and involved agents who
were military personnel, Nazi officials, clerks, janitors, and
housewives, as well as "businessmen" in a network of corporations (both real and dummy companies) throughout Europe. A
similar Red Orchestra was established in the United States, and,
as noted in previous chapters, its agents succeeded in penetrating to the highest levels of the federal government. A few top
agents were exposed in high-profile cases — Alger Hiss, Harry
Dexter White, Victor Perlo, the Rosenbergs — but, according to
both Communist defectors and U.S. intelligence officials, dozens
of Red cells involving hundreds of high-level Soviet agents were
never exposed.* Many of these agents were not engaged merely
in the lower level aspects of espionage such as stealing state
secrets and reporting on military plans and weapons develop-

ment. They were performing a more critical role for the Kremlin as "agents of influence": misinforming and misdirecting America's leaders and actually influencing and formulating U.S. policies concerning the most sensitive areas of our national security.

The Art of War by Sun Tzu has long served as a primary textbook for Soviet military and intelligence strategists. Written over 2,000 years ago, it is one of the most famous studies of strategy ever written. The Communists have especially focused on Sun Tzu's lessons on strategic deception and the supreme importance of espionage and intelligence. They are completely familiar with what Sun Tzu described as the "five sorts of spies": Native spies; internal spies; double spies; doomed spies; and surviving spies. "Native spies are those from the enemy country's people whom we employ," explained Sun Tzu. "Internal spies are enemy officials whom we employ. Double spies are enemy spies whom we employ. Doomed spies are those of our own spies who are deliberately given false information and told to report it to the enemy. Surviving spies are those who return from the enemy camp to report information." [6]

"When all these five types of spies are at work and their operations are clandestine, it is called the 'divine manipulation of threads' and is the treasure of a sovereign," [7] continued China's master strategist. The Communists adapted and greatly expanded on the ancient sage's doctrines, creating a global apparatus

---

*On February 14 and 15, 1957, former Soviet NKVD agent Alexander Orlov testified before the Senate Internal Security Subcommittee ("Scope of Soviet Activity In The United States," Part 51). Orlov claimed knowledge of 38 espionage rings in the U.S., with only two exposed as a result of the revelations of Whittaker Chambers and Elizabeth Bentley. Decades later, in the 1990s, evidence was still seeping out to confirm those charges of penetration of the U.S., including some of our most sensitive institutions and high-level positions. The recently released "Venona intercepts" — decoded secret Soviet transmissions collected in the 1940s — verified that Harry Hopkins, top adviser to President Franklin Roosevelt, was a Soviet agent. Ditto for atomic bomb scientists Robert Oppenheimer and Theodore Hall. But the identities of many of the Venona agents are still unknown.

with capabilities and long-term plans for world conquest that would have astounded Sun Tzu.

The Net That Covers the World

In 1955, British intelligence expert and author E. H. Cookridge aptly described the global Soviet apparatus as "the net that covers the world," in his book by that title. As he pointed out, the Communists had at that time established a worldwide militant organization of tens of millions of members, operating aggressively in virtually every country toward a centrally directed common objective — an accomplishment without parallel at any time in history. Besides controlling these millions of disciplined members, who could be ordered into coordinated global action on short notice, the Communist leaders had developed an intelligence apparatus of unparalleled, massive proportions. Cookridge noted:

> The number of men and women employed by the Soviet government on intelligence work has been estimated at about 250,000 — this quite apart from the internal political police. The number is at least ten times larger than that of agents used by all Western nations combined. But even this is only part of the Communist secret army.... A suggestion that there are 750,000 men and women in the world — semiprofessional agents, informants, fifth-columnists, fellow-travelers, and sympathizers — whom the Soviet secret service succeeded in ensnaring in some way into the spy net — is probably an underestimate. It is a formidable army, combined with a quarter of a million of full-time agents and officials, and led by an *elite* of 10,000 to 12,000 trained master spies.[8]

"No other nation," Cookridge noted, "devotes anything approaching the proportion of its manpower and resources to secret service work as do the Soviet Union and the satellite countries."[9] Likewise, no other nation comes close to matching the size of the internal secret police forces required by the Communists to maintain their Total State. Through innumerable movies, documentaries, novels, articles, and history books, Hitler's dreaded

Gestapo has been cast as the epitome of evil incarnate in the long drama of human existence. It has become synonymous with totalitarian brutality and malevolence, and rightly so. Yet most Americans have never even heard of Stalin's even more murderous and evil NKVD. Historian Martin Malia points out that German National Socialism, for all of its cruelty and viciousness, was "distinctly less murderous than Communism." [10] A major reason for this can be seen in the relative strength of the Nazi and Soviet secret police organs at the time of the Hitler/Stalin Pact: In 1939, Hitler's Gestapo employed a total of 7,500 people; Stalin's NKVD employed 366,000!

During the 1940s, '50s, and '60s, the U.S. Congress and many state legislatures held extensive investigative hearings into Communist penetration and subversion in the United States. These official inquiries produced a large number of important reports that included testimony from top military and intelligence authorities, as well as Communist defectors. Reports by the Committee on Un-American Activities of the House of Representatives, such as "The Communist Infiltration of the Motion Picture Industry" (1947), "Communist Political Subversion" (1956), "Soviet Total War" (1956), and "Communist Target — Youth" (1960) provided explosive, detailed information about the Soviet attack on America. As did reports of the Senate Internal Security Subcommittee (SISS), such as "The Institute of Pacific Relations" (1951), "Exposé of Soviet Espionage" (1960), and "The Soviet Empire" (1965). The voluminous 1953 SISS report entitled "Interlocking Subversion in Government Departments" labeled the Communist operations in our government "a conspiracy" and concluded:

> Policies and programs laid down by members of this Soviet conspiracy are still in effect within our government and constitute a continuing hazard to our national security. [11]

The massive scope and insidious nature of the Communist offensive was so far beyond what most Americans imagined that

FBI Director J. Edgar Hoover stated in 1956 that "the individual is handicapped by coming face to face with a conspiracy so monstrous he cannot believe it exists." [12] That handicap, however, was largely the work of the CFR-dominated media, which made sure that the American public remained largely unaware of the shocking information uncovered by the congressional investigations. The same media subversives attacked the congressional investigators and characterized proper concern over Communist and socialist advances as "right-wing paranoia."

Many Tentacles, One Brain

In 1960, the Kremlin hosted the Congress of 81 Communist Parties from around the world. Those parties boasted a collective strength of more than 40 million members. But their real strength then, as now, lay in their ability to get *non-Communists* to do their work for them. In the U.S., as elsewhere, the Communists created hundreds of front organizations and penetrated virtually all existing organizations and institutions, with the intent of gradually gaining significant influence, if not total control. Labor unions were especially targeted because they offered: 1) huge sources of funds, in the form of members' dues; 2) major political clout to elect sympathetic politicians and influence legislation and policy; 3) an important conduit of propaganda for class warfare; 4) the ability to paralyze governments and economies through strikes; and 5) the ability to mobilize large numbers of non-Communists (in marches and demonstrations) to give the appearance of popular support for Communist causes.

Similarly, the Communists and their various Marxist-socialist brethren have, during the past century particularly, targeted the colleges and universities — with amazing success. They have gained such influence in academia that from the 1960s onward they have been able to generate mass demonstrations of students, and even violent riots, by exploiting emotional issues such as war, nuclear weapons, the environment, homosexual rights, feminism, civil rights, race, etc.

One of the most knowledgeable analysts of Communism is

Jimmy Clabough of Brooklyn, New York. Mr. Clabough, a careful scholar of Communist literature and strategy, who has been attending and monitoring Communist meetings in the New York City area for years, says the Red network in this country is as strong as ever. "Look at the records of all of the so-called experts who keep assuring us that 'the Cold War is over,'" he says. "These are the same voices — the Kissingers, the Kennans, the McNamaras, the *New York Times* and *Washington Post* — who have always been *disastrously* wrong on every major call concerning Communism. The Clinton 'Chinagate' scandals were the tip of the iceberg. Communist activities in New York City alone are increasing at a furious rate. They are practicing the old 'united front' strategy of finding 'hot button' issues that they can exploit with every group imaginable: the homeless, gays, environmentalists, feminists, ethnic minorities, clergymen, New Agers, labor unions, etc. By appealing to these issues, they have developed large cadres of what I call Enviro-Leninists, Homo-Leninists, Femi-Leninists, Afro-Leninists, Peacenik-Leninists, Guru-Leninists, and Labor-Leninists. And they so expertly manipulate and orchestrate these various elements that the average television viewer or newspaper reader doesn't recognize the Communist coordination behind the scenes. As Lenin said: 'We must build Communism with non-Communist hands.'" [13]

This was precisely the message of Soviet Premier Konstantin Chernenko, when, in his June 1983 address to the Central Committee of the Communist Party of the Soviet Union (CPSU), he made this noteworthy remark:

> The battle of ideas in the international arena is going on without respite. We will continue to wage it vigorously ... our entire system of ideological work should operate as a well-arranged *orchestra* in which every instrument has a distinctive voice and leads its theme, while *harmony is achieved by skillful conducting.* [14] [Emphasis added.]

As we will show in this and following chapters, despite the

supposed "collapse" of Communism, that global orchestra has continued playing, with the same "skillful conducting" continuing from the background. There are still official Communist Parties operating in most countries and dozens more socialist parties run by "former" Communists. Meanwhile, in the 1990s, Russia and China reestablished friendly relations and began openly cooperating on many economic and military fronts.*

What many readers will find most extraordinary is that it is often difficult to discern whether it is the Communist leaders who are in charge of conducting this orchestra, or the CFR one-worlders, since they both are so frequently standing arm-in-arm at the same podium, moving their conductor's batons in perfect synchronization. And always, the "harmony" they seek is that which leads ineluctably to their mutual goal of world government.

To the massive, worldwide, militant network of the Communists, the CFR Insiders have added their own formida-

---

*Some of the most clear-sighted analysts of global affairs predicted this decades ago. Soviet defector Anatoliy Golitsyn and John Birch Society founder Robert Welch were ridiculed by both liberals and conservatives for contending that the so-called "Sino-Soviet Split" was entirely a strategic deception from the start, aimed at playing the West for suckers. Their careful research, reasoned analysis, and alarming predictions have proven true. Golitsyn's books, *New Lies for Old* [15] and *The Perestroika Deception*, [16] are immensely important for an understanding of this deception. Robert Welch's printed exposé of the phony Sino-Soviet split began in the August 1971 *Bulletin* of The John Birch Society and was developed in subsequent *Bulletins*. For example, in the December 1971 *Bulletin*, he observed: "If you have any doubt that these wars or threats of wars are all arranged by the Communists, with the actual fighting subject to being turned off or on by the Communists at will, then you are a long way from recognizing the kind of world you are living in. You might even swallow the now increasing rumor of some kind of border military conflict being produced by the bitterness between Red China and Soviet Russia. Of course they could no more be real enemies than could the two hands of one human body directed by one brain. But neither Moscow nor Peking would have the slightest hesitation about getting a few hundred thousand of their respective subjects killed in such a 'war,' in order to make their 'feud' look real, if the Insiders who write the script for this worldwide show decided that such an act would be worth the trouble."

ble global resources, including: presidents, prime ministers, and other government officials; billions of dollars from tax-exempt foundations and corporate globalists; prestige and brain power from numerous think tanks and universities; the tremendous impact of their one-world media cartel; and the growing power of their global rent-a-mob, otherwise known as the NGO (Non-Governmental Organization) lobby. Together they apply simultaneous "pressure from above and below" in a strategy that is known in Communist circles as "revolutionary parliamentarianism."

Pressure From Above and Below

The one-world architects know that they must create the appearance of popular support for their global designs in order to pave the way for national governments to surrender political power to the UN. To accomplish this surrender, they have devised a giant pincer strategy in the form of a huge NGO network (pressure from below) on the one hand, and sympathetic political and corporate leaders (pressure from above) on the other. The NGOs clamor for "world governance," and their orchestrated clamor is portrayed as the collective voice of the peoples of the world expressing a global consensus. The political and corporate leaders — according to plan — then "respond" to the "will of civil society."

The use of this pincer strategy to seize power was explained by Communist Party "theoretician" Jan Kozak. In his instructions for "revolutionary parliamentarianism," written in the early 1950s, Kozak detailed how he and his fellow Communist conspirators overthrew a democratically elected, mainly non-Communist government in Czechoslovakia and turned it into a Communist dictatorship — *legally*. [17]

Kozak explained how his Communist minority in parliament (in coalition with socialists and "liberals") worked in concert with the street-level activists and grassroots revolutionaries. Utilizing demonstrations, strikes, rallies, petitions, threats, and — sometimes — sabotage, the radicals (like the NGOs today) provided "pressure from below." Meanwhile Kozak and his co-conspirators provided coordinated "pressure from above" to get parliament to institute Communism piecemeal, by centralizing power and taking over more and more functions that had previously been left to local governments and the private sector. It is important to understand that this takeover was accomplished by a small minority. But this minority was highly *organized* and disciplined. And it was also highly skilled in the art of deception, in creating the false appearance of having overwhelming numbers on their side. The opposition was psychologically outmaneuvered and made to believe that "resistance is futile." They surrendered without firing a shot. The Communists won that war because *they were the only side fighting*; their opponents didn't even realize they were under attack!

A similar operation is underway today on a global scale. The war is on, but for the most part only one side is fighting. The UN-CFR axis is organizing NGOs, churches, educational institutions, labor unions, business groups, and other organizations into a force that it calls "global civil society." At the UN's World Civil Society Conference in Montreal in 1999, UN Secretary-General Kofi Annan explained to the professional NGO activists their new "partnership" with the UN. Annan explained that the NGOs must serve as "strategic partners in policy — in areas where you can persuade your Governments to work through the United Nations. You can tell them that our goals are your goals, and that you want them to give us the means to achieve those goals." [18]

Kofi Annan is not the mastermind of this UN pincer strategy, of course; he is merely a factotum carrying out the program for the Insiders who have posted him as their front man. The magnitude of this global pincer strategy and the incredibly deceptive processes employed in the pursuit of their monstrous goals is mind-boggling. To paraphrase (and modify) Sun Tzu, when all of these elements are at work and their operations and/or connections are clandestine, it is justly called the "diabolic manipulation of threads."

Orchestrating the "Disarmament" Concert

This diabolic manipulation and conspiracy are very apparent when one looks beneath the surface of the global "peace" and "disarmament" campaigns during the last half of the 20th century. These campaigns support a primary objective of the UN's founders — providing the UN with a monopoly of force. Recall that the primary impetus, ostensibly, for creating the UN was to "put an end to war" through an organization which would provide "collective security." As we have already seen, it was the CFR one-world brain trust, together with the Communists, that designed, organized, and launched the UN. And it was the same cabal that authored the State Department policy documents, *Freedom From War* and *A World Effectively Controlled By the United Nations*.[19]

The global "disarmament" campaign — which is, in truth, a program to *transfer* arms from private individuals and individual nation-states to the UN — continues unabated. In fact, it is accelerating. In May 2000, thousands of activists from across the planet gathered at the United Nations in New York for the "Millennium Forum." Disarmament was very much on the agenda. The Forum was the formal rent-a-mob warm-up to prepare the NGO militants for coordinated action at the Millennium Summit of world leaders, which would follow in September. Addressing the NGO activists, UN Secretary-General Kofi Annan welcomed them as "the new superpower," leaders of the new international "civil society," and "implementing partners" in the work of the UN.[20] But contrary to the manufactured image, these NGOs certainly do not represent civil society, and most are not independent.

A key disarmament document advanced at the UN's Millennium Forum, and later at the Millennium Summit, was *The Hague Agenda for Peace and Justice for the 21st Century*,[21] which was praised by Secretary-General Annan. The person in charge of presenting the Hague Agenda document at the Forum was Cora Weiss, president of the private Hague Appeal for Peace and Justice, Inc. "There are only three documents that you need ... to be an informed, effective member of organized civil society,"

Weiss told the Forum attendees. "The Charter of the United Nations, the [Universal] Declaration of Human Rights, and *The Hague Agenda for Peace and Justice for the 21st Century*." [22] My colleague and fellow senior editor at *The New American*, William Norman Grigg, who attended that UN session, noted: "Neither the Declaration of Independence nor the U.S. Constitution was among Weiss' indispensable texts, and once her background is understood it will become clear why neither of our founding documents made the cut." [23]

Cora Weiss is both a member of the CFR and a veteran, hardcore Leninist. She is the daughter of Samuel Rubin, a longtime member of the Communist Party, U.S.A., and heads a tax-exempt foundation that bears her father's name. The Samuel Rubin Foundation is the chief financial angel behind the Institute for Policy Studies (IPS), a very influential Washington, D.C. "think-tank" which has long served as a major front for Soviet KGB activities. The chairman of IPS is Cora Weiss' husband, Peter Weiss, a radical attorney who is a member of the Communist-front National Lawyers Guild. Like Tom Hayden, Jane Fonda, and other pro-Communist traitors, Cora Weiss made the pilgrimage to Hanoi during the Vietnam War and organized pro-Vietcong demonstrations. In 1969, she returned from North Vietnam two days before Christmas and held a major press conference where she reported that American POWs were treated well and housed in "immaculate" facilities. Weeks later, at a press conference she held in the Cannon House Office Building in Washington, D.C., Weiss scoffed at the claims of two former POWs — Lieutenant Robert Frishman and Seaman Douglas Hegdahl. Frishman and Hegdahl had testified before Congress concerning the inhumane treatment they had experienced at the hands of the Reds. Weiss made light of their injuries, and referred to our POWs as "war criminals." [24]

As self-appointed high priestess of disarmament at the Millennium Forum, Weiss declared to the UN assemblage: "I propose the activation of Chapter VII, article 47 of the UN Charter, which provides for a Military Staff Committee to assist the

Security Council for the maintenance of international peace."[25] The activation of Chapter VII would require a standing UN military with the power to "take such action by air, sea or land forces as may be necessary to maintain or restore international peace and security."[26]

In keeping with the schemes of the global strategists, both at Pratt House and in the Kremlin, the *Hague Agenda* proclaims that "it is time to redefine security in terms of human and ecological needs instead of national sovereignty and national borders."[27] Which, naturally, will require the "creation of standing UN peace forces for use in humanitarian interventions" and the implementation of "demobilization programs" around the world to "reclaim and destroy weaponry" not under UN control.[28] This refers not only to nuclear arms and other weapons of mass destruction, but also to "light weapons, small arms and guns"[29] — meaning those held by private citizens, as well as those under control of national military forces. (More on the UN drive for personal disarmament in Chapter 9).

Joining Cora Weiss (CFR, IPS) on the board of directors of the Hague Appeal for Peace and Justice, Inc. are: Adele Simmons (CFR and president of the John D. and Catherine T. MacArthur Foundation); World Federalist Movement officials Tim Barner and William Pace (CFR); and Peter Weiss (IPS). Funding for the Hague Appeal is provided by the usual CFR-dominated sources: Ford Foundation, Carnegie Corporation of New York, Samuel Rubin Foundation, Stewart R. Mott Charitable Trust, billionaire George Soros (a CFR director), *The Nation* magazine, Institute for Policy Studies, Greenpeace International, UNESCO, UNIFEM, and the World Federalist Association.[30]

The Hague Appeal is an international coalition of 180 organizations, most of which have been involved in the radical "peace and disarmament" movement for decades.* The Hague Appeal received favorable support from the CFR media cartel during the Forum, which was bracketed for months before and after with a coordinated release of disarmament appeals in all the usual CFR transmission belts: the *New York Times, Washington Post, Los*

Angeles Times, Foreign Affairs, Foreign Policy, Christian Science Monitor, etc.

Why This Orchestration Works!

Why do the CFR elites go through such elaborate charades, creating these multitudes of radical front groups (or co-opting existing ones) and funding them with piles of money? And why all of the orchestrated media support? The CFR elites know, of course, that they wouldn't get very far if they were honest and straightforward about their intent: "People of the world: Our global political, economic, and social arrangements are all wrong. However, our elite group of superior thinkers have a plan. All you have to do is relinquish all political and financial power to us so we can fix everything. Trust us." Wouldn't work, obviously.

However, what if they employ a different strategy? What if they fund a gaggle of radical groups, with various elements calling for the transfer of power in one area or another to international authorities? What if they also fund another gaggle of even *more radical* groups to make the first gaggle appear "moderate" and "reasonable"? And suppose they saturate the print and broadcast media with the antics and propaganda of these groups for a sufficient length of time. And suppose that this propaganda clamors for government to address outrageous problems while ignoring any possible danger to freedom in the new "arrangements." Then the pressure from below will reach the point that the Insiders above can have their political agents in Congress and the White House respond to the "will of the people" with "compromise" legislation. These "compromise" solutions always move the whole political arena further leftward, toward ever bigger, more oppressive government.

In his 1968 book *The Strawberry Statement: Notes of a College*

---

*These include Amnesty International, the American Friends Service Committee, Friends of the Earth, Pax Christi, the International Fellowship of Reconciliation, Parliamentarians for Global Action, UNICEF, the Women's International League for Peace and Freedom, the World Order Models Project, and the WorldWatch Institute.

Revolutionary, radical activist/author James Kunen made an interesting admission about this process. Concerning the campus riots then rocking the nation, he wrote:

> In the evening, I went up to the U. to check out a strategy meeting. A kid was giving a report on an SDS [Students for a Democratic Society] convention. He said that ... at the convention, men from Business International Round Tables ... tried to buy up a few radicals. These men are the world's leading industrialists and they convene to decide how our lives are going to go.... They offered to finance our demonstrations in Chicago. We were also offered ESSO (Rockefeller) money. They want us to make a lot of radical commotion so they can look more in the center as they move to the left. [31]

Another similar revelation was provided by Jerry Kirk, who, as a student, was active in the SDS, the DuBois Club, the Black Panthers, and the Communist Party. In a 1970 interview, Kirk said:

> Young people have no conception of the conspiracy's strategy of "pressure from above and pressure from below".... They have no idea that they are playing into the hands of the Establishment they claim to hate.... The radicals think they are fighting the forces of the super-rich, like Rockefeller and Ford, and they don't realize that it is precisely such forces which are behind their own revolution, financing it, and using it for their own purposes. [32]

Understanding the objectives, it was not surprising that the *Hague Agenda* and the UN Millennium events were accompanied by a deluge of disarmament propaganda — courtesy of the Pratt House mediacracy. Simon and Schuster, one of America's largest book publishers, brought out William Shawcross' new paean to the UN, *Deliver Us from Evil: Peacekeepers, Warlords, and a World of Endless Conflict.* [33] Written largely from the perspective of Kofi Annan, whom the left-wing Shawcross obviously adores (and with whom he traveled the world), the book repeatedly indicts the U.S. for its miserly refusals to surrender more of our sovereignty, money, and military to the noble UN. Glowing reviews followed in the CFR media choir.

The CFR's *Foreign Affairs* (which *Time* has dubbed "the most influential journal in print" and *Newsweek* has called the "preeminent" journal of its kind) and the Carnegie Endowment's *Foreign Policy* both provided several issues running of globalist disarmament forensics. In the September/October 2000 issue of *Foreign Affairs*, timed for the Millennium Summit, Jonathan Schell led off with "The Folly of Arms Control," in which he argued for complete nuclear disarmament as envisioned in the 1946 Baruch Plan. [34] And he reminded "the great and good" that the U.S. is obligated under Article VI of the Nonproliferation Treaty (NPT) to "pursue negotiations ... [for] nuclear disarmament, and on a treaty on general and complete disarmament under strict and effective international control." [35] The same issue of *Foreign Affairs* featured an article by Russian Minister of Foreign Affairs Igor Ivanov warning that any U.S. move toward deploying a missile defense system would jeopardize NPT, ABM, CTBT — the whole edifice of arms control treaties. [36] Also in the same issue, General Andrew J. Goodpaster (CFR) offered boilerplate Pratt House "Advice for the Next President," echoing the Schell and Ivanov appeals for disarmament, and urging the use of NGOs to "mobilize understanding." [37]

Writing in 1975, retired Admiral Chester Ward, a veteran CFR member who had grown sharply critical of the organization wrote:

> Once the ruling members of CFR have decided that the U.S. Government should adopt a particular policy, the very substantial research facilities of CFR are put to work to develop arguments, intellectual and emotional, to support the new policy, and to confound and discredit, intellectually and politically, any opposition. The most articulate theoreticians and ideologists prepare related articles, aided by the research, to sell the new policy and to make

it appear inevitable and irresistible. By following the evolution of propaganda in the most prestigious scholarly journal in the world, *Foreign Affairs*, anyone can determine years in advance what the future defense and foreign policies of the United States will be.[38]

Millennium Summit Pressure

As the UN Millennium Summit got underway, the pressure from above *and* below increased. Following the pattern from past Summits, it was a well-honed, multi-level, multi-pronged, multi-dimensional attack aimed at multiple targets. Prime targets, of course, were the heads of state in attendance; if they could be induced to sign the disarmament treaties, declarations, and resolutions, it would add to the international momentum and legitimacy of the UN disarmament agenda. Other intended targets, however, were the U.S. public and the U.S. Congress, as well as the U.S. governmental, academic, and intellectual cadres who follow, influence, and make foreign policy — and then help sell it to the public.

The UN's glossy *UN 2000* report, which was provided to all Summit participants, included an essay by President Clinton's Ambassador to the UN, Richard C. Holbrooke (CFR, TC). Mr. Holbrooke parroted the globalist hymn to enlarge and empower the UN, calling for a major boost in the world body's military and police capacities. It also featured similar bilge by billionaire eco-socialist and CNN founder Ted Turner, whose UN Foundation has contributed more than $250 million in support of UN programs and activities. Joining them in this orgy of praise for the UN were such one-world luminaries as: former Norwegian Prime Minister Gro Harlem Brundtland, now Director-General of the UN's World Health Organization; Chris Patten (TC), who played a key role in the betrayal of Hong Kong to Red China and who now serves as a member of the European Commission; former Socialist President of Ireland Mary Robinson, now UN High Commissioner for Human Rights; left-wing author William Shawcross; and Bjorn Stigson, president of the environmental extremist World Business Council for

Sustainable Development.[39]

Among the profusion of programs circulating at the Summit, the Middle Powers Initiative (MPI) is particularly noteworthy. Claiming to represent the non-nuclear "middle-power" countries of the world, it describes itself as "a carefully focused campaign established by a network of international citizens organizations to encourage ... leaders of the nuclear weapons states to break free from their Cold War mindset" and embrace disarmament — as defined by the MPI and the UN.[40] But, as we shall see, MPI's "independence" is all illusion; while posing as a "citizens network," MPI is, in reality, nothing less than a front group for the one-world internationalists.

Independence Sham

MPI's primary spokesperson is New Zealand Prime Minister Helen Clark, whose Labour Party is affiliated with the Socialist International. The eloquent Mrs. Clark championed the MPI disarmament campaign both at the UN Summit and at the Gorbachev Foundation-sponsored "State of the World Forum," which ran concomitantly with the UN affair, a few blocks away at the Hilton Towers. Many UN leaders and heads of state jockeyed back and forth between the UN and the Gorbachev confab, where they shmoozed and "brainstormed" with corporate titans, academics, NGO rabble-rousers, and New Age gurus. As it turns out, Gorbachev's State of the World Forum is also one of the original eight co-sponsors of the MPI, as well as a funder of the group.

And we see the same repetitious pattern emerge in the MPI case: funding for the Initiative comes from the Rockefeller Foundation, Samuel Rubin Foundation, and the W. Alton Jones Foundation. MPI's International Steering Committee includes Comrade Peter Weiss, and it included the late Senator Alan Cranston (TC, WFA), a veteran one-worlder. Other "Establishment" activists at the Initiative include General Lee Butler, General Andrew J. Goodpaster, and former Secretary of Defense Robert Strange McNamara (all CFR). The "anti-Establishment" activists at MPI include a host of revolutionary radicals. Among the MPI co-sponsors are the Parliamentarians for Global Action, the Women's International League for Peace and Freedom, the Nuclear Age Peace Foundation, and the International Peace Bureau.[41] All of these groups have been long connected to the KGB-created-and-controlled World Peace Council (WPC), which, since its founding in 1949 by Communist mass-murderer Joseph Stalin, has served the dual purpose of leading the drive for U.S. disarmament and providing support for terrorist groups and regimes worldwide.*

Both the Establishment and anti-Establishment activists were eager to cite the fact that the World Court at the Hague had issued an opinion on July 8, 1996 that: "There exists an obligation to ... bring to a conclusion negotiations leading to nuclear disarmament in all its aspects under strict and effective inter-

---

*One of the most informative studies on the WPC, *The War Called Peace: The Soviet Peace Offensive*, was published in 1982 by the Western Goals Foundation. The study accurately notes: "Since 1950, when it launched the Stockholm Peace Appeal, the World Peace Council (WPC) has been the Soviet Union's single most important international front organization." During the 1960s and '70s, the WPC played a crucial role in organizing the anti-Vietnam War protests throughout the U.S. and stirring up anti-American demonstrations throughout the world. It has led, albeit often from the background, most of the "popular" disarmament campaigns, such as those supporting the ABM, SALT, INF, and CWC treaties, and the crusades against building a U.S. missile defense system. The WPC has supported, with financial aid and propaganda, terrorist organizations such as the PLO, ANC, UDT, and SWAPO. In fact, the WPC has included leaders of terrorist groups among its top officers. Which is hardly surprising considering that the WPC's longtime president, Romesh Chandra, was a member of the Central Committee of the Communist Party of India. The Soviet "control agent" over Chandra for many years was KGB officer Aleksandr Berkov, who was later replaced by fellow KGB officer Igor Belyayev. Although Chandra was the WPC's front man, Berkov and Belyayev actually called the shots — as directed by Moscow. WPC national affiliates, such as the U.S. Peace Council (USPC), were and are controlled by national Communist parties. The WPC and USPC closely coordinate their activities with other KGB-connected groups, such as the Institute for Policy Studies, Women's International League for Peace and Freedom, the Women's Strike for Peace, the Center for International Policy, the Center for Defense Information, Citizens Committee for a Sane World, and others.

national control."[42] They prattled that the nuclear weapon states are "flouting the World Court" and the rule of law by not disarming. They cited "eminent" scholars who argued that the U.S. and the other nuclear states risk running afoul of "the Nuremberg Principles" and "international humanitarian law."[43] They posed as the moral voice of the majority of the world's non-nuclear powers while rebuking the major powers for endangering the planet because of chauvinistic adherence to narrow national and ideological interests.

Of course, the MPI does not represent the "middle power" states at all; its whole purpose (and the reason that it has been so bountifully funded and promoted) is to provide orchestrated pressure from below so that the Insiders of the "weapons states" will have the excuse to do what they have wanted to do all along. Our home-grown internationalists realize that by having the disarmament pressure appear to come from an independent citizens network, the motives and agendas of those who must implement the changes will not be seriously challenged.

As a journalist covering the UN Millennium Summit, the Gorbachev State of the World Forum, and a number of additional programs that took place in New York City in September 2000, this reporter had a front-row seat to this amazing spectacle. The diabolic "manipulation of the threads" was both fascinating and frightening to behold. It was not the first time that I had observed this phenomena; I had seen it in operation at previous summits.

Still, it was evident that, with practice, the Kremlin-Pratt House one-worlders are perfecting their pincer strategy. They have become very adept at managing their rangy NGO rent-a-mob, which, on cue, either chants and demonstrates in the streets, or comes inside the halls of power and negotiates like a genuine "superpower." At the same time, they have assembled an amazing array of politicians-and-professors-for-hire, who can be counted on to spout the proper globalist slogans, and reporters who reliably retail every line of internationalist propaganda handed to them.

With the orchestra so lavishly funded and skillfully conducted, they are able to give the appearance that their position truly does "represent the will of global civil society." Politicians who might normally do battle are completely outgunned and overwhelmed; there is no way they can match, by themselves, the intellectual firepower of the assembled think tanks and universities that have been preparing their positions for months — or even years. And when their congressional offices are besieged with an orchestrated campaign of telephone calls, e-mails, faxes, and letters; while CNN, C-Span, and the other networks are all spewing forth the same story — even the stalwart begin to crumble before such an onslaught. That is what has been happening, and what we can expect to see a great deal more of, as the advocates of "global democracy" continue to press their fraudulent and totalitarian agenda.

We hasten to add, however, that this totalitarian agenda can be stopped, and it must. In fact, the plans of this cabal have been disrupted many times through well-organized exposure of the hidden agendas and the phony orchestration. The good news is that these deceptions cannot stand the light of day. The bad news is that credible evidence to support this story will never reach sufficient numbers of Americans through disorganized action. However, the existence of strong *organizational* leadership opens up real opportunities. For more on the antidote, the reader may wish to jump to Chapter 14. However, there is still much more to the story. The following chapters will examine some of the other prominent strategies of this cabal.

Chapter 6

Enviromania

World Federalists believe that the environmental crisis facing planet earth is a global problem and therefore calls for a "global" solution — a worldwide United Nations Environmental Agency with the power to make its decisions stick. [1]
— World Association of World Federalists, 1972

[T]he great enemy is not the Soviet Union but the rapid deterioration of our planet as a supporting structure for civilized life. [2]
— George F. Kennan (CFR), *Washington Post* column,
November 12, 1989

Global warming, ozone depletion, deforestation and over-population are the four horsemen of a looming 21st century apocalypse. As the cold war recedes, the environment is becoming the No. 1 international security concern. [3]
— Michael Oppenheimer (CFR),
New York Times, March 27, 1990

We've got to ride the global warming issue. Even if the theory is wrong, we will be doing the right thing in terms of economic and environmental policy. [4]
— Timothy Wirth (CFR),
former U.S. Senator and Under Secretary of State,
now head of Ted Turner's UN Foundation

In searching for a new enemy to unite us, we came up with the idea that pollution, the threat of global warming, water shortages, famine and the like would fit the bill.... All these dangers are caused by human intervention.... The real

enemy, then, is humanity itself.[5]
— The Council of the Club of Rome, 1991

The [UN] *Security Council recently expanded the concept of threats to peace to include economic, social and ecological instability.*[6]
— "The New World Army," *New York Times* editorial,
March 6, 1992

Global warming, ozone depletion, deforestation, species extinction, wildlife habitat destruction, resource exhaustion, overpopulation. Since the 1960s, these and a host of other supposed environmental "crises" have exploded onto the world scene, mobilizing millions of people in a global crusade to "save the planet." This writer was involved as a true believer in the early period of this global movement, and, as a high school senior and student body secretary, helped plan and organize a 1970 school ceremony for the first Earth Day: a demonstration in which students donned gas masks, as a "consciousness-raising" protest against air pollution, and symbolically buried an automobile carburetor.

In the three decades since that time, the environmental movement has grown into a global green juggernaut involving millions of activists and wielding enormous political, social, and economic power. Contrary to popular misconceptions, this has not been a healthy development for "Mother Earth" or her human inhabitants. As my colleague William Norman Grigg has rightly noted, "the environmental movement is animated by a desire to regiment human society rather than 'save the planet.' The movement's economic outlook is socialist, its political ambitions are totalitarian, and its religious affinities are unmistakably pagan."[7]

The Big Green agenda is about power and control, not clean air and saving whales. While the vast majority of pedestrian-level environmentalists may genuinely care about local ecology issues and really believe in the apocalyptic scenarios regarding the so-called "ozone hole" and the alleged dangers from greenhouse gases, clearly the elites guiding these concerned cadres know such threats are bogus or vastly exaggerated. Certainly, the scientific evidence does not support the charges that these alleged "crises" are so imminent and of such planet-threatening magnitude as to justify totalitarian solutions.

In fact, the overwhelming weight of *real* science and the bulk of honest scientists argue that genuine environmental problems are best solved not by draconian governmental fiat but by market forces and the enforcement of private property rights. Conversely, it is also true that the worst environmental degradation on the planet has taken place under those Communist and socialist regimes where free markets and property rights have been most ruthlessly suppressed.

It is not the purpose of this study to address or refute the myriad absurd claims of the enviro-extremists; that has already been done by many eminent scientists and scholars.* It is, instead, our purpose here to show *why* the Establishment opinion cartel insists on ignoring the clear verdicts of science and enshrines as oracles the charlatans whose eco-science has been repeatedly exposed as error-ridden or completely fraudulent.

Earth Summit Eyewitness
This blatant deception and censorship by the "ruling class journalists" was especially crucial to the "success" of the 1992 UN Conference on Environment and Development (UNCED), the so-called Earth Summit, in Rio de Janeiro. This writer can claim the dubious distinction of being, perhaps, the only "non-greenie" journalist amongst the thousands of reporters and media personalities who converged on this global orgy of environmental extremism.

Providentially, I met up with one of the few other "contrarian" souls attending the Summit almost immediately upon exiting my plane onto the sweltering tarmac of the Rio airport. As the long passenger lines from the various airliners converged under the airport's shade cover for the two-hour Customs process, I had the good fortune to "converge" with Dr. Dixy Lee Ray, who had just

THE UNITED NATIONS EXPOSED

deplaned from another aircraft. Dr. Ray, who died in 1993, was one of my heroes: a genuine, eminent scientist who boldly challenged the absurd claims and dangerous proposals of the environmental fanatics and calmly disregarded the vicious, personal attacks that she received in return.

As a distinguished professor of zoology, author and commentator, former chairman of the Atomic Energy Commission, former governor of the state of Washington, and recipient of many awards (including the United Nations Peace Prize), one might be forgiven for naively assuming that this woman would be mobbed by reporters seeking her learned opinion on the weighty matters under discussion at the Summit. Hardly! Dr. Ray was virtually

*See, for instance, *Rational Readings on Environmental Concerns*, edited by Jay H. Lehr (Van Nostrand Reinhold, 1992); *The State of Humanity,* edited by Julian L. Simon (Blackwell, 1995); *Earth Report 2000: Revisiting the True State of the Planet*, edited by Ronald Bailey (McGraw-Hill, 2000); *Environmental Gore: A Constructive Response to Earth in the Balance*, edited by John A. Baden (Pacific Research Institute, 1994); *Ecology, Liberty and Property: A Free Market Environmental Reader*, edited by Jonathan H. Adler (Competitive Enterprise Institute, 2000); *Trashing the Planet*, by Dixy Lee Ray (Regnery, 1990); *Environmental Overkill*, by Dixy Lee Ray (Regnery, 1993); *Science Under Siege: How the Environmental Misinformation Campaign Is Affecting Our Laws, Taxes, and Our Daily Lives*, by Michael Fumento (New York: W. Morrow, 1996); *Polluted Science: The EPA's Campaign to Expand Clean Air Regulations*, by Michael Fumento (Washington, D.C.: AEI Press, 1998); *Sound And Fury: The Science and Politics of Global Warming*, by Patrick J. Michaels (Cato Institute, 1992); *The Satanic Gases: Clearing the Air About Global Warming*, by Patrick J. Michaels and Robert C. Balling (Washington, D.C.: Cato Institute, 2000); *The Heated Debate: Greenhouse Predictions Versus Climate Reality*, by Robert Balling (San Francisco: Pacific Research Institute for Public Policy, 1992); *Hot Talk, Cold Science: Global Warming's Unfinished Debate*, by S. Fred Singer (The Independent Institute, 1997); *The Ultimate Resource 2*, by Julian L. Simon (Princeton University Press, 1998); *Hoodwinking the Nation*, by Julian L. Simon (Transaction Publishers, 1999); *Free Market Environmentalism*, by Terry L. Anderson and Donald R. Leal (St. Martin's Press, 2001); *Ecocide In the USSR: Health and Nature Under Siege*, by Murray Feshbach and Alfred Friendly, Jr. (Basic Books, 1992); "East Europe's Dark Dawn," *National Geographic*, June 1991; *Environmental Politics: Public Costs, Private Rewards*, by Michael S. Greve and Fred L. Smith, Jr. (Praeger, 1992); and *Undue Influence*, by Ron Arnold (The Free Enterprise Press, 1999) ignored, as were other noted scientists and scholars, while the CFR Establishment press drooled over every sacred syllable uttered by the likes of Fidel Castro, Mikhail Gorbachev, Jerry "Governor Moonbeam" Brown, then-Senator Al "I invented the Internet" Gore, Jacques Cousteau, and Maurice Strong.

During the course of the Summit, I had the opportunity to meet with, interview, and compare notes with Dr. Ray several times. I noted that with her background in zoology she should be better prepared than most for the profusion of weird specimens populating the conference. "I've never seen a bigger zoo," the feisty scientist responded, in a comment intended to convey both the absurdity and seriousness of what was transpiring at the UN confab.

Although ignored by most of the media (and even pointedly censored and rebuked by some) at Rio, Dr. Ray did successfully expose some of the dangerous UNCED policies and proposals. Through her columns and live talk-radio interviews from the Earth Summit, and by her speeches and explosive book exposé following the event, she alerted many Americans to the perils of the global green agenda. In *Environmental Overkill*, she wrote: "First, we must recognize that the environmental movement is not about facts or logic. More and more it is becoming clear that those who support the so-called 'New World Order' or World Government under the United Nations have adopted global environmentalism as a basis for the dissolution of independent nations and the international realignment of power." [8]

The opinions of other prominent scientists were also censored or suppressed by the Insider-run media. Shortly before the convening of the Earth Summit, a group of more than 250 distinguished scientists, including 27 Nobel Laureates, released a statement called the *Heidelberg Appeal to Heads of States and Governments*. The statement, which was subsequently signed by hundreds of additional scientists worldwide, said, in part: "We are, however, worried at the dawn of the twenty-first century, at the emergence of an irrational ideology which is opposed to scientific and industrial progress and impedes economic and social development."[9] This private ad hoc group appealed to government officials to base ecological proscriptions "on scientific criteria and not on irrational preconceptions," and carried a warning "to the authorities in charge of our planet's destiny against decisions which are supported by pseudoscientific arguments or false and non-relevant data."[10]

Forgive the political naïveté of these well-meaning scientists. But appealing to venal politicians and the prostitute press on the basis of facts is almost like trying to sell compassion to Mafia thugs or morality to the studio execs of Hollywood Babylon. What was the reaction of the CFR media cartel to the *Heidelberg Appeal*? Predictable: They ignored it.

The same blackout occurred later when an even larger group of scientists signed a petition opposing the half-baked "science" undergirding the incredibly dangerous UN Kyoto Protocol on global warming. Headed by Dr. Frederick Seitz, former president of the National Academy of Sciences and president emeritus of Rockefeller University, the petition was signed by more than 18,000 scientists, including thousands of meteorologists, climatologists and atmospheric scientists. The scientists' statement said, in part:

> We urge the United States government to reject the global warming agreement that was written in Kyoto, Japan in December 1997, and any other similar proposals. The proposed limits on greenhouse gases would harm the environment, hinder the advance of science and technology, and damage the health and welfare of mankind....
>
> There is no convincing scientific evidence that human release of carbon dioxide, methane, or other greenhouse gases is causing or will, in the foreseeable future, cause catastrophic heating of the Earth's atmosphere and disruption of the Earth's climate. Moreover, there is substantial scientific evidence that increases in atmospheric carbon dioxide produce many beneficial effects upon the natural plant and animal environments of the Earth.[11]

Nonstop Propaganda and Censorship

But the "ruling class journalists" are more than willing to play the scientist numbers game when it suits the one-world agenda. Before, during, and after Rio, the media mavens trumpeted the supposed findings of the UN's Intergovernmental Panel on Climate Change (IPCC).[12] Then-Senator Al Gore, who led the U.S. Senate delegation to Rio, repeatedly cited the "authoritative" IPCC report in his fervent pleas of support for the global warming treaty. At his major press conference at the Rio Hilton, this writer challenged his citation of the IPCC report and his repeated ludicrous claim that 98 percent of the scientific community endorsed the global warming idea as fact. The IPCC report had been fraudulently altered, I pointed out, and many of the scientists who had worked on the project had publicly disavowed its political agenda disguised as science. This easily verified fact had been reported (albeit in "small print") in the "mainstream" press. Gore evaded the tough question like a true politician, stating: "I don't want to open a debate on this, but let me say that I will stay after [the press conference] if you like...."

Thanks to Senator Steve Symms (R-Idaho), who took the microphone following Al Gore, I was able to ask Gore a follow-up question, zeroing in on the well-documented IPCC fraud and pointing out that the Gallup poll of climatologists and meteorologists taken a few months earlier found that only *19 percent, not 98 percent*, believed in global warming.[13] Again Gore evaded, snidely remarking that there are a lot of people who "still argue that NASA staged the moon landing in a movie lot." I replied that the poll I had just cited was not a survey of wild-eyed cranks, but, on the contrary, represented the vast majority of climatic scientists, including internationally recognized authorities like Hugh Ellsaesser at Lawrence Livermore Laboratory, William Reifsnyder at Yale, Nathaniel Guttman at the National Climatic Data Center, Robert Balling, director of the Arizona Climatology Laboratory, and many others. Senator Gore, who otherwise never missed an opportunity to pontificate on his favorite subject, was suddenly under great pressure to leave.

"Well, we've really got to go," he said.

Although Gore's evasiveness and slippery exit were frustrating, they were not surprising; it was precisely what one would have expected of him. What was harder to take (though not totally unexpected) was the reaction of the press corps. It was obvious to this correspondent — and should have been, as well, to all others present — that my questions had caught him off balance. I had refuted his claims with fact, backed up with citations and sources. I had even challenged one of his prized documents as fraudulent. He was caught in a lie and was clearly uncomfortable. This is the kind of "blood in the water" situation that normally sets off the shark sensors of journalists and sends them into a "feeding frenzy." If Senator Symms, a conservative, had been similarly caught, you can be sure the shark pack would have been all over him in a split second. That didn't happen with Gore, of course, because the horde of "journalists" in attendance had come not as news reporters but as advocates and propagandists. They were there to regurgitate and retail as gospel whatever globaloney the UN and its proponents dished out.

Allow us to provide a few more examples. One of the major scare stories that had received a major buildup prior to Rio, and was a key focal point of the Summit, concerned the alleged massive destruction of the Amazon rain forest. According to the militant enviro-lobby and its media allies, we could expect cataclysmic global environmental consequences unless UN authority over the world's forests was established. So, again, one might naively think that the man of the hour would be Professor Evaristo Eduardo de Miranda, the world's leading expert on Amazon deforestation. Dr. Miranda, an ecologist at the University of São Paulo, is a former consultant to the UN who heads Brazil's center for monitoring the Amazon region by satellite. His laboratory was the only source for complete satellite data on the status of Amazon deforestation.

But to the U.S. media, Dr. Miranda and his fellow scientists didn't exist. Small wonder: His data did not support the apocalyptic paradigm the Insider-managed media were selling. In fact,

Dr. Miranda's data showed that the studies sponsored by the United Nations Food and Agriculture Organization, the World Bank, World Wildlife Fund, and the Conservation Foundation were exaggerating the rate of deforestation by 300 to 400 percent and grossly misrepresenting other data. [14]

Moreover, much of the destructive deforestation decried by the green extremists was the result of the socialist policies of Brazil's socialist government. The solution, Dr. Miranda pointed out, would not be found in *international* socialist policies implemented by the UN's bureaucracy. Moreover, he noted, not all deforestation is bad; converting some of the massive jungle for farming, livestock, timber harvest, and other productive uses is a *good* thing and necessary for food, jobs, and economic progress. [15]

Another expert "pariah" at Rio was Dr. Alexander Bonilla of Costa Rica. A world-famous ecologist and former recipient of the United Nations' top environmental honor, the GLOBAL 500 Award, Dr. Bonilla was a natural to respond to questions about "biodiversity" and "sustainable development," which were major watchwords at the Summit. However, as with Drs. Ray and Miranda, Dr. Bonilla's science did not fit the reigning paradigm. The outspoken scientist urgently warned of the danger posed by the "greening of the Reds." Even more than in the U.S. and Europe, he noted, the Communists and "former" Communists in Latin America had poured into the environmental movement, where they exploited environmental issues to promote Marxist ideology and "class struggle." [16]

Dr. Bonilla was angry and disturbed over the usurpation of science by those who would use it for purely political purposes. "We have many poor people with very substandard living conditions," he explained. "They need jobs, decent housing, clothes, food, drinkable water, things that can be provided in a manner compatible with sound economic and ecological practices." [17] But the environmental leftists, he said, want to stop all economic development, in the name of environmental protection. This will consign many people to lives of grinding poverty, sickness, illiteracy, and early death. "The knowledge and technology is available to enable a stewardship of natural resources that allows both prosperity and environmental integrity," Bonilla asserted. [18]

As expected, Dr. Bonilla's message was deemed unimportant by the "ruling class journalists"; instead, the American people needed to hear and see and read the blatherings of "experts" like Castro, Gorbachev, and Gore.

The New York-Moscow Green Axis

As in the other areas we have examined, the one-world Insiders, both in New York and in Moscow, have been working hand in hand to excite and exploit environmental fears in the service of building world government. Over and over again, we see these supposedly opposing forces supporting the same subversive, totalitarian programs and agenda.

Environmentalism offers the would-be global dictators unparalleled opportunities to exercise their statist ambitions. Three of the broad primary objectives they expect to realize through their environmental agenda are:

- Abolition of private property, the keystone of every socialist political-economic system (see next chapter).
- Global regimentation, with draconian regulation, in minute detail, of (in the words of one of their favorite eco-programs) "every person on earth."
- World government, with legislative, executive, and judicial powers, including military and police to enforce "world law."

The internationalist elite of the New York-Moscow Axis have been working in tandem to convince the peoples of the world that, in the words of the World Federalist Association, "Global Problems Require Global Governance." Through the influence of their symbiotic power networks, this one-world slogan has become universally adopted by Communists, socialists, feminists, environmentalists, human rights activists, disarmament advocates, and others worldwide. As usual, the coordinating brain center is Pratt House, the CFR.

Previously we noted that CFR braintruster Lincoln P. Bloomfield, in his 1962 study for the CFR-dominated Kennedy State Department, *A World Effectively Controlled by the United Nations*, had conceded that it would be difficult to bring about a merger between the U.S. and the Soviet Union. Obviously, Americans would not go for union with a murderous, totalitarian system. That is why the threat of nuclear annihilation, "mutually assured destruction," had to be built into a credible threat more to be feared than Communism itself. Then, at the critical point, the Soviets would come to their senses and realize that only "collective security," under which national armaments were transferred to UN authority, offered a viable future. The Kremlin would mellow and democratize. However, Bloomfield saw that this scheme posed a major problem. He wrote: "if the communist dynamic were greatly abated, the West might lose whatever incentive it has for world government." [19]

Indeed, if the nasty, blood-soaked Reds convincingly demonstrate that they are "mellowing," then much of the pressure for surrendering our arms evaporates. Obviously another sufficiently grave threat (or threats) must be found to substitute for, or augment the nuclear holocaust fear. As Bloomfield saw it, the drive for world government would require "a crisis, a war, or a brink-of-war situation so grave or commonly menacing that deeply rooted attitudes and practices are sufficiently shaken to open the possibility of a revolution in world political arrangements." [20]

Dr. Bloomfield is not alone in recognizing the utility of war and crisis in the service of totalitarianism. Another Insider strategist who has expounded on this subject is the late Herman Kahn (CFR), physicist/futurist founder of the Hudson Institute. In his essay, "World Federal Government," co-authored with Anthony J. Wiener, Kahn acknowledges that building world government requires "intense external dangers." [21] Echoing Bloomfield, Kahn stated that "a world government could only be created out of war or crisis — an emergency that provided an appropriate combination of the motivations of fear and opportunity." [22] The

Kahn/Wiener essay so impressed the leaders of the World Federalist Association that they have reprinted and promoted it.[23]

Still another voice in the crisis choir is Brian Urquhart, a former UN under secretary-general and now a full-time UN propagandist at the Ford Foundation. Urquhart has lamented, "There are moments when I feel that only an invasion from outer space will reintroduce into the Security Council that unanimity and spirit which the founders of the Charter were talking about."[24] Mr. Urquhart's one-world colleagues have actually considered the feasibility of creating such a unifying extra-terrestrial "threat." That was one of the considerations pondered by the "Special Study Group" (SSG) convened in 1963 by the same Pratt House gang in the Kennedy administration who commissioned Bloomfield's study.[25] The SSG produced a secret report that created a storm of controversy when it was anonymously released in 1967 as the *Report From Iron Mountain*.[26]*

According to the *Iron Mountain* report, the SSG considered whether "such a menace would offer the 'last, best hope of peace,' etc., by uniting mankind against the danger of destruction by 'creatures' from other planets or from outer space."[27] But the group decided such far-out scenarios lacked "credibility." Ditto for most other contrived "menaces." However, they decided, "the environmental-pollution model" offered hopeful potential.[28] "It may be," said the *Report*, " ... that gross pollution of the environment can eventually replace the possibility of mass destruction by nuclear weapons as the principal apparent threat to the survival of the species."[29]

The line adopted by the CFR Establishment press was that the *Report From Iron Mountain* was a hoax, a "brilliant satire." But was it? At the very time that they were dismissing the report as

---

*The available evidence indicates that Herman Kahn and his CFR-laden Hudson Institute may have formed the core of the SSG, or that the SSG may have been entirely a Kahn/Hudson operation. See Gary Allen's articles "Think Tanks: Where the Revolution Is Being Planned" and "Making Plans: For a Dictatorship in America" in *American Opinion* magazine, March and April 1971, respectively.

a delightful joke, the Pratt House illuminati were implementing the game plan it proposed. Through their power and influence in government, academe, the media, tax-exempt foundations, and Wall Street, they were furiously building the threat of environmental destruction into "a credible substitute for war capable of directing human behavior patterns in behalf of social organization."[30] Three years after the publication of *Iron Mountain* the first Earth Day was held, launching a global crusade that has had a dramatic impact on our world — politically, economically, socially, philosophically, morally, and religiously.

Recall that according to Dr. Bloomfield (see Chapter 2), "the order we examine may be brought into existence as a result of a series of sudden, nasty, and traumatic shocks."[31] The Iron Mountain gang concurred, noting that the new "war substitute" must provide an "immediate, tangible, and directly felt threat of destruction."[32] Thus, a nonstop series of nasty and traumatic shocks has been provided by the Insider-financed and -directed environmental movement. Those shocks have been aimed at convincing a significant share of the population of the Western countries that our planet faces imminent, cataclysmic consequences unless immediate, global action is taken — action that includes global regulation of environmental "menaces."

For three decades we have been assaulted with an incessant bombardment of environmental doomsday propaganda. At every turn, eco-destruction awaits us: The oceans are dying; the rain forests are disappearing; the deserts are growing; species are being driven to extinction; critical resources are being depleted; CO_2 is increasing; the earth is warming; the polar ice caps are melting; carcinogens are everywhere; pesticides are killing us. Crises! Crises! Crises!

We Are All One
But mere *crises* are not enough; they must be *GLOBAL CRISES!* Traditionally, *war* has been the ultimate crisis for mankind. During war the people yield vast powers to the government for the welfare and survival of the tribe, city, or nation. The envi-

ronmental "crises" we face, say the one-world eco-saviors, are *global crises*, presenting a *global threat* as deadly as war. Obviously, handling this threat is beyond the capabilities of individual nation states. Ergo, we must have *global government* with *global powers*.

This was the theme of Mikhail Gorbachev's celebrated "End of the Cold War" speech in Fulton, Missouri, in 1992. "The prospect of catastrophic climatic changes, more frequent droughts, floods, hunger, epidemics, national-ethnic conflicts, and other similar catastrophes compels governments to adopt a world perspective and seek generally applicable solutions," he declared. This could only be accomplished, said Gorbachev, through "some kind of global government." "I believe," said the CFR-approved "former" Communist, "that the new world order will not be fully realized unless the United Nations and its Security Council create structures ... which are authorized to impose sanctions and make use of other measures of compulsion." [33]

Gorbachev's Fulton speech (which perfectly reflected the CFR line — and was probably written by Pratt House wordsmiths) signaled a new stepped-up phase in the drive for global "interdependence" and "convergence." That drive includes an enormous propaganda campaign saturating the American public with the idea that our environmental problems are too immense to be dealt with by our present system of independent, sovereign nation states. Thus we increasingly find ourselves confronting such pre-fabricated slogans as "Global Problems Require Global Solutions," "Global Problems Require Global Governance," and "Think Globally, Act Locally."

Amongst environmentalists and many other one-world "grievance" agitators, these slogans have become incessant mantras. "The first law of ecology tells us that 'everything is connected to everything else,'" proclaims environmental radical Jeremy Rifkin in his book *Entropy: Into the Greenhouse World.* [34] This thesis of global "interconnectedness," "unity," and "oneness" — a new "paradigm shift" — now permeates all discussion of things economic, political, social, environmental, moral, and spiritual —

thanks to the promotion it has received from the Insider elite. School children are inculcated with this message from their textbooks. Children and adults receive daily doses of *inter*dependence from television "news" and "nature" programs. This is a conscious, subversive effort to reorient the public to a "one-world" view.

Professor of international law and one-world architect Benjamin Ferencz asserts that "antiquated notions of absolute sovereignty are absolutely obsolete in the interconnected and interdependent global world of the 21st century." [35] This is also the message of New Age political activists Corinne McLaughlin and Gordon Davidson. In *Spiritual Politics: Changing the World From the Inside Out*, they write: "A systems approach is needed, as all our problems are interconnected and interdependent, facets of one single crisis — essentially a crisis of perception. This crisis is part of a cultural shift from a mechanistic worldview to a holistic and ecological view, from a value system based on domination to partnership, from quantity to quality, from expansion to conservation, from efficiency to sustainability." [36]

In the same vein, New Age futurist and best-selling author Alvin Toffler approvingly notes that the "Third Wave" era, in which we are now living, "gives rise to groups with larger than nationalist interests. These form the base of the emerging globalist ideology sometimes called 'planetary consciousness.'" [37] Fellow globalists Jessica Lipnack and Jeffrey Stamps develop this thesis in their book *Networking*. In this emerging world view, they say, "nature's ecological orchestra is revered as one unified instrument, inner development is valued as a correlate to social involvement, and the planet is understood to be an interconnected whole." [38] But this is not "nature's" orchestra we are hearing; it's the same Pratt House-orchestrated choir singing the same anti-national sovereignty, pro-world government refrain — with a decidedly neo-pagan spiritual twist added. (This "spiritual" dimension of the globalist agenda will be more closely examined in Chapter 12).

If we "follow the money," we quickly see that the funding for the groups and individuals singing this tune comes from the usual sources: the big CFR-dominated tax-exempt foundations and corporations.[39] The tune is amplified in the political realm by CFR politicians like Senators John Kerry, Charles Schumer, John D. Rockefeller, John Chafee, and Joseph Lieberman, and Representatives Richard Gephardt, Lee Hamilton, Barney Frank, Jim Leach, Sam Gejdenson, and Charles Rangel. Newt Gingrich, the CFR's prize "conservative," invites Alvin Toffler (repeatedly) to address the House of Representatives and even pens a glowing introduction to one of the futurist's works of Marxoid flummery.[40]

And the CFR media cartel dutifully publicizes the apocalyptic scenarios of the doomsayers and praises them as courageous "prophets." Fright peddlers and one-world apostles such as Gorbachev, Rifkin, Toffler, Ferencz, et al., are favorably reviewed, sympathetically quoted, and provided with national media platforms to trumpet their nonsense and disinformation. Their twaddle is assigned as required reading to millions of students as though it is gospel. As at Rio, genuine scientists and scholars representing the authentic voice of scientific consensus are ignored or even vilified when they refute the hysterical nonsense and claptrap of the environmental gurus. Because of this blatant bias of the controlled media, these lunatic ravings and New Age mystic musings are no longer relegated to the wacky fringes of society, where they belong; they are expounded by supposedly "serious" think tanks, "respected" journals, and "mainstream" politicians, *and form the basis for international treaties and federal policies and law.*

The Work of Decades

This "cultural shift," as McLaughlin and Davidson put it in *Spiritual Politics*,[41] has not happened overnight; it has been the patient work of more than a generation. Earth Day 1970 marked the launch of an ongoing offensive by an "ecology movement" that the Insiders had been building for years. 1972 marked another major watershed. In that year, the Club of Rome, an international coterie of one-world elitists (including many of the usual CFR regulars) came out with a much-heralded study, *The Limits to Growth*. This eco-socialist jeremiad proclaimed: "Entirely new approaches are required to redirect society toward goals of equilibrium rather than growth." [42] In order to save the earth, said the Club report, "joint long-term planning will be necessary on a scale and scope without precedent." [43] A "supreme effort" by all would be required "to organize more equitable distribution of wealth and income worldwide." [44]

The authority of *The Limits to Growth* was presented as beyond question. After all, it was produced by researchers using "sophisticated" computer models at the "prestigious" Massachusetts Institute of Technology. Added to this was the stature of the scientific, intellectual, political, and corporate celebrities associated with the esteemed Club of Rome. These "impressive" cachets notwithstanding, the *Limits* study was about as "scientific" as Chicken Little's claims that "the sky is falling." The main difference is that Chicken Little was a poor fool who actually believed her own hysterical alarms. The Club of Rome Insiders are peddling Chicken Little hysteria in order to panic and stampede all the barnyard animals into their New World Order corral.

Interestingly, that same year, 1972, Gus Hall, National Chairman of the Communist Party of the United States (CPUSA), released a book entitled *Ecology* with a similar message. "Human society cannot basically stop the destruction of the environment under capitalism," said Comrade Hall. [45] "Socialism is the only structure that makes it possible." [46] He continued: "Socialism corrects the basic flaw of capitalism. It sets human society on a new path. The means of production, factories, mines and mills become the property of the people. They operate and produce only to fulfill human needs.... This is the foundation for a new set of priorities, for new values.... What is involved is a 'conflict of values.'" [47]

1972 was also the year of the first "Earth Summit," the United Nations Conference on the Human Environment, held in

Stockholm, Sweden. Serving as secretary-general of that event was Canadian billionaire-socialist Maurice Strong (whom we will see, later on, become a high-level Insider). The conference was hosted by Swedish Prime Minister Olof Palme, one of the many leaders of the Socialist International in attendance. An immediate outcome of that summit was the creation of the United Nations Environment Program (UNEP), with Mr. Strong as its first executive director. Other summit results included a socialist-environmentalist manifesto called the Stockholm Declaration,[48] consisting of 26 principles, and the Stockholm Plan of Action,[49] a set of 109 (mostly Marxist) recommendations. One of the key intellectuals advising the conference and helping write its reports was Rockefeller University microbiologist Rene Dubos.*

That same year, Dubos came out with the celebrated book *Only One Earth*, which was co-authored with the British Fabian Socialist Barbara Ward (Lady Jackson).[50]

Thus, in 1972, the same eco-socialist "marching orders" were given to the hard-core Communist cadres, the worldwide socialist parties, and the great global mainstream of environmentalists and concerned citizens. In the years since those reports by the Club of Rome, the Communist Party, the UN, and Dubos/Ward, a deluge of similar and increasingly militant reports and books appeared from the Communist-socialist left paralleling, and at times converging with, the themes espoused in reports, articles, and books by the CFR "capitalist" elites. Although these "opposing sides" may attack each other rhetorically, what's important is the bottom line: Both sides are advocating central planning (socialism) and internationalism (world government). The Red-Green orchestra was playing furiously.

By the mid-1980s, we see U.S.-Soviet "convergence" in full swing, with Soviet dictator Mikhail Gorbachev and U.S. leaders engaged in large-scale cooperative propaganda efforts to push the same global environmental agenda. Gorbachev's subsequent replacement by Boris Yeltsin, and then Vladimir Putin, did not derail the CFR-Kremlin cooperation in this ongoing venture; in

---

*Dubos coined the slogan "Think Globally, Act Locally."

fact, it accelerated the agenda. Comrade Gorbachev, acting ostensibly as a private citizen, launched his "global brain trust" (his words), the Gorbachev Foundation, staffed in Moscow with 150 "former" Communist apparatchiks, and with affiliated institutes in the U.S. and other nations. During the 1990s, which leading world-order theorist Professor Richard Falk (CFR) said would be the "decade of transformation,"[51] Gorbachev was in constant motion, along with the leading lights of Pratt House, pushing the CFR-Kremlin one-world line.

In his 1992 book *Voting Green*, Rifkin wrote: "[T]he new Green vision places the environment at the center of public life, making it the context for both the formulation of economic policies and political decisions."[52] That was penned to coincide with the UN's Earth Summit. And the CFR media orchestra made sure that that message was delivered repeatedly to the American public, to opinion molders, and to policy makers and legislators by a gaggle of different messengers. This kind of orchestrated saturation is essential if you are going to effect a real "cultural shift" or "paradigm shift."

A cascade of enviro-Marxist offerings mushroomed out of nowhere with the same theme. On the plane to Rio de Janeiro and at the Earth Summit itself, everywhere I looked, delegates, activists, and reporters were ravenously devouring (and later parroting) the contents of a host of new books and reports. *The State of the World*, an annual environmental fright report put out by the Worldwatch Institute (WI), was everywhere cited as holy writ.[53] Worldwatch is headed by Lester Brown (CFR), whom the *Washington Post* has admiringly described as "one of the world's most influential thinkers."[54] His website notes that he founded WI in 1974 "with support of the Rockefeller Brothers Fund."[55] And the WI annual reports acknowledge that "the Rockefeller Brothers Fund and the Winthrop Rockefeller Trust provide core funding for the *State of the World* series."[56]

Another tome that excited the Earth Summit greenies, while garnering rave reviews from the Establishment media, was *Changing Course*, by Stephen Schmidheiny and the Business

Council for Sustainable Development (BCSD).[57] The BCSD is loaded with corporate-socialist one-worlders, such as Maurice R. Greenberg, chairman of American International Group, Inc. Mr. Greenberg is vice-chairman of the CFR and his AIG is a CFR corporate member.

One of the most celebrated books to come out at the time of the Summit was produced by then-Senator Al Gore. In *Earth In The Balance: Ecology and the Human Spirit*, Gore insisted that "the effort to save the global environment" must become the "single shared goal [and] the central organizing principle for every institution in society."[58] The book is a perfervid piece of socialist eco-propaganda larded with an incredible number of errors, ludicrous claims, and blatant misrepresentations. But it was exactly what the Pratt House globalists wanted, and it was a relatively easy matter for them to provide the hype necessary to turn it into a bestseller. Gore, a protégé of Communist billionaire Armand Hammer,[59] led the U.S. Senate delegation to Rio and was launched on his way to becoming Vice President of the United States.

Trilateral Road to Rio
More important than the Gore book, though read by a far smaller, elite audience, was the revealing Trilateral Commission book *Beyond Interdependence: The Meshing of the World's Economy and the Earth's Ecology*, by Canada's Jim MacNeill, Holland's Pieter Winsemius, and Japan's Taizo Yakushiji.[60] David Rockefeller (then head of the CFR and Trilateral Commission) and Maurice Strong teamed up to write, respectively, the foreword and introduction to the Trilateral book. "... I have been privileged to work closely with the principal author, Jim MacNeill, for over two decades," wrote Strong. "He was one of my advisors when I was secretary general of the Stockholm Conference on the Human Environment in 1972. We were both members of the World Commission on Environment and Development and, as secretary general, he played a fundamental role in shaping and writing its landmark report, *Our*

Common Future [a socialist/environmentalist manifesto also known as The Brundtland Report]."[61] What's more, revealed Strong, MacNeill "is now advising me on the road to Rio,"[62] where Strong served a dual role, as the UN impresario and the Insiders' on-site manager.

Beyond Interdependence served as the Trilateral game plan for Rio, and it had Strong's full endorsement. "This book couldn't appear at a better time, with the preparations for the Earth Summit moving into high gear," said Strong.[63] To stress its importance, he said it would help guide "decisions that will literally determine the fate of the earth."[64] According to this head summiteer, the Rio gathering would "have the political capacity to produce the basic changes needed in our national and international economic agendas and in our institutions of governance...."[65] In his estimation, *"Beyond Interdependence* provides the most compelling economic as well as environmental case for such reform that I have read."[66]

MacNeill and his co-authors advocated "a new global partnership expressed in a revitalized international system in which an Earth Council, perhaps the Security Council with a broader mandate, maintains the interlocked environmental and economic security of the planet."[67] "The Earth Summit," wrote MacNeill and his cohorts, "will likely be the last chance for the world, in this century at least, to seriously address and arrest the accelerating environmental threats to economic development, national security, and human survival."[68]

Of course, all of the official preparatory meetings and negotiations leading up to the Earth Summit were really just so much spectacle for public consumption. And the Rio gathering itself was additional "consensus" sideshow to provide an aura of planetary "democracy" for a program that was already worked out in detail by the one-worlders, with their CFR brain trusts at the World Resources Institute, Worldwatch Institute, World Order Models Project, the Business Council for Sustainable Development, etc., long before. The objective? The obvious one was to give impetus to the global environmentalist agenda. But an important additional objective was to prepare the world to accept a broad new UN mandate (without rewriting its charter): The UN was not just about peacekeeping anymore.

Ronald I. Spiers (CFR) was one of many globalist agents who prepped public opinion and policy makers for what was to come, when he wrote, in the March 13, 1992 *New York Times*: "The [United Nations] Trusteeship Council should be changed from a body dealing with the vestiges of colonialism to one dealing with the environment, becoming in effect the trustee of the health of the planet."[69] Surprise! That's precisely what happened at Rio.

An earlier purveyor of this line, the venerable CFR "wise man" George F. Kennan, explained in a *Washington Post* column appearing on November 12, 1989 that we now live "in an age where the great enemy is not the Soviet Union but the rapid deterioration of our planet as a supporting structure for civilized life."[70] Kennan, a Princeton University professor and former U.S. Ambassador to the Soviet Union, was the author of our nation's phony Cold War policy of "containment" of Communism.

Jessica Tuchman Mathews (CFR, TC), then vice president of the World Resources Institute, followed with an article in the July/August 1990 *EPA Journal* asserting that "environmental imperatives are changing the concept of national sovereignty," and "multipolarity [is] replacing the bipolar U.S.-U.S.S.R. axis around which nations used to array themselves."[71] Moreover, she wrote, "it is likely that international problem-solving in the decades ahead will for the first time depend on collective management, not hegemony. And it is to precisely this form of governance that global environmental problems will yield."[72]

Gorbachev's Toxic Globaloney

Mikhail Gorbachev, who is the darling of new world order promoters, and was one of the superstars of the Earth Summit, had also been thumping this theme for a couple of years. Addressing the 1990 Global Forum in Moscow, he called for "ecologizing" society and said: "The ecological crisis we are experiencing today — from ozone depletion to deforestation and disastrous air pollution — is tragic but convincing proof that the world we all live in is interrelated and interdependent." [73]

"This means," Gorbachev continued, "that we need an appropriate international policy in the field of ecology. Only if we formulate such a policy shall we be able to avert catastrophe. True, the elaboration of such a policy poses unconventional and difficult problems that will affect the sovereignty of states." [74] In a 1994 interview with the significant title, "From Red to Green," in the Insider-funded *Audubon* magazine, Gorbachev stated: "We must change all our values.... What we are talking about is creating new forms of life on the basis of new values." [75]

In a 1995 interview with the environmental magazine *Grassroots*, Gorbachev insisted that the only hope for saving our planet lay in "the development and implementation of an Earth Charter, a body of international ecological laws that would guide the actions of individuals, corporations and governments ... the time has come for a code of ethical and moral principles that will govern the conduct of nations and people with respect to the environment." [76]

But what are these "new values" and "moral principles" that Mr. Gorbachev insists that all humanity must embrace? That is an important question to answer, since he is playing such a key leadership role in this process. Besides heading up his Gorbachev Foundation and State of the World Forum, Mr. Gorbachev (Nobel Laureate, *Time* magazine's "Man of the Decade" [77]) is also head of Green Cross International, of which Global Green USA is the American affiliate. And he was chosen at Rio by his good buddy Maurice Strong to lead the drafting of the Earth Charter.

Let's take a look at the values and principles of the "Prophet of Perestroika." This is the same Gorbachev who, in November 1987, proclaimed: "In October 1917, we parted with the Old World, rejecting it once and for all. *We are moving toward a new world, the world of Communism. We shall never turn off that road.*" [78] (Emphasis added.) "Perestroika," he said then, "is a continuation of the October Revolution." [79] By which he means V. I.

Lenin's bloody, murderous Bolshevik Revolution. As we will see below, Gorbachev is an unrepentant, unregenerate, militant, atheist Communist. (And, as we will see in Chapter 12, that has not hindered in the least his ascent into the ranks of the UN's premier spiritual leaders who are confecting the diabolical new Global Ethic, or world religion.)

In 1989, Gorbachev declared: "*I am a Communist, a convinced Communist*. For some that may be a fantasy. But for me it is my main goal." [80] The following year, even as he was being hailed as the "man who ended Communism," he reiterated this conviction, stating, "*I am now, just as I've always been, a convinced Communist.*" [81] He has never repudiated these or his many other similar statements. And a close examination of his speeches and statements that *appear* to show a "new" Gorbachev actually show him to be still a hardcore Leninist. Just as Hitler revealed his real self in *Mein Kampf*, for all who were willing to see, Gorbachev has made quite clear where he stands, and for what he stands.

Are the CFR cognoscenti promoting Gorby illiterates? Are they unaware that his "ex-Communist" act is a ruse? Of course not; they are *fully* aware of the deception involved here. It is the Pratt House plutocracy that has been his main sponsor and the primary force assisting his deception.*

Given his unrepentant convictions, it is a simple matter to see why Gorbachev so enthusiastically supports the global enviro-Leninist regimens emanating from the UN. Such as Agenda 21.

---

*In his famous book *Perestroika*, he plainly admitted: "We are not going to change Soviet power, of course, or abandon its fundamental principles, but we acknowledge the need for changes that will *strengthen socialism*." [82] (Emphasis added.) In the same revered text he explained that "according to Lenin, socialism and democracy are indivisible," and the "essence of perestroika lies in the fact that it *unites socialism with democracy* and revives the Leninist concept of socialist construction both in theory and in practice." [83] (Emphasis in original.) Thus, when he declares for "democracy," he means "democracy" within the Leninist conception and definition of the term, something quite the opposite of that which most Americans assume he is talking about.

Agenda 21's Terrifying Agenda

This mammoth program for global social engineering and eco-tyranny is a massive blueprint for regimenting all life on Planet Earth in the 21st century — in the name of protecting the environment. *Agenda 21: The Earth Summit Strategy to Save the Planet* (EarthPress, 1993), one of the UN-approved editions of the program, makes this brazen assertion:

> Effective execution of Agenda 21 will require a profound reorientation of all human society, unlike anything the world has ever experienced — a major shift in the priorities of both governments and individuals and an unprecedented redeployment of human and financial resources. This shift will demand that a concern for the environmental consequences of every human action be integrated into individual and collective decision-making at every level. [84]

With breathtaking audacity, the document continues:

> There are specific actions which are intended to be undertaken by multinational corporations and entrepreneurs, by financial institutions and individual investors, by high-tech companies and indigenous people, by workers and labor unions, by farmers and consumers, by students and schools, by governments and legislators, by scientists, by women, by children — in short, by every person on Earth. [85]

If Gorbachev is a "socialist," a "Communist," a "Leninist" — which he says he is, and vindicates that claim with many actions — it is perfectly understandable that he would be very pleased with the direction that the United States is going with the UN environmental agenda. As a Leninist, he is comfortable with *long-term* strategy, and, as his idolizing biographer, Gail Sheehy, noted, he has long been known for "his emulation of Lenin's policy of two steps forward, one step backward." [86]

But Comrade Mikhail, as we've noted, is getting plenty of help from "our" side. He and his Russian colleagues are provided with continuous tutoring and infusions of cash from world order heavyweights such as George Soros (CFR), Zbigniew Brzezinski (CFR, TC), George Shultz (CFR, TC), Henry Kissinger (CFR, TC), David Rockefeller (CFR, TC), and Richard N. Gardner* (CFR, TC).[87]

It was Professor Gardner who penned the now-famous article, "The Hard Road to World Order," in the April 1974 issue of *Foreign Affairs*. One of the boldest calls for world government ever to appear in the CFR's journal, it proposed building the "house of world order" through "an end run around national sovereignty, eroding it piece by piece."[88] What's more, it set out the CFR Insider plans for exploiting fears about environmental calamity as a vehicle for expanding the UN's power. In this 1974 article, Gardner wrote:

> The next few years should see a continued strengthening of the new global and regional agencies charged with protecting the world's *environment*. In addition to comprehensive monitoring of the earth's air, water and soil and of the effects of pollutants on human health, we can look forward to new procedures to implement the principle of state responsibility for national actions that have transnational environmental consequences, probably including some kind of "international environmental impact statement"....[89] [Emphasis in original.]

Together with Gorbachev and his "former" Communist cronies in the Kremlin, the Pratt House one-worlders intend to fasten a global enviro-Leninist world government upon the planet Earth. And they are far along the way to accomplishing this.

---

*Gardner also tutored then-Governor Jimmy Carter in foreign policy "issues" for two years to prepare him for the presidency.[90]

Chapter 7

The UN's War on Private Property

Private land ownership is also a principal instrument of accumulation and concentration of wealth and therefore contributes to social injustice.... Public control of land use is therefore indispensable....[1]
— United Nations "Habitat I" Conference Report, 1976

In one word, you reproach us with intending to do away with your property. Precisely so; that is just what we intend.[2]
— Karl Marx, *The Communist Manifesto*, 1848

Property is theft![3]
— P. J. Proudhon, the "Father of Anarchy," 1840

Property *struck the first blow at* Equality; *...* the supporters of Governments and property are the religious and civil laws; *therefore, to reinstate man in his primitive rights of Equality and Liberty, we must begin by destroying all Religion, all civil society, and finish by the destruction of all property.*[4] (Emphasis in original.)
— Adam Weishaupt, founder of the Order of the Illuminati, 1776

According to Karl Marx, "the theory of the Communists may be summed up in the single sentence: abolition of private property."[5] That's pretty plain, and it's directly out of the *Communist Manifesto*. It has been the rallying cry of collectivists of all stripes — communists, socialists, anarchists, fascists — and has guided the most ruthless and bloody regimes of the past century. Lenin, Stalin, Mao, Ho Chi Minh, Ceausescu, Tito, Gomulka,

Castro, Pol Pot, Mengistu, Ortega, and dozens of other Communist dictators and satraps all fervently espoused that Marxian precept and applied it with a vengeance. And in so doing, they produced mountains of corpses and rivers of blood unequalled in all history.

Conversely, the champions of freedom have ever recognized that private property is essential both to human liberty and to the material well-being and economic advancement of all classes of people. "Let the people have property," observed Noah Webster, "and they will have power — a power that *will* for ever be exerted to prevent a restriction of the press, and abolition of trial by jury, or the abridgement of any other privilege."[6] (Emphasis in original.) Justice Joseph Story, who was appointed to the Supreme Court by President James Madison and became one of America's most revered jurists, put it this way: "That government can scarcely be deemed to be free when the rights of property are left solely dependent upon the will of a legislative body, without any restraint. The fundamental maxims of a free government seem to require that the rights of personal liberty and private property should be held sacred."[7]

"It is the glory of the British constitution," said Samuel Adams, "that it hath its foundation in the law of God and nature. It is an essential, natural right, that a man shall quietly enjoy, and have the sole disposal of his own property."[8] Moreover, said Adams, "Property is admitted to have an existence even in the savage state of nature.... And if property is necessary for the support of savage life, it is by no mean less so in civil society. The utopian schemes of levelling, and a community of goods, are as visionary and impracticable as those which vest all property in the Crown are arbitrary, despotic, and in our government, unconstitutional."[9]

In his famous encyclical *Rerum Novarum*, written in 1891, Pope Leo XIII stated: "We have seen that this great labor question cannot be solved save by assuming as a principle that private ownership must be held sacred and inviolable. The law, therefore, should favor ownership, and its policy should be to induce as many as possible of the humbler class to become owners." "Men always work harder and more readily," he continued, "when they work on that which belongs to them; nay, they learn to love the very soil that yields, in response to the labor of their hands, not only food to eat but an abundance of good things for themselves and those that are dear to them." [10]

In our own day, this same powerful truth was expounded clearly by the great economist Friedrich A. Hayek. "What our generation has forgotten," he said in his 1944 Nobel Prize-winning classic, *The Road to Serfdom*, "is that the system of private property is the most important guaranty of freedom, not only for those who own property, but scarcely less for those who do not. It is only because the control of the means of production is divided among many people acting independently that nobody has complete power over us, that we as individuals can decide what to do with ourselves." [11]

It is easy, then, to see why those who have totalitarian ambitions always attempt to destroy private property. Because, like Hayek, they understand that as long as "the control of the means of production is divided among many people acting independently," their plans for total power will remain frustrated. The millions of farmers, homeowners, businessmen, shopkeepers, artisans, laborers, and professionals who own their own property form a natural obstacle to tyrannical aspirations. If people are allowed to own their land, grow their food, manufacture whatever products they choose, live in homes of their own, and freely exchange their goods, services, and labor — why, they just might not meekly yield to the dictates of central planners, whether of the fascist, communist, or socialist variety!

So whom do you think the folks at the United Nations and their Insider sponsors choose to follow: Adams, Webster, Leo XIII, and Hayek? Or Marx, Mao, Lenin, and Stalin? You guessed it: Time after time after time, they've chosen the path of power, slaughter, tyranny, and destruction, rather than liberty, morality, and justice. As we will see next, with an examination of a few of the UN's eco-Marxist programs.

The UN Gets Into the Act

We begin with "Habitat I," the Conference Report of the United Nations Conference on Human Settlements, held in Vancouver, Canada, during June 1976. The Preamble of this important document, endorsed by the United States and the other participating nations, declares:

> Land ... cannot be treated as an ordinary asset, controlled by individuals and subject to the pressures and inefficiencies of the market. Private land ownership is also a principal instrument of accumulation and concentration of wealth and therefore contributes to social injustice.... Public control of land use is therefore indispensable....[12]

The main body of the text then proposes the following Marxist policies, among others:

> Recommendation D.1 Land resource management
>
> (a) Public ownership or effective control of land in the public interest is the single most important means of ... achieving a more equitable distribution of the benefits of development whilst assuring that environmental impacts are considered.
>
> (b) Land is a scarce resource whose management should be subject to public surveillance or control in the interest of the nation....
>
> (d) ... Governments must maintain full jurisdiction and exercise complete sovereignty over such land with a view to freely planning development of human settlements....[13]

Then there is Agenda 21, the massive environmental manifesto that came out of the 1992 UN Earth Summit. As we saw in Chapter 6, this is a monstrous socialist scheme for micromanaging every square centimeter of the planet's surface — not to mention the air and space above it and the ground and seas below it. This green communist manifesto holds that "land must be regarded primarily as a set of essential terrestrial ecosystems and only secondly as a source of resources."[14] We must develop new social systems, it says, because "traditional systems have not been able to cope with the sheer scale of modern activities." These new systems will "have as their goal both the effective management of land resources and their socially-equitable use."[15]

Agenda 21 states further: "All countries should undertake a comprehensive national inventory of their land resources in order to establish a system in which land will be classified according to its most appropriate uses...."[16] Moreover: "All countries should also develop national land-management plans to guide development."[17]

Another frightful creature to emerge from the Rio Earth Summit (UNCED) was the Global Biodiversity Assessment (GBA). The GBA is a huge, 1,140-page instrument that claims to provide a "scientific" basis for implementing the Convention on Biological Diversity. "Property rights are not absolute and unchanging," it informs us, "but rather a complex, dynamic and shifting relationship between two or more parties, over space and time."[18] And the UN ecocrats are determined to make any property rights they don't abolish outright as "complex, dynamic and shifting" as possible. "We should accept biodiversity [i.e., plants and animals] as a legal subject, and supply it with adequate rights. This could clarify the principle that biodiversity is not available for uncontrolled human use."[19] Translation: We must assign legal "rights" to animals, trees, bugs, bushes, weeds, birds, fishes, even mountains, and then appoint "custodians," "guardians," or "trustees" (all of whom must be watermelon Marxists, of course) to look out for and speak for these rights.

"Contrary to current custom," says the GBA, "it would therefore become necessary to justify any interference with biodiversity, and to provide proof that human interests justify the damage caused to biodiversity."[20] In other words, under this socialist scheme, a "guardian" or "stakeholder" (someone claiming to represent a plant or animal species on the property) can assert a priority right over that of the actual property owner, and force the owner to "prove" that any activity he contemplates for "his" property will not adversely impact the flora and fauna which constitute the "biodiversity" in that "ecosystem."

Two other alien entities spawned at the Earth Summit were the UN Commission on Sustainable Development and an international NGO with quasi-official functions known as the Earth Council. These organizations coordinate the activities of national councils on biodiversity, which have been established to implement Agenda 21. The Earth Council is presided over by Maurice Strong, Secretary-General of the Rio Earth Summit, a director of the World Economic Forum, a member of the Commission on Global Governance, and a director of the Gorbachev Foundation.

U.S. Pressure From Above

In 1993, President Clinton (CFR) created the President's Council on Sustainable Development (PCSD) by executive order. The PCSD joined five Cabinet members with the leaders of the Sierra Club, the Natural Resources Defense Council, the Environmental Defense Fund, and the Nature Conservancy and charged them to "develop policy recommendations for a national strategy for sustainable development that can be implemented by the public and private sectors."[21] They were to use as their guide the UN Convention on Biodiversity, which Clinton signed in June 1993 (but which the Senate has yet to ratify).

In 1995 the PCSD issued its report, *Sustainable America, A New Consensus*, which stated:

> Privately owned lands are most often delineated by boundaries that differ from the geographic boundaries of the natural system of which they are a part. Therefore, individual or private decisions can have negative ramifications ... that result in severe ecological or aesthetic consequences to both the natural system and to communities outside landowner boundaries.[22]

That same year, President Clinton demonstrated how such internationalist socialist policies can play out when he brought in a team of UN bureaucrats (at U.S. taxpayer expense) from the

UNESCO World Heritage Committee (WHC). Their mission was to close down a proposed gold mine on private property in the vicinity of Yellowstone National Park, which the UN lists as a World Heritage Site. Militant eco-fanatics together with the Clinton-Gore administration had been trying for years to stop the Crown Butte Mining Company from starting operations there. The company had jumped through all of the costly and convoluted state and federal environmental impact analyses and presented no risk to the park or surrounding area.

But before Crown Butte could begin operation, the UNESCO-WHC "scientists" came up with a finding that allowing the project to go forward would be ecologically disastrous. That was the only pretext President Clinton needed to issue an executive order stopping all new mining permits within a 19,000-acre area of federal land near Yellowstone. The UNESCO delegation went even further, seeking to review all policies involving mining, timber, wildlife, and tourism within an area of nearly *18 million acres* surrounding the park, including millions of acres of private land. They and their U.S. enviro-Leninist allies want to create the "Greater Yellowstone Ecosystem," an enormous "biodiversity reserve." This is part of the UN's global Wildlands Project, aimed at "re-wilding" literally half of the U.S. land area.

Wildlands are constructed of habitat zones called "core areas," in which human activity is increasingly restricted and ultimately (virtually) eliminated. The core areas are then linked to restrictive "buffer zones." These areas are then connected by networks of "wildlife corridors."

It's important to recognize that this U.S.-UN eco-entanglement didn't begin with Bill Clinton and it won't end now that he has left office. George Bush the Elder (CFR) occupied the White House in 1992, and his main representative at the Earth Summit that year was EPA Administrator William Reilly (CFR), a militant greenie. Before coming on board the Bush team, Reilly had served as president of both the Conservation Foundation and the World Wildlife Fund-U.S. And he had served as executive director of a land-use task force chaired by Laurance S.

Rockefeller, which promoted Marxist land-use controls and expropriation.

Reilly's contempt for private property was evident not only from the EPA policies he promulgated, but also from his own words. In his introduction to the 1985 book *National Parks for a New Generation*, for example, he advocated "greenline parks." Under this concept, closely akin to the UN schemes, privately owned land adjacent to federal or state parks could be declared part of the park system by executive fiat and its use restricted to conform to park purposes — in blatant disregard and violation of constitutional protections against such abuse.

In addition, Reilly argued that the "mainstream" American attitude toward property rights in land has been "the right of citizens to exercise dominion over land they own," but if "parks are to be protected ... the tradition of park stewardship must gradually be extended beyond park boundaries, to domains where mainstream attitudes about private property and freedom of action still prevail today."[23]

This "watermelon Marxism" — green on the outside, red on the inside — has been promoted and supported *continuously* in the highest levels of our federal government, through both Republican and Democratic administrations, by the CFR Establishment. And the same one-world coterie also has continuously provided the "pressure from below" as well.

More Establishment Radicals

Take, for instance, watermelon Marxist Jeremy Rifkin, whose book, *Entropy: Into the Greenhouse World,* we mentioned in the previous chapter. It was published by Bantam New Age Books, a division of Bantam Books, one of the largest Establishment publishing houses, and was highly praised in the CFR press. And who is Mr. Rifkin? A radical activist in the Vietnam anti-war movement, he was a founder of the Johnny Appleseed Brigades. In 1976 he headed up the Peoples Bicentennial Commission (PBC), a thoroughly Marxist operation funded by the usual tax-exempt foundations and the federal government. He has lectured for the KGB-front Institute for Policy Studies (IPS) and written for the radical socialist *Mother Jones* magazine. All of which, of course, has qualified him to join the august company of savants who participate in the Gorbachev State of the World Forum palavers. It also guarantees him Insider foundation funding for his Washington, D.C.-based Foundation on Economic Trends.

And what type of economics does Comrade Rifkin espouse? Because of the worsening greenhouse crisis, he says in *Entropy*, "For the first time in our country's history we will have to deal with the ultimate political and economic question — redistribution of wealth."[24] (Though rest assured it is not his or Mr. Rockefeller's wealth he wants to redistribute.) Under the system he favors, "The long-accepted practice of private exploitation of 'natural' property is replaced with the notion of public guardianship."[25]

This is also the message of Peter Bahouth, the former head greenie at Greenpeace. Now he is director of the Turner Foundation, where he ladles out millions of dollars to his comrades at Greenpest, Fiends of the Earth, the Environmental Defense Fraud, and other eco-fascist extortionists. The Turner Foundation insists that property rights are responsible for a host of problems associated with urban and suburban sprawl and further insists that state governments must impose more restrictions on property rights. "States must insist localities determine ... defined urban growth boundaries,"[26] says a recent Foundation statement. Indeed, says the Foundation, "politically potent bubbles about free markets and property rights must be popped."[27]

The Turner Foundation, of course, is the eco-hobbyhorse of Citizen Ted Turner, whose multi-million dollar palatial estates on several continents are not to be counted among the private property bubbles to be popped by Turner's Greenpest lackies. Turner, Rockefeller, and other members of the ruling elite smugly believe that their money and political clout will protect them from the Marxist programs they are foisting on us lesser folk of

the middle class. As Marx pointed out in his *Manifesto*, his immediate target was "not the abolition of property generally, but the
abolition of bourgeois property." [28]

Yes, it is the property of the *bourgeois* — the middle class —
that is the principal target of Marx and his present-day disciples.
We have already seen the "future" envisioned by these one-world
corporate socialists. It is an Orwellian nightmare world in which
Soviet Commissars luxuriate in their Black Sea villas and the
upper-level Communist *nomenklatura* enjoy pampered, privileged lives — while the vast majority of the Russian people exist
in misery and grinding poverty.

But the Pratt House billionaires already possess greater
wealth and enjoy more luxury than their Soviet counterparts
could ever dream of, you say. True, but the Communist elite
enjoy something that the top Insiders crave more than wealth
and luxury: power — raw, unchallenged power. The power of the
master over the slave. The power of the tyrant over the masses.
Blocking their path to totalitarian power is the middle class.
Thus the ongoing attack on *middle class property* by the would-
be global overlords and their watermelon Marxist minions.

Chapter 8

The UN's International
Court of Criminals

*[The proposed International Criminal Court] repudiates
the Constitution, the Bill of Rights, and the Declaration of
Independence and cancels the 4th of July.... What are the limits on the ICC? There are none. It's insane!* [1]
> — Professor Charles Rice,
> Notre Dame University School of Law

*With the stroke of a pen, President Bill Clinton has a last
chance to safeguard humankind.... He must simply sign a
treaty, finalized in Rome in 1998, to create a permanent
International Criminal Court.* [2]
> — Robert S. McNamara (CFR, TC) and Benjamin B.
> Ferencz, *New York Times* op-ed, December 12, 2000

*The United States is today signing the 1998 Rome Treaty
on the International Criminal Court.* [3]
> — President Bill Clinton (CFR, TC), December 31, 2000

On December 31, 2000, David Scheffer (CFR), President Clinton's
Ambassador for the International Criminal Court, signed the ICC
Rome Treaty for the United States. This was an incredibly radical, revolutionary act, which will bring devastating consequences
for the American people, if they allow the U.S. Senate to ratify it.
If ratified and implemented, this brazenly treasonous scheme by
the CFR Insiders would rend asunder our constitutional protections and cause American citizens to be vulnerable to prosecution
before international UN tribunals for alleged violations of lawless
UN "laws." If convicted by this UN kangaroo court system,
American citizens could be subjected to whatever penalties the

ICC judges decree, including imprisonment wherever the black-robed globalists may decide to send them.

Regardless of whether one views the prospect of the ICC sympathetically or with horror and revulsion, it must be admitted by all who are fair-minded that U.S. accession to this treaty would represent a momentous, colossal change to our judicial and constitutional system. Who but a totalitarian would argue that a change of this magnitude should be even contemplated, let alone attempted, without an informed debate and a genuine public consensus? Yet there has been no public debate of this issue. Would Americans embrace this attack on their most precious rights if there had been? Obviously not, which is why the entire crusade for the ICC has been carried out by the Insiders as a massive stealth campaign, aimed at *imposing* UN judicial rule on an unsuspecting America.

Ask yourself: Did you see the development of the ICC covered on the evening news on NBC, ABC, CBS, and CNN? Did you see the supposed merits and real dangers debated on *Face the Nation*, *Nightline*, *The Capital Gang*, *Hardball*, *60 Minutes*, *Larry King Live*, or *20/20*? Of course you didn't, because those debates never happened. At the time that President Clinton announced the U.S. signing of the Rome Treaty, probably not one U.S. citizen in 100 had heard of the document, and not one in a thousand had any inkling of what it entailed.

The organized forces for world government, however, had been *intensely* active for several years preparing to spring the ICC trap. Pro-ICC articles were appearing in the internationalist journals, pro-ICC studies were issued by globalist think tanks, a fortune in foundation grants was provided to pro-ICC academics and NGOs to attend international conferences and symposia — all of this was taking place on an enormous scale, while most Americans were completely in the dark.

The op-ed quoted above by Robert McNamara and Benjamin Ferencz appeared in the *New York Times* during the closing days of the Clinton administration. It is a typical example of the means by which the one-world Insiders signal their political agents and intelligentsia to act on an issue of serious import to their global agenda.* Similar editorials, op-eds, articles and commentaries appeared in the *Washington Post, Christian Science Monitor,* and many other Establishment print and broadcast propaganda organs, while, at the same time, the mammoth, pro-ICC, NGO network intensified its lobbying for the UN. All of the usual chorus voices began hymning in unison, creating the false impression that a new "consensus" had formed, that "enlightened" political leaders now accepted the virtuous and unanswerable arguments of the selfless representatives of "global civil society." Hereafter, only hopeless, heartless, Neanderthal, "sovereigntists" would oppose the creation of this desperately needed institution that is designed (we are told) to establish "the rule of law" globally, "stop the culture of impunity," and bring to justice the world's most terrible criminals.

American Criminal Justice System
But should we Americans toss out our own justice system or allow it to be subsumed in some global ICC system on the basis of promises by the UN and its champions? Do any of the UN's member

---

*As Defense Secretary under both JFK and LBJ, Mr. McNamara (CFR, TC) was a principal architect of the insane doctrine of Mutually Assured Destruction (MAD) and the disastrous U.S. debacle in Vietnam. Following those efforts, which were fiascoes for America, but bonanzas for the Insiders, McNamara went on to serve the CFR cabal as head of the World Bank, where he lavished billions of dollars taken from U.S. taxpayers on Communist and socialist regimes throughout the world.

Professor Ferencz of Pace University, an inveterate one-worlder and author of many books promoting disarmament and world government, is one of the early architects and proponents of the ICC. His books *Defining International Aggression* (1975), *An International Criminal Court — A Step Toward World Peace* (two volumes, 1980), *Enforcing International Law* (two volumes, 1983), and *PlanetHood: The Key to Your Future* (1991) greatly influenced the development of the ICC Statute, as did he personally. Professor Ferencz was the recognized *eminence griese* at the UN's ICC Summit in Rome, and it was due to his personal, vigorous lobbying that the undefined crime of "aggression" was included in the ICC Statute.

regimes now have in place *better* justice systems than we enjoy under the U.S. Constitution? Ha! The thought is ludicrous!

One doesn't have to do an extensive study of foreign jurisprudence to know that it would be a very bad idea to run afoul of the ruling authorities in Red China, Russia, Cuba, Syria, Iraq, Iran, Rwanda, Nigeria, and dozens of other tyrannical regimes throughout the world, where concepts of due process, the rule of law, and constitutional rights do not even exist.

Even in many Western European countries such as France, Germany, and Italy, rights that Americans take for granted — jury trial, habeas corpus, speedy trial, the right to counsel — are weak to nonexistent. During the Rome conference, ICC proponents frequently pointed to the Yugoslav war crimes tribunal as a model. That is a chilling thought to anyone familiar with the Tribunal prosecutor's position that five years is a reasonable time for a defendant to wait in prison for a trial. Other ICC advocates frequently cite the European Court of Human Rights as a model for the ICC. But this supranational judicial body has ruled in various cases that pretrial detention of three, four, or even seven years is acceptable!

The American criminal justice system is far from perfect, but in comparison to what exists in most of the rest of the world, it stands out as a shining beacon. And this is so in spite of the fact that over the past half century it has been mangled and transmuted into a system that would be completely unrecognizable to the framers of our Constitution. As originally conceived, virtually all criminal law was left to the purview of state and local governments. There were no federal laws regarding murder, rape, robbery, theft, vandalism, fraud, and other ordinary criminal matters. The central government was restricted to prosecuting treason, espionage, malfeasance of office, and other matters directly related to the federal government.

Over the past few decades, however, the federal government's reach has been drastically lengthened through a massive onslaught of federal legislation, presidential executive orders, and judicial decrees. The damage to our freedoms and constitutional order springing from the federal judiciary has been cata-strophic. The federal courts, especially since the New Deal, have been running amok, acting as a super-legislature in matters as diverse as abortion, education, the environment, pornography, race relations, sexual conduct, sedition, employer-employee rela-tions, religious practice, local police, state prisons, housing, etc.

Some of our early founders recognized the potential for these tragic developments long, long ago. Writing in 1821, toward the end of his life, Thomas Jefferson predicted the dire conse-quences America might suffer as a result of judicial usurpation: "It has long ... been my opinion ... that the germ of dissolution of our federal government is in the constitution of the federal judiciary ... working like gravity by night and by day, gaining a little today and a little tomorrow, and advancing its noiseless step like a thief over the field of jurisdiction, until all shall be usurped from the States, and the government of all be consoli-dated into one. To this I am opposed, because when all govern-ment ... shall be drawn to Washington as the center of all power, it will render powerless the checks provided ... and will become as venal and oppressive as the government from which we separated." [4]

Jefferson's pessimistic view was based upon his sober assess-ment of the corruptibility of human nature. He was warning, in the citation above, of the dangers inherent in the *natural ten-dency* in human beings and institutions toward greater and greater corruption, not against any particular combination of individuals then scheming to overturn our system of govern-ment. However, as gloomy as his projections were, it is doubtful that even he could have imagined the outrageous and seditious usurpations of our federal judiciary. And it is certain that he and every other Founding Father, along with generations of earlier Americans, would stand in dumfounded disbelief to learn that America's leaders today are seriously proposing that the people of the United States be subjected to the jurisdiction of an *inter-national judiciary*.

The Campaign for an ICC

The vast majority of Americans today are blissfully ignorant of the fact that such a radical proposal is even under consideration. But the truth is that it is perilously close to becoming a reality. And unless the American public becomes sufficiently alerted, alarmed, and activated to oppose this incredibly subversive scheme, it will become reality.

The formal campaign for an ICC was launched in the summer of 1998 at a United Nations summit convened in Rome. The month-long conference concluded on July 17th with the announcement that 120 nations had voted in favor of approving the new "Rome Statute of the International Criminal Court" and that it would enter into effect and *become binding upon the entire planet* as soon as it was formally ratified by 60 nations. The ostensible targets of the new ICC are dictators, tyrants, and other nasty practitioners of "genocide, war crimes, aggression and crimes against humanity." But the UN membership is replete with murderous dictators, tyrants, and the worst practitioners of these and other heinous crimes. The likes of Fidel Castro, Yasir Arafat, Sam Nujoma, Mikhail Gorbachev, Li Peng, Vladimir Putin, and other bloody-handed thugs have always been welcomed and honored at the United Nations.

The Real Targets of the ICC

Who, then, are the real targets of the ICC proponents? Those who stand in the way of their proposed "new world order," naturally. That includes, of course, so-called "right-wing dictators," like General Augusto Pinochet, who has never been forgiven by the international Socialist-Communist-Insider cabal for overthrowing the brutal Communist regime of their favored *leftwing* dictator: Salvador Allende in Chile. In 1998, while the 82-year-old Pinochet was visiting England for medical treatment, he was arrested and held on a warrant issued by Baltazar Garzon, an investigative magistrate from Spain. Judge Garzon, a Marxist activist, was pursuing a revolutionary political agenda, not seeking justice for real crimes. Many legal authorities condemned Garzon's action for violating established canons of international law. Eduardo Fungarino, Spain's chief government prosecutor, filed a court motion charging that the judge had broken many legal procedures in issuing the arrest order, and that Garzon had "an absolute lack of jurisdiction" over alleged crimes committed outside of Spain against citizens of other countries.[5]

However, the Insider-controlled prostitute press would not allow these inconvenient facts, and others of equal importance in the case, to come to the attention of the American people.* Instead, we were treated to a nonstop diet of shrill editorials and shrieking demonstrators demanding not only that Pinochet be drawn and quartered, but that a permanent international tribunal, the ICC, be established to bring "dictators" of his ilk to justice.

But the phony "human rights" activists demanding Pinochet's scalp could not care less about genuine violations of human rights and real justice for bloody dictators. At the time of Pinochet's arrest in England on the Spanish warrant, Communist dictator Fidel Castro was welcomed to Spain and PLO terrorist leader Yasir Arafat was a guest of the Clinton White House. Likewise, Jiang Zemin, the butcher of Tiananmen Square, as well as the bloody-handed Soviet tyrants Mikhail Gorbachev, Boris Yeltsin, and Vladimir Putin — and virtually every other mass-murdering despot of the left — have been conspicuously ignored by the self-righteous frauds leading the ICC choir.

However, anti-Communist military leaders and heads of state like Pinochet are not the only — or even the chief — targets of the ICC. The *primary* target of the ICC architects is the United States and the American people. This was conspicuously obvious

---

*For an in-depth look at the orchestrated global campaign to "get" Pinochet, together with a thorough analysis of the charges leveled against him, please see: "Patriot Enchained," *The New American*, September 13, 1999; and "Persistent Persecution of Pinochet," *The New American*, April 10, 2000 at *www.thenewamerican.com/focus/pinochet/*.

at the ICC Summit in Rome, where America-bashing was the order of the day.

As one who was in Rome "at the creation," this reporter can attest firsthand to the fact that the long-standing hatred toward the United States by the vast majority of the pathetic regimes that comprise the UN menagerie is still alive and well. Day after day, throughout the ICC conference, the U.S. was subjected to tirades and condemnations — by official delegates as well as by NGOs — for supposed past and present sins. In fact, from the nonstop anti-U.S. invective one might imagine that America is the principal, if not the sole, source of evil in the world. The billions of dollars that we have ladled out over the past half-century to these countries and the UN itself have purchased us not an iota of good will.

There were calls at the Rome conference for prosecuting Presidents Bush (George W.'s father) and Clinton for war crimes. A handbill distributed at the summit by the Society for Threatened Peoples, one of the Marxoid groups among the NGO horde, charged the U.S. with these past "war crimes": "Dropped 15 million tonnes of bombs in the Vietnam War, conducted air raids on Cambodia, supported Indonesia's annexation of East Timor, backed right-wing death squads in Guatemala in the early eighties." [6]

Months before the Rome conference had even begun, the UN Commission on Human Rights had targeted the U.S. with a purely political attack alleging that this country unfairly applies the death penalty. The Insiders' White House agent Bill Clinton aided the scheme by inviting UN human rights monitor Bacre Waly Ndiaye to America to meet with U.S. officials and inspect our prisons. In September and October 1997, Mr. Ndiaye came to the U.S. and visited prisons in Florida, Texas, and California. The *New York Times* reported:

> For Mr. Ndiaye, the visit to the United States is important because of the *precedent it sets* [emphasis added].
>
> "I am really hoping that with this visit, the United States

Government will show the way to other countries which have been resistant to United Nations mechanisms," he said.[7]

Mr. Ndiaye's U.S. precedent-setting tour provided the Insider-funded NGO radicals at Amnesty International, Human Rights Watch, the ACLU, and the Lawyers Committee for Human Rights with a propaganda bonanza. The Insider media cartel retailed all their lurid charges of the horrors of the American justice system. In April 1998, shortly before the ICC Summit, the UN Commission on Human Rights released a report based on the Ndiaye investigation. The report charged that application of the death penalty in the United States is tainted by racism, economic discrimination, politics, and an excessive deference to victims' rights.[8]

The Commission also accused the U.S. of being in violation of the 1966 UN Covenant on Civil and Political Rights and called on the U.S. to suspend all further executions until U.S. state and federal laws were brought into compliance with "international standards."[9] This provided the NGO cabal with another golden opportunity for a round of media-enhanced attacks on the U.S. legal system. One of the aims of this report and its companion NGO campaign was to sow seeds of doubt and guilt in American public opinion concerning the fairness of American justice; this would make the upcoming ICC proposals for an international system seem much more reasonable. It also gave the Clinton administration an opportunity to strike a moderate pose while advancing this radical agenda. The Clintonites said, in effect, "Well, we think these UN charges are exaggerated but we recognize that the U.S. justice system isn't perfect. We want to be a good example to the rest of the world and cooperate with the UN."

This was all a colossal, insidious charade, of course. Not to mention the epitome of hypocrisy. At the very time that Kofi Annan's Commission was denouncing the U.S. justice system, the sainted Mr. Annan was suppressing information that he had been a key silent accomplice in the Rwandan genocide. Lt.-Gen. Romeo Dallaire, the former commander of Canada's UN "peacekeeping" mission to Rwanda in 1994, revealed that he had sent a fax to Annan's office warning that Rwandan security officials had been ordered to "register" the (predominantly Christian) Tutsis as an obvious prelude to mass liquidation. Annan's office ordered Dallaire to "assist in the recovery of all weapons distributed to or illegally acquired by civilians," which, in effect, meant disarming the intended victims![10] So Mr. Annan, whose Commission was chastising the U.S. for gross abuses, was himself involved in one of the most atrocious genocides in world history. Likewise, many of the UN representatives at Rome who cited the Commission report in their denunciations of the U.S. were representing some of the most repressive and brutal regimes in the world.

We don't mean to imply that all of the U.S. bashing at Rome was emanating from Third World countries, Communist satrapies, or UN agencies. Canada, Norway, Britain, Germany, Italy, and other U.S. "allies" vied for top anti-U.S. honors, too. On the final day of the conference, when the very minimal objections of the U.S. to the ICC were soundly defeated, the assembled delegations erupted in a tumultuous and defiant display of anti-American jubilation — which was joined by much of the press corps, including "American" reporters.

Naturally, the U.S. NGOs topped all others in attacking their homeland. As Reuters reported, "the American NGOs were the scourge of the United States,"[11] at the conference. On July 8th, *Terra Viva*, one of the major NGO newspapers that has become "must reading" at UN summits, carried this headline in large print: "Police Brutality Deeply Rooted in US" The story announced the release of a Human Rights Watch report charging a national epidemic of police brutality.[12] The 440-page report, entitled *Shielded From Justice: Police Brutality and Accountability in the United States*,[13] was time-released for maximum effect on the conference. Human Rights Watch spokesman Richard Dicker, who was one of the top NGO strategists at Rome, seemed never to be satisfied if not hurling vitriol at the U.S. But that has not hindered him or his group from receiving hundreds of thousands of dollars from the Ford Foundation, which has enabled the group to push the ICC agenda.[14]

NGO Evolution-Revolution

The revolutionary role of the NGOs at the Rome summit is one of the biggest untold stories of that event. As CFR staffer Jessica T. Mathews approvingly noted in *Foreign Affairs*, ever since the 1992 Earth Summit in Rio de Janeiro, NGOs have been exercising more and more influence at UN conferences.[15] But the Rome experience marked a watershed in the incredible evolution of NGO power. At the ICC Conference, the NGOs were given unprecedented access and privileges and accorded a status almost on a par with official state delegations. NGO experts and officials, inflamed with their own self-importance, regularly addressed the ICC Plenary Session as though they were official heads of state. They remonstrated, cajoled, and chastised the assembled plenipotentiaries to adopt NGO positions, which always argued for larger jurisdiction and more power for the Court. NGO briefing papers, reports, resolutions, press releases, and legal opinions flooded the conference. The NGO Coalition for an International Criminal Court (CICC) was given a large suite of offices within the FAO (the UN's Food and Agriculture Organization) conference building itself, just down the hall from the main meeting room, so that the NGO activists — who outnumbered the official delegates — could overwhelm the conferees with "good cop-bad cop" lobbying tactics.

World Federalist Association leader William Pace (CFR), Richard Dicker, and other CICC spokesmen incessantly reminded the world press and the assembled dignitaries that they were vested with the moral authority of "over 800 NGOs worldwide representing all sectors of global society." It was, of course, a gigantic confidence game; the NGO "diversity" amounted to a choice of your favorite flavor of socialism. Take your pick: Castroite, Trotskyite, Marxist, Stalinist, Leninist, Maoist, Gramsciite.

Certainly among the most influential of the NGOs was the

Rome-based Transnational Radical Party (TRP), an openly Communist organization that boasts Mayor of Rome Francesco Rutelli and European Commissioner Emma Bonino among its members,[16] both of whom played prominent roles at the ICC confab. Together with its sister organization, No Peace Without Justice, the TRP and other NGOs organized daily demonstrations and panel discussions, in addition to ICC-related broadcasts on its radio program, Radio Radicale. As the host country and the nation with the largest delegation — 58 delegates, as compared to the next largest, the U.S., with 40 — Italy was in the driver's seat. The Prodi government and Mayor Rutelli gave every advantage to the NGO radicals, granting permission for streets to be blocked for marches and demonstrations and even allowing NGO militants to set up a continuous propaganda stage partially blocking the entrance to the FAO/ICC conference site. On July 14th (Bastille Day, of course) Mayor Rutelli granted the TRP and its CICC allies an especially rare privilege: a torchlight march through the Via Sacra (Sacred Way), a path through the temple ruins that reportedly has only been opened twice this century.

The Transnational Radical Party headquarters in Rome was the center for many NGO activities that spilled out of the FAO complex. At that venue, Judge Richard Goldstone, former prosecutor for the UN war crimes tribunals for Rwanda and Yugoslavia, presented a report promoting the ICC.[17] Not surprisingly, the report was produced by a task force headed by Goldstone and sponsored by the Twentieth Century Fund. This American Insider foundation has been funding radical, left-wing causes for much of this century. Accompanying Judge Goldstone was Morton Halperin (CFR), the notorious Marxist activist and longtime associate of the Institute for Policy Studies. President Clinton attempted to place Halperin in a sensitive, top Defense Department post, but the Senate, prodded by exposure of his subversive background, refused to confirm him. Halperin stayed on for awhile in other capacities in the Clinton regime, before moving on to a position in the CFR's Studies Department, and then an appointment as vice president of the Twentieth Century Fund.*

Of course, leading the clamorous "global civil society" cabal** was the World Federalist Movement, whose representative, William R. Pace (CFR), ran the NGO show. The World Federalists (headed by CFR veteran John B. Anderson), who have long advocated world government, clearly have mastered the fine art of demagoguery and mob control. However, they do not exercise their leadership by virtue of strategic vision, tactical genius, or moral suasion. They have been accorded the piper status by those who pay for the tunes. It costs a great deal of money to assemble a horde of activists, fly them around the globe, set them up with accommodations and entertainment in one of the most expensive cities in the world, and equip them with all the resources they need to effectively push a coordinated, pre-arranged agenda. Even more than at previous summits, the NGO "citizen lobbyist" campaign at Rome was completely the creation of the same old Pratt House coterie: the CFR and its foundation, corporate, think-tank network.

---

*In Rome, Halperin and Goldstone joined one-worlders Ben Ferencz, John Roper (Royal Institute for International Affairs), and Marino Busdachin (Secretary-General of No Peace Without Justice) at the Transnational Radical Party offices to help make the pitch for global governance. In January 2001, the CFR announced that Halperin would be rejoining the group's staff to "direct a project on democracy." [18]

**Among the many other groups comprising the storied "diversity" of the NGO claque were: Parliamentarians for Global Action; European Law Students Association; Women's Caucus for Gender Justice; Caribbean Association for Feminist Research and Action; American Bar Association; International Federation of Lawyers; International Women's Rights Action Watch; Beyond Borders; the Carter Center; Maryknoll Society Justice and Peace Office; Center for Reproductive Law and Policy; National Association of Democratic Lawyers; OXFAM UK; Earth Action International; Pax Christi International; Sisterhood Is Global Institute; Global Policy Forum; Gray Panthers; Vietnam Veterans of America Foundation; Washington Office on Latin America; International Association of Democratic Lawyers; International Association of Judges; International Commission of Jurists; Women's Action Group; International Council of Jewish Women; World Council of Churches; and the World Order Models Project.

If you wish to take the time to do so, you can research the individual NGOs and the grants they received. But there is no need to do so, since these "anti-Establishment" rabble-rousers admit their dependence on the globalist Establishment "sugar daddies." According to the Coalition for an ICC website home page, "Substantial funding for the CICC communications project has been received from private foundations, progressive governments, participating organizations of the Coalition, and private individuals, including major grants from the European Union, the Ford Foundation, and the MacArthur Foundation." [19]

The principle NGO press conferences in Rome were presided over by CFR handler William Pace, and his lieutenants Richard Dicker and Professor Rhonda Copelon, a lesbian legal scholar from City University of New York, affiliated with the Women's Action Group. Likewise, they and a select cadre of hardcore radicals led the daily strategy sessions at the NGO office suite. These events, which this writer attended, usually featured 50 to 100 or more NGO activists of the Femi-Leninist, Enviro-Leninist, Afro-Leninist, Homo-Leninist, Lesbo-Leninist stripe. This motley menagerie of uncivil specimens, always spouting hateful diatribes and Marxist cant, by no means can legitimately claim to represent "global civil society." But their CFR paymasters are hellbent on legitimizing this false claim, because these misfits and miscreants are essential components in their "pressure from below" strategy.

Shaping a Consensus

The enormity of the deception and the immense resources and coordination of this global network are amazing to behold. But even the astounding NGO-Insider spectacle at Rome fails to provide a full appreciation of the fact that it was but a part of a much larger scheme. The Rome gathering was the culmination of a multi-year program of PrepComs (Preparatory Committee meetings) that had been carefully orchestrated to arrive at the contrived global "consensus" that is now being celebrated by the votaries of "world order." The final PrepCom meeting, held from

March 16th through April 3rd, 1998 in New York, was a mini-preview of the Rome summit, with all the major actors, from UN officials and pro-ICC national delegates, to NGO activists, honing their skills, practicing their parts, and coordinating their activities with their Insider media allies.

In order to get all of the cadres marching in sync, and to create the appearance of popular support, the Insiders had to set up a host of ongoing programs throughout the country before, during, and after the Rome summit. One of the major events attended by this writer was an ICC symposium at the luxurious Biltmore Hotel in Los Angeles on February 26, 1998. The CFR leadership was obvious. The moderator of the program was Dr. Edwin M. Smith (CFR), professor of international law at the University of Southern California and formerly an appointee to the U.S. Arms Control and Disarmament Agency by President Clinton (CFR). The main speaker for the program was Ambassador Scheffer (CFR), formerly an adjunct professor of international law at Georgetown University Law Center, President Clinton's alma mater. The program was sponsored by the United Nations Association; the World Federalist Association; Amnesty International; the American Civil Liberties Union; the American Bar Association; Friends of the United Nations; B'nai Brith; and the law firms of Gibson, Dunn, and Crutcher, and Milbank, Tweed, Hadley, and McCloy. CFR members play prominent, if not dominant, leadership roles in all of these organizations.

These individuals and organizations are engaged in what Professor George C. Lodge (CFR) calls "quietly assembling global arrangements" and "shaping a consensus." Lodge, who is a professor at the Harvard Business School and a trustee of the Carnegie Endowment for International Peace, writes in his 1995 book, *Managing Globalization in the Age of Interdependence*, that there are "energetic and creative individuals in government, interest groups, and corporations [who] are quietly assembling global arrangements to deal with crises and tensions. For the most part, they work outside of legislatures and parliaments and are screened from the glare of the media in order to find common interests, shape a consensus, and persuade those with power to change." [20]

Professor Thomas R. Dye of Florida State University described this same "consensus shaping" process many years earlier in his 1976 book *Who's Running America?* Dye noted that the CFR and its related "policy-planning groups are central coordinating points in the entire elite policy-making process." He went on to describe how they function:

> They bring together people at the top of the corporate and financial institutions, the universities, the foundations, the mass media, the powerful law firms, the top intellectuals, and influential figures in the government. They review the relevant university- and foundation-supported research on topics of interest, and more importantly they try to reach a consensus about what action should be taken on national problems under study. Their goal is to develop *action recommendations* — explicit policies or programs designed to resolve or ameliorate national problems. At the same time, they endeavor to build consensus among corporate, financial, university, civic, intellectual, and government leaders around major policy directions. [21] [Emphasis in original.]

The Proposed ICC

The proposed ICC has proceeded through this process, and has gone from "action recommendation" to "consensus" to (almost) full realization. The ICC is breathtakingly audacious on many counts but the most amazingly brazen claim, and one unprecedented even for so outrageous an outfit as the United Nations, is the assertion by the UN that once the Rome Statute is ratified by 60 countries (a completely arbitrarily selected number, by the way: totals ranging from 30 to 90 were considered), the newly established court will then have compulsory jurisdiction over *all* countries, even those that refuse to ratify it. This is, of course, a revolutionary and flagrant violation of the most fundamental principle of treaty law, namely, that *a treaty is an agreement that is binding only upon those who are party to the treaty.* Yet the ICC zealots had no qualms of conscience in repeatedly and piously invoking "the rule of law" to advance their totally lawless proposal.

By December 31, 2000, when President Clinton signed the ICC treaty, 27 nations had ratified the document, and the court's advocates were predicting that the requisite 60 ratifications would be obtained by 2002. The new court is to be headquartered in The Hague, Netherlands, which is already host to the World Court, the UN tribunal that was set up in 1945 to try cases between nations. The new ICC would try *individuals* who are accused of violating international laws.

Dr. Charles Rice, professor of law at Notre Dame University, has termed the ICC "a monster," both in concept and reality, noting that it effectively "repudiates the Constitution, the Bill of Rights, and the Declaration of Independence and cancels the 4th of July." "In our system," Professor Rice explains, "law is supposed to be a rule of reason which, in a sense, controls the state and compels the state to operate under the law." [22] But the super-jurisdictional ICC, he points out, has no legitimate basis for its claimed authority, no protections against abuses, no accountability, and virtually no limits to its jurisdiction. "What are the limits on the ICC?" he asks, and then answers, "There are none. It's insane!" [23]

What do esteemed legal scholars like Professor Rice find so monstrous about the ICC? Let's take a look at the kinds of crimes the new ICC would claim jurisdiction over, and then briefly examine the structure and procedures of the court as laid out in the Rome Statute.

The 166-page Rome Statute claims universal jurisdiction for the ICC to try individuals charged with genocide, war crimes, crimes against humanity, and aggression, anywhere on earth. In the first place, these four "core" crimes are so vaguely defined and were so contentiously debated at the Rome summit that no reasonable claim to consensus can be made concerning even the definition of these crimes, which is the most basic requirement for just laws. Which means the definition of the crimes will be left completely to the arbitrary interpretation of the ICC judges. (In the case of the crime of "aggression," no definition was even included in the statute.)[24]

But the severe definitional problems associated with these four "core crimes" don't even begin to hint at the nightmarish possibilities that would be unleashed under a global ICC system. First of all, there is no question that, once formally established, many other additional "crimes" will be added to the ICC's jurisdiction. We already have promises on that score from the drafters of the Rome Statute.

In 1993, Connecticut Senator Christopher Dodd (CFR) introduced a resolution calling for the establishment of the ICC to combat "unlawful acts such as war crimes, genocide, aggression, terrorism, drug trafficking, money laundering, and other crimes of an international character."[25] Mikhail Gorbachev and other one-world luminaries have called for adding "ecological crimes" to the jurisdiction of the ICC.[26] At the Rome ICC Summit, many delegates insisted that these and a vast array of other crimes — piracy, child pornography, kidnapping, political assassination, religious persecution, discrimination based on sexual orientation, etc. — be included. The delegates were repeatedly assured by the Summit leaders that these could be added later, but were told they should not jeopardize the establishing of the ICC by insisting on inclusion of all these other crimes at the beginning.

So, as if an ICC with global jurisdiction over the four "core crimes" were not bad enough, the dials have been preset for a vast expansion of court jurisdiction. But what about the ICC system itself? Some of the most egregious threats that are built into the system include:

- No right to trial by jury.
- No right to a speedy trial.
- Judges, prosecutors, and counsel drawn from murderous totalitarian and authoritarian regimes with juridical views completely at odds with Western concepts of law and justice and

specifically hateful of America and Americans.

- No appeal of an ICC decision, except to the same ICC court.
- A person convicted under the ICC may be sentenced to prison anywhere in the world the ICC chooses.
- An ICC prosecutor may decide to bring charges against an individual based upon accusations provided by NGOs, such as the ACLU, the Environmental Defense Fund, the National Gay and Lesbian Task Force, etc.

In other words, under an ICC regime, an American citizen, whether in the United States or abroad, could be accused of a crime by a member of some militant group, then indicted, extradited, tried, and convicted by prosecutors and judges from North Korea, Zambia, Mongolia, China, Iraq, Cuba, Turkey, or Russia. And then sentenced to serve time at some undisclosed prison in Zimbabwe, Kosovo, Albania, Cambodia, or Algeria.

U.S. Leaders Support ICC

Any reasonable American quickly realizes that Professor Rice was indeed accurate in describing the proposed ICC regime as "a monster." And therein lies much of our problem: Average Americans cannot conceive that anything so patently absurd and obviously injurious to American interests could ever be adopted by our elected leaders. Besides, they reason, even if the U.S. Senate ratifies the ICC statute, the U.S. government would never allow wild abuses of the ICC against American citizens. And, as the U.S. is indisputably the most powerful nation on earth, we have no reason to fear that the ICC could force its jurisdiction on us in any case harmful to our interests.

But, as we pointed out in Chapter 1, depending on U.S. courts and elected officials to guard against abuses under a UN regime is a dangerously misplaced hope. Many of them are already on record as favoring global institutions with legislative, executive, and judicial powers that could override U.S. sovereignty and supersede our constitutional checks and balances.

Every American should take note of the fact that the primary objection posed by U.S. Ambassador David Scheffer (CFR) and the U.S. State Department at the ICC Summit was the concern that U.S. Armed Forces personnel serving abroad might stand in danger of being accused of war crimes under the ICC statute.[27] This is a very real concern, of course, but far from the only or most important concern. The official U.S. position appears to be that if this one major area of concern can be addressed with some exemption or written assurance, then the U.S. could live with the ICC — all in the interest of showing U.S. respect for the "rule of law" worldwide.

This is like leaders of a church girls camp agreeing to allow the League of Reformed Rapists to run their camp — as long as the League provides written certificates attesting to the reform of its members and guarantees that the "ex-rapists" will not force themselves on girls under, say, 13 years of age. Or police officials agreeing to merge with the Mafia in a "joint crime-fighting effort," as long as Mafia dons agree to have their extortion squads stop breaking the legs of shopkeepers (for a few weeks, at least) and to nix the use of dum-dum bullets by their hit men.

It ought to be obvious to all that you don't establish justice and fight crime by inviting the worst criminals and terrorists to join the prosecution, sit on the judiciary, and staff the police. Yet that is precisely what the ICC would do.

And America's opinion cartel is more than ready to accept this monstrosity. The main organs of the CFR-dominated media (*New York Times*, *Washington Post*, ABC, CBS, NBC, CNN, etc.) have supported the ICC. The massive NGO rent-a-mob, from radical enviros to so-called human rights activists, are eagerly pushing this agenda. That is to be expected.

However, what should be most alarming to Americans is that many of our top officials — together with their co-conspirators in the Insider media, foundations, and think tanks — are *leading* the whole movement to subject the United States to international jurisdiction under the ICC. As mentioned in Chapter 1, members of the U.S. Supreme Court have already stated that in the 21st century they will be relying on other international sources for their decisions.[28] Many of America's leading law journals and "legal authorities" have adopted an "internationalist" view of the law which holds that U.S. law must yield to wider "global legal mandates."

The federal executive branch has intervened several times in state criminal matters at the behest of the UN. In November 1998, U.S. Secretary of State Madeleine Albright (CFR) urged the state of Texas to yield to a World Court decision and the appeals of "global civil society" and overturn the death penalty in the case of Joseph Stanley Faulder.[29] This U.S. concession was an important part of the Insiders' calculated plan gradually to concede U.S. sovereign jurisdiction in criminal matters. This is not merely a grab for power by UN globocrats, third-world dictators, Communist commissars, and fuzzy-headed Marxist academics; it is a colossal grab for global judicial power by one-world votaries within our own government and other centers of power in our society.

A Global Constabulary

And, naturally, it doesn't stop with an ICC. A global judiciary presupposes a global constabulary, both to arrest accused "criminals" and to enforce the Court's rulings. Thus the same Pratt House thought cartel that has brought us the ICC monster is pushing hard for an international police corps. Writing in *Foreign Affairs* in 1997, New York University professor of law Theodor Meron (CFR) told his one-world comrades that, "from now on, international criminal tribunals must be more effectively supported by police power." Professor Meron continued:

> Just as there can be no national justice without a police force, there can be no effective international justice without arrests, subpoenas, investigations, and a reliable enforcement mechanism. The international community's inability to create such a mechanism, whether for ad hoc criminal tribunals or for the proposed international criminal court, threatens all efforts to create a system of international criminal justice. But we must not give up in despair.[30]

149

In December 2000, senior government officials from more than 150 countries converged on Palermo, the capital of Sicily, for a UN conference ostensibly aimed at stepping up the global fight against "transnational organized crime." The event, led by UN Secretary-General Kofi Annan and UN Under Secretary-General Pino Arlacchi, featured 20 heads of government and unveiled a new UN convention against the scourge of organized crime.

Mr. Arlacchi, the UN's top globocop and the driving force behind the gathering, has been lionized by the Establishment media as "the world's mafia buster." Reputedly a top expert on the Sicilian Mafia, Arlacchi has been criticized by others who dispute his exaggerated and premature claims of victory over the mob. "To talk of the death of the Mafia is unwise — it is just sleeping,"[31] said Maria Falcone, in a report by *The Daily Telegraph* of London. Miss Falcone, sister of famed anti-Mafia investigator Giovanni Falcone, who was assassinated by a Mafia bomb in 1992, says, "How can you say that the Mafia is over when some of the biggest bosses, including the biggest, Bernardo Provenzano, are still at large?"[32]

Good question. Even more important questions concern the UN's direct and indirect roles in helping establish and expand the global crime syndicates. Over the past decade, for instance, tens of billions of dollars that the IMF has pumped into Russia have been funneled into the Russian Mafia, fueling the massive growth of this ruthless criminal behemoth, which the UN now points to as a prime target of its current crusade.*

At best, this would be evidence of gross incompetence. But any reasonably intelligent analysis of the available evidence points directly to conspiracy by the world government advocates to create the problem in order to justify the "solution," which, as usual, involves the transfer of more power to the UN.

---

*See the following articles from *The New American*: "Crime Fighters Converge," August 22, 1994; "G-Men Going Global?" January 23, 1995; "Enemy Within the Gates" and "Russian Mafia: Organized Crime is Big Business for the KGB," February 19, 1996; "Russia's Global Crime Cartel," May 27, 1996; "Drug War on the West," April 10, 2000 at www.thenewamerican.com/focus/russia/.

Of course, by any reasonable standard, we would have to acknowledge that many, if not most, of the regimes that comprise the UN General Assembly are themselves criminal enterprises, thugocracies in which the cleverest and most ruthless thugs have clawed their ways to the top. Certainly that is the case as regards such "respectable" UN member states as Russia, China, Belarus, Ukraine, Yugoslavia, Montenegro, Albania, Georgia, Cuba, Iran, Iraq, Syria, Libya, Zimbabwe, and dozens of other regimes where the organized crime cartels are mere extensions of the governments' police-state apparatuses. The UN has served well to cover the official criminal dealings of these governments, especially the central roles played by the Communist regimes of Russia, China, and Cuba over the past three decades in directing and overseeing the largest narcotics operations in the world.*

Mr. Arlacchi, as the UN's head of drug control and crime prevention, has been a key player in providing this cover to the criminal regimes involved. Now, according to Arlacchi, the UN must be empowered to deal with the global crime "crisis." One of the UN's Palermo proposals calls for the creation of a UN fund to help poorer states fight the crime syndicates. "This is the new UN," said Arlacchi, "We are trying to create the UN of the future." [33]

The would-be globocops also insist that since organized crime is now a "transnational phenomenon," the nations of the world must "harmonize" their criminal codes and crime-fighting methods and efforts. "What we are trying to do here is set some strong universal standards for the fight against crime," said Arlacchi at the Palermo conference. "If we don't do that then criminals simply move their headquarters from those countries that are fighting the problem to those that aren't." [34]

In this, Arlacchi is parroting the Establishment party line that the CFR brain trust began promoting in earnest during the

---

*See: Joseph Douglass, *Red Cocaine: The Drugging of America and the West* (1999). Also the following articles from *The New American*: "Danger! KLA in the USA," May 24, 1999; "Narco-Terrorism: Drug War on the West," and "Narco-Dollarization," April 10, 2000, at www.thenewamerican. com/focus/drugs/.

1990s. *Foreign Affairs* has been the lead conduit, as usual. Typical is this offering from CFR factotum Jessica T. Mathews in the journal's January/February 1997 issue: "Globalized crime is a security threat that neither police nor the military — the state's traditional responses — can meet. Controlling it will require states to pool their efforts and to establish unprecedented cooperation ... thereby compromising two cherished sovereign roles. If states fail, if criminal groups can continue to take advantage of porous borders and transnational financial spaces while governments are limited to acting within their own territory, crime will have the winning edge." [35]

Organized crime isn't the only excuse the one-worlders have for grabbing global police powers; terrorism is another. Writing in the Summer 2000 issue of *Foreign Policy* (the Carnegie Endowment's sister journal to the CFR's *Foreign Affairs*), Robert Wright opined: "The most compelling incentive for broader and deeper supranational governance may come from terrorism and crime.... Policing will increasingly need to be a cooperative international venture, and increments of national sovereignty will have to be surrendered." [36]

Similar paeans to global policing in law journals, law enforcement periodicals, and academic publications have been preparing the legal community, the law enforcement community, politicians, and opinion molders for this planned transformation of the UN into a planetary "Globocop."

Thus we have counterparts to the Palermo conference and the UN crime convention purporting to offer solutions to the problem of terrorism. Which, again, would be laughable, except that the matter is so deadly serious. For, as in the case of organized crime, the member regimes of the UN who piously intone of the need to combat terrorism are some of the major promoters and sponsors of terrorist groups worldwide. Those prime sponsors include: Russia, China, Cuba, Syria, Iran, Iraq, Libya, Algeria, North Korea — to name a few.

The Insider-Communist cabal is accelerating the drive to install their planned system of global injustice. They intend to control not only the judges and the courts but also the prosecutors and the police. If we allow them to succeed, we will soon be shackled in a state of affairs too horrible to imagine: a global gulag in which the most vicious criminals are the jailers.

But now that Bill Clinton is out of the White House, we don't have to worry on this score, right? We wish that were so; unfortunately it isn't. The Bush administration has been less than comforting on this issue. In an October 12, 2000 meeting hosted by the Council on Foreign Relations, CFR member Condoleezza Rice — who was then George W. Bush's foreign policy advisor — was asked whether a Bush administration would support the ICC. Dr. Rice replied, in part: "Governor Bush has not yet taken a position on the [ICC]. I will tell you that I think there are concerns for a country like the United States.... I was deeply disturbed that someone would think it necessary to investigate whether NATO had committed war crimes in the bombing of Kosovo." [37] In other words, she was repeating for CFR Team B the same "red herring" issue that Mr. Scheffer offered as an objection for CFR Team A. The plan, obviously, is for this false issue to be resolved as a way to soften U.S. opposition to the ICC. Perhaps NATO troops will be given immunity from ICC prosecution in exchange for accepting prominent roles as ICC "enforcers."

It should be plain that the ICC cannot be made acceptable by any amending or reforming. It is not just flawed around the edges but at the very core. It is not wrong just in particulars, but in principle.

It must be opposed and rejected *en toto*. We must heed James Madison who warned:

> ... it is proper to take alarm at the first experiment on our liberties. We hold this prudent jealousy to be the first duty of citizens, and one of [the] noblest characteristics of the late Revolution. The freemen of America did not wait till usurped power had strengthened itself by exercise and entangled the question in precedents. They saw all the consequences in the principle, and they avoided

the consequences by denying the principle. We revere this lesson too much, soon to forget it. [38]

The ICC would be a disaster even if it were proposed by *honorable* men. But as the proposed agency of a criminal conspiracy against freedom and justice, it should be rejected out of hand.

Chapter 9

Civilian Disarmament

When the Cambrian measures were forming, They promised perpetual peace.
They swore, if we gave them our weapons, that the wars of the tribes would cease.
But when we disarmed They sold us and delivered us bound to our foe,
And the Gods of the Copybook Headings said: "Stick to the Devil you know." [1]

— Rudyard Kipling,
"The Gods of the Copybook Headings"

I am a United Nations fighting person.... I would fire upon U.S. citizens who refuse or resist confiscation of firearms banned by the U.S. government. [2]

— from a "Combat Arms Survey" given to members of
the United States Marine Corps, 1994

It's high time to gun down the 2nd Amendment.... America will continue to have its own versions of the killing fields as long as there are millions of handguns floating around waiting for another psychopath with a grudge. [3]

— Walter Shapiro, *USA Today* columnist,
anti-gun diatribe for September 17, 1999

I think the country has long been ready to restrict the use of guns ... and now I think we're prepared to get rid of the damned things entirely — the handguns, the semis and the automatics. [4]

— Roger Rosenblatt essay in *Time*, August 9, 1999

The incredibly audacious schemes for national disarmament set forth in *Freedom From War*, *Blueprint for the Peace Race*, the Gorbachev-CFR Global Security Project, and other programs discussed in Chapter 2 are transparent plots to subject all the nations of the world, including the United States of America, to a global military-police state under an empowered United Nations. This is perfectly clear from any reasonable reading of the documents themselves.

Please understand this critically important point: These proposals do not advocate "world disarmament," as is generally supposed, based on the "peace" rhetoric used to promote them. Instead they propose to *transfer* world armaments from the nation states to the global superstate envisioned by the one-world Insiders and their Communist-socialist cohorts.

This represents the most gigantic, naked grab for power this world has ever seen. No previous world power or dictator has ever enjoyed such vast, unchecked power. Not Napoleon or Queen Elizabeth; not Stalin, Mao, or Hitler.

These proposals amount to giant "trust me" schemes that are so facially fraudulent as to be ludicrous. They could be compared to the situation in which city officials get together with Mafia kingpins and announce that they are going to join forces to fight the crime and violence that are ripping the community apart. Under any circumstances, such a proposal would rightly be viewed as absurdly dangerous and a betrayal of office by those elected to uphold justice. The sanity and integrity of the officials involved would be immediately suspect.

However, there would be no lingering doubts about integrity if it became known to citizens that the mayor is involved in a multi-million dollar business deal with a mafia-owned dummy corporation, the police chief's election campaign is being financed by mob-controlled unions, the district attorney's former law firm (in which his wife and brother are still partners) is the main counsel for the chief mafia don, and all the top judges are driving Rolls Royces and springing gangsters from jail, on the flimsiest of excuses, faster than they can be apprehended. This would especially be the case if the officials involved are so flagrantly arrogant that they are regularly seen socializing in public with leading mafiosi and are regular "guests" at gang-owned restaurants, brothels, and casinos.

Under such circumstances, only the most dimwitted or willfully blind would fail to see that the city is facing a campaign of systemic corruption conceived and orchestrated by a criminal conspiracy. And if the police chief appoints a notorious mob hit-man, with an arrest record as long as his arm, to head a "task force" of convicted felons to go about the city disarming all the citizens — in the interest of peace and security, of course — it should then be crystal clear that the good citizens had better organize immediately and sweep the criminals from office, if they hope to have any chance of saving themselves and their community. In the face of such overwhelming evidence, only total fools, complete cowards, or corrupt souls who had already joined the conspiracy would fail to heed the call to battle.

We are, almost literally, at that very point today. Not only are the one-world Insiders pushing relentlessly for national disarmament, but for individual disarmament as well. For many decades the same globalists who have lobbied ceaselessly for empowering the UN — the Ford, Rockefeller, and Carnegie foundations, the CFR, etc. — have carried on a continuous campaign against personal ownership of firearms.

Who is really calling the tunes and setting the agenda for the gun control "citizens network"? As usual, if you really want to know, *follow the money*. Handgun Control Incorporated, the National Council for a Responsible Firearms Policy, the Center to Prevent Handgun Violence, the ACLU, the National Council of Churches, and other groups that have led this campaign have been dependent upon these Insider feed troughs for funding. And they have depended on the CFR-dominated media cartel to disseminate their disinformation, while demonizing guns, gun owners, and all organized resistance to personal disarmament.

However, what even most of the organized gun-rights forces have failed to realize until very recently — and what some are still oblivious to — is the fact that the program for disarming the individual private citizen, depriving him of his means of self-defense, is directly tied to the United Nations and the program for national disarmament. The Second Amendment to the U.S. Constitution, which guarantees "the right of the people to keep and bear arms, shall not be infringed," has to go. Free people with the means to defend themselves are viewed by the United Nations as a threat to "peace."

They Want *Your* Gun

The same militant anti-gun organizations that are pressing for ever more restrictive limitations on private gun ownership have obtained NGO status at the UN and have been busy during most of the 1990s developing the UN's gun control plans. And though their opening wedge cleverly suggests that they are targeting "illicit" civilian possession of "military" weapons, it is clear that their real agenda is outright confiscation of all civilian-owned firearms, including handguns, rifles, and shotguns.*

In May 2000, hordes of NGO activists converged on New York City to attend the UN "Millennium Forum," a giant rehearsal session to prepare the global rent-a-mob for its role as the voice of "civil society" at the upcoming "main event," the Millennium Summit of world leaders, which would be gathering at the UN in September. At their May confab, the NGO leaders produced their Millennium Forum Action Plan which, among other things, calls on the UN "to expand the United Nations Arms Register, including specific names of arms producers and traders, in order to show production and sale of *small arms and light weapons.*" [5] (Emphasis added.)

For those familiar with the UN's record over the past several years in promoting an increasingly hostile attitude toward individual private ownership of firearms, this is a clear call for accelerated pressure on national governments to ratchet up their gun control efforts at all levels. Well aware of Mao Zedong's dictum that "political power grows out of the barrel of a gun," the one-world revolutionaries are accelerating their pressure from above and below to restrict (and eventually outlaw) private ownership of firearms and concentrate all power in the hands of government.

In his report to the heads of state attending the Millennium Summit, entitled *We the Peoples: The Role of the United Nations in the 21st Century,* Secretary-General Kofi Annan asserts that

---

*Some of the most rabid anti-gun propagandists have occasionally vindicated the fears of freedom-loving Americans by admitting that their attacks on handguns or "assault weapons" are merely incremental steps in a piecemeal onslaught on all private firearm ownership. The *Washington Post*, for example, in an August 19, 1965 editorial, stated: "We are inclined to think that every firearm in the hands of anyone who is not a law enforcement officer constitutes an incitement to violence."[6] The *Post* has given no evidence of having changed this totalitarian bent in the years since. Likewise, Joyner Sims, deputy commissioner for the Florida State Health Department, offered this gem, as quoted by the *Chicago Tribune*, on October 31, 1993: "The goal is an ultimate ban on all guns, but we also have to take a step at a time and go for limited access first. Lawmakers are scared to death of this issue. If we create anger and outrage on a national level, it would really help the local folks."[7]

Nelson T. Shields, who preceded Sarah Brady as chairman of Handgun Control, Inc., was quoted in *The New Yorker*, July 26, 1976, as saying: "We're going to have to take one step at a time, and the first step is necessarily ... going to be very modest.... And the final problem is to make the possession of *all* handguns and *all* handgun ammunition — except for the military, policemen, licensed security guards, licensed sporting clubs, and licensed gun collectors — totally illegal."[8] (Emphasis in original.) The *Los Angeles Times* opined, in an editorial for November 8, 1993, that "we must severely constrict if not virtually end the private possession of guns.... This country does not need one more gun in circulation; in fact, it needs about 200 million less."[9] Michael K. Beard, president of the Coalition to Stop Gun Violence, made this admission in an interview: "Our goal is to not allow anybody to buy a handgun.... The stated goal of the most active supporters of restrictions, aside from the 'moderate' goals they often espouse in the heat of legislative battle, is to abolish gun ownership totally."[10] The campaign to disarm American citizens has intensified in recent years, rising to near hysteria following the Columbine school shootings. The ultimate objective of this media-driven campaign was given full voice by "comedienne" Rosie O'Donnell, who declared on her nationally televised talk show of April 21, 1999: "I don't care if you want to hunt, I don't care if you think it's your right. I say, 'Sorry.' It is 1999. We have had enough as a nation. You are not allowed to own a gun, and if you do own a gun I think you should go to prison."[11]

"small arms proliferation is not merely a security issue; it is also an issue of human rights and development." [12] He went on:

> Even if all arms transfers could be eliminated, however, the problem posed by the many millions of illicitly held small arms already in circulation in the world's war zones would remain.... Controlling the proliferation of illicit weapons is a necessary first step towards the non-proliferation of small arms. These weapons must be brought under the control of states....[13]

Further, he announced, "The United Nations is convening a conference on the illicit trade in small arms and light weapons in 2001." [14] NGO activists and government delegates alike have made it very clear in disarmament forums already held by the UN that virtually all private ownership is considered illicit.

The first notice most Americans received concerning the UN plan for targeting firearms came on May 24, 1994, when they opened their newspapers to a story by Associated Press reporter Charles J. Hanley on a new UN stealth gun control initiative for the whole world. The AP article reported:

> So quietly that even the gun lobby hasn't noticed, the United Nations is beginning to set its sights on global gun control.
> The U.N. Disarmament Commission has adopted a working paper, a basis for future debate, that proposes tighter controls on the gun trade in the United States and other member nations as a way of combating international arms trafficking. [15]

That same day, the *Washington Times*, in an article entitled "U.S. OKs study of U.N. gun control," reported:

> The Clinton administration has agreed to participate in a discussion of ways for the United Nations to control the manufacture of guns and their sales to civilians.
> This represents the first U.N. effort to foster regulation of the multi-billion-dollar trade in small arms....
> The U.N. working paper declares that governments individually

are "impotent" to deal with global arms trafficking and proposes "harmonization" of gun control standards around the world to make trafficking easier to spot and prevent.

"The arms permitted for civilian use ... should be subject to controls at all points in the chain, from production and/or acquisition up to the time they are sold to an individual. From then on they should remain subject to monitoring and control," the paper says.

Any "harmonization" would inevitably mean tightening controls on the loosely regulated U.S. gun business....[16]

Concerning the above story, we should note, first of all, the ploy commonly used in selling UN schemes, which invariably involves portraying the current U.S. Insider administration (whether Republican or Democrat) as the coy and reluctant lover. Thus it is reported that "the Clinton administration has *agreed* to participate" in the UN gun grab conference, implying that Clinton and his one-world CFR crew running the executive branch of the most powerful country in the world are yielding to reason and the entreaties of the "world community."

Behind-the-Scenes Leadership
In truth, the Clinton administration was working furiously behind the scenes *leading* the UN effort. This has been standard procedure, in both Republican and Democrat administrations, since World War II. The Insider-chosen occupant of the White House feigns opposition to the UN treaty, or at least expresses "grave concern" about some clause or provision (as, for instance, in the case of the Genocide Convention, the Law of the Sea Treaty, or the treaty for an International Criminal Court), so that when the administration embraces the treaty during the final push for ratification, we are supposed to be satisfied that all of our concerns have been addressed by a president who is looking out for American interests.

U.S. involvement in the UN gun control plot came long before the Clinton administration, but, in the words of Harlan Cleveland, that involvement has been carried out "mostly below the surface of public attention."* Recall that the 1961 *Freedom From War* plan is a three-stage program for the complete disarming of nation states and the simultaneous *arming* of the United Nations. In its own words, *Freedom From War* states:

> In Stage III progressive controlled disarmament ... would pro-

---

*It quickly became apparent that the Insiders intended that the UN gun-grab conference not rise above "the surface of public attention." Considering this campaign's brazen assault on the U.S. Constitution, American national sovereignty, and the fundamental human right to self-defense, it is understandable that both the UN and the Clinton administration would want to keep this subversive initiative as quiet as possible and would be reluctant to discuss it. Officials at the U.S. State Department and the UN rebuffed repeated attempts by this writer to obtain a copy of the working paper or to discuss it in detail. First we were told that the AP and *Washington Times* reports were erroneous and exaggerated, and that concern was overblown. Unconvinced, we insisted we would like to judge for ourselves by examining the document.

At the State Department, after several office transfers, we were informed that Ambassador Stephen Ledogar, the U.S. representative on the Disarmament Commission, was out of the country and no one else knew how to obtain a copy of the document. At the UN, after six departmental transfers, we reached the director of the UN Disarmament Commission, a Mr. Sohrab Kheradi, who informed us that the report would not be released until mid-July (1994). However, under our persistent entreaties, Mr. Kheradi agreed that he would arrange for *The New American* to receive a pre-release copy forthwith. Days passed, but still no working paper. More calls to the UN and more promises to send the report. Weeks passed. Finally, we reached the Secretary of the Disarmament Commission himself, Mr. Kuo-chung Lin, who had been away on vacation. Mr. Lin assured us that the concerns stirred by initial news coverage of the working paper were "based on a misunderstanding" of the nature and significance of the report. "This is only the report of the chairman of the Working Group for *discussion* over the next two years," he explained. "It doesn't establish any policy or have any binding effect." But is it not true, we asked, that its purpose is to bring about the establishment of policy that will have "binding effect"? No, no, he laughed. Its purpose is simply to encourage "debate and discussion." [17]

Of course, as a UN official from Communist China, where debate and discussion can land you in prison, and where unarmed dissenters are unceremoniously squashed beneath the tracks of army tanks, Mr. Lin's cavalier attitude toward attacks on the Second Amendment is understandable, even expected. It is the attitudes and actions of *American* officials, who collude with the likes of Comrade Lin, that are far more troubling.

ceed to a point where *no state would have the military power to challenge the progressively strengthened U.N. Peace Force....*

The manufacture of armaments would be prohibited except for those agreed types and quantities to be used by the U.N. Peace Force and those required to maintain internal order. *All other armaments would be destroyed or converted to peaceful purposes.* [18] [Emphasis added.]

"*All* other armaments would be destroyed." Notice that no provision is made to exempt arms owned by private citizens. An innocent oversight? Hardly. The UN itself, as we've already seen, is hardly sympathetic to private gun ownership. That's to be expected, since the Insiders who designed it and support it, along with all of the Communist regimes and most of the non-Communist countries who make up the UN membership, share a statist hostility toward civilian possession of arms. Anyone familiar with the UN's history in this matter, as well as the history of its legal interpretation of treaties, will recognize that private arms are targeted for destruction under the term "all other armaments." We can expect that this terminology in *Freedom From War* and other agreements, conventions, and treaties will be cited as legally requiring the U.S. to disarm its civilian population. All under the guise of following "the rule of law."

To initiate the *Freedom From War* program, President Kennedy signed Public Law 87-297 (H.R. 9118), creating the United States Arms Control and Disarmament Agency (ACDA). According to that legislation, "as used in this Act, the terms 'arms control' and 'disarmament' mean 'the identification, verification, inspection, limitation, control, reduction, or elimination, of armed forces and *armaments of all kinds* under international agreement ... to establish *an effective system of international control....*'" [19] (Emphasis added.)

In its "Second Annual Report to Congress" (February 1963), the ACDA presented a simple graphic depiction (see top of next page) demonstrating its proposed three-stage disarmament process. [20] Observe that in Stage III, as explained in *Freedom*

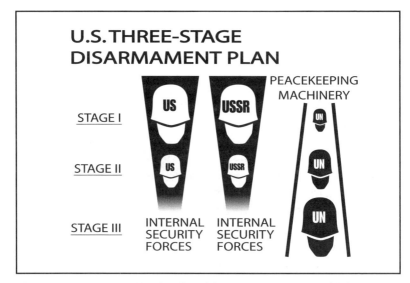

This diagram appeared in the 1963 "Second Annual Report to Congress" of the U.S. Arms Control and Disarmament Agency.

From War and *Blueprint for the Peace Race*, the U.S. armed forces cease to exist and only "internal security forces" — i.e. those to be used against American citizens — are permitted. Of course, under this scheme, the UN "peacekeeping machinery" will be superior to the "internal security forces" and will be able to dictate the "laws" that will be enforced.

Authors of *Freedom From War*

Official responsibility for developing and initiating the disarmament program outlined in *Freedom From War* goes to President Kennedy and his Secretaries of State (Dean Rusk) and Defense (Robert S. McNamara), both of whom were members of the CFR. The real authors of *Freedom From War* and Public Law 87-297, however, were John J. McCloy, the chairman of the CFR, and Arthur H. Dean, a CFR director — together with Valerian Zorin, their Soviet counterpart.[21]

McCloy, Kennedy's chief disarmament adviser and negotiator with the Soviets, entered the Establishment through the Wall

Street law firm of Cravath, Swaine and Moore, and later became a senior partner at Milbank, Tweed, Hadley, and McCloy, a firm closely tied to the Rockefeller family. He served as an Assistant Secretary of War under FDR and as U.S. High Commissioner to occupied Germany. He headed the World Bank, Chase Manhattan Bank, the Ford Foundation, and, most importantly, from 1953–1970 was chairman of the Council on Foreign Relations. He was an adviser to nine presidents and sat on the boards of directors of many corporations. He and a small group of CFR confederates "selected" the presidential candidates for both the Republican and Democrat parties, and then selected the cabinets, ambassadors, and other top appointments of the winning contestant. [22] Few would dispute journalist Richard Rovere's characterization of McCloy in the May 1962 *Esquire* magazine as "chairman of the American Establishment." [23]

McCloy's blue-chip résumé, however, included a few red flags. While serving in the War Department, McCloy approved an order permitting Communist Party members to become officers in the U.S. Army. [24] He defended identified Communist John Carter Vincent and supported pro-Communist atomic scientist J. Robert Oppenheimer. [25] In 1946, FBI head J. Edgar Hoover warned President Truman of an "enormous Soviet espionage ring in Washington," and expressed concern over the "pro-Soviet leanings" of McCloy, Dean Acheson, and Alger Hiss. [26] Hiss, of course, was later exposed as a Soviet agent. He was also a member of the CFR and one of the main architects of the United Nations.

Assisting McCloy in drafting *Freedom From War* and the statute for the Arms Control and Disarmament Agency was Arthur H. Dean. [27] Dean was chairman of the U.S. delegation for two years to the UN disarmament conferences in Geneva.

A junior partner at Sullivan & Cromwell, Dean became the senior partner when the prestigious law firm's headman, John Foster Dulles (a CFR founder), was appointed to fill a vacant Senate seat. [28] Dean was also vice-chairman of the Institute of Pacific Relations (IPR), the Communist-run outfit most responsible — together with our State Department — for turning China over to the Communists in 1949.[29] When IPR member Alfred Kohlberg tried heroically to expose the treason within IPR, it was Dean who scuttled the investigation.[30] In 1952, the U.S. Senate Judiciary Committee issued a scathing report on the IPR, citing it as "an instrument of Communist policy, propaganda and military intelligence."[31] The Senate report also concluded:

> Members of the small core of officials and staff members who controlled IPR were either Communist or pro-Communist....
>
> The effective leadership of the IPR used IPR prestige to promote the interests of the Soviet Union in the United States....
>
> The IPR was a vehicle used by the Communists to orientate American far eastern policy toward Communist objectives.[32]

With the above information in mind, we direct the reader's attention to *The Wise Men*, the glowing 1986 hagiography of McCloy and five of his globalist CFR cohorts, authored by Walter Isaacson (CFR) and Evan Thomas (CFR).[33] This one-world apologia provides many admissions against interest, including a very significant photograph on page 605 showing McCloy and Soviet dictator Nikita Khrushchev chest deep in the waters of Khrushchev's swimming pool, in a warm, comradely embrace, with Khrushchev's arm around McCloy's neck.

So, let us summarize some of the ground we've just covered: The *Freedom From War* scheme for disarming the U.S. (nationally and individually) can be traced back directly to a Russian Communist (Valerian Zorin) and two top Pratt House one-worlders with extensive ties to Communist intelligence operations, one of whom cavorted in a swimming pool with the "Butcher of Budapest," the Communist dictator who bellowed at the U.S., "We will bury you."

Yet Dean and McCloy, with the help of their CFR associates in the media, passed themselves off as Republicans, and conservative, anti-Communist Republicans at that!

Destructive Duo: Clark and Sohn

Still another important key to understanding the true nature and history of the Kennedy-CFR disarmament plan, and its successor incarnations, is the team of Establishment Wall Street lawyer Grenville Clark and Harvard law professor Louis B. Sohn (CFR). John J. McCloy had been strongly influenced by Grenville Clark at a military training camp during the summer of 1915.[34] Clark was a vice president and founder of the United World Federalists (UWF, which later changed its name to the World Federalist Association).[35] The UWF/WFA, which has been one of the most hardcore groups advocating world government, was actually conceived at a private Conference on World Government in 1946 at Clark's home in Dublin, New Hampshire.[36]

"It has been well said," according to Mr. Clark, "that in our modern age the obdurate adherence to national sovereignty and national armed forces represents a form of insanity which may, however, be cured by a species of shock treatment."[37] He spelled out that "shock treatment" in *World Peace Through World Law*, a detailed plan for socialist world government through a revised UN Charter.[38]

This text, co-authored with Professor Sohn and published in 1958 by Harvard University Press, is venerated by all "world order" advocates. It proposes a global superstate in which a "world police force" known as the United Nations Peace Force would be invested with "a coercive force of overwhelming power."[39] "This world police force," wrote Clark and Sohn, "would be the only *military* force permitted anywhere in the world after the process of national disarmament has been completed."[40] (Emphasis in original.)

However, these architects of "world order" would not be satisfied with a monopoly of *military* power. They believed that "even with the complete elimination of all [national] *military* forces there would necessarily remain substantial, although strictly limited and lightly armed, internal police forces and that these police forces, supplemented by civilians armed with sporting rifles and fowling pieces, might conceivably constitute a serious threat to a neighboring country in the absence of a well-disciplined and heavily armed world police."[41] (Emphasis in original.)

Thus, Chapter 3, Article 13 of the Clark/Sohn UN scheme mandates that "the strength of the internal police forces of any nation shall not exceed two for each 1000 of its population," [42] and Article 14 orders strict controls on the possession of arms and ammunition by police and private citizens:

> No nation shall allow the possession by its internal police forces of any arms or equipment except of the types permitted by the regulations adopted by the General Assembly ... and in no case shall the number of revolvers and rifles combined exceed one for each member of the internal police forces, the number of automatic rifles one for each hundred members of such forces, and the ammunition supplies 100 rounds per rifle or revolver and 1,000 rounds per automatic rifle. No nation shall allow the possession by any public or private organization or individual of any military equipment whatever or of any arms except such small arms as are reasonably needed by duly licensed hunters or by duly licensed individuals for personal protection. [43]

Care to speculate as to how difficult it would be under the envisioned UN regime to become "duly licensed" for hunting or personal protection? Try next to impossible, based upon the known animus of the one-world elite toward popular ownership of firearms, and the established record on this matter of the Communist, socialist, and authoritarian regimes that constitute the overwhelming majority in the UN.

The Clark/Sohn plan also would eliminate the "problem" of private citizens' access to ammunition by providing that "no nation shall produce or allow the production of any explosives except insofar as the General Assembly may authorize...." [44] Moreover, "every nation shall obtain a special license from the [UN] Inspector-General for ... [t]he operation by it or by any public or private organization or individual ... engaged in the production of any light arms, ammunition ... or of tools for any such production." [45]

It also provides that "no nation shall produce or allow the production of *any arms*, weapons or military equipment *whatever*, or of *tools* for such production, except" (emphasis added), and then goes on to list those few exceptions: internal police and the tiny minority of "duly licensed individuals." [46]

In "Annex I" of the Clark/Sohn program, we are told: "Finally, this Annex makes provision for *enforcement measures against individuals*, organizations and nations who may commit violations of the Annex or of any law or regulation enacted thereunder." [47] (Emphasis added.) And, presaging the International Criminal Court, which would not be formally launched until 40 years later (1998), it states: "All penal proceedings against individuals and private organizations would be brought by a new legal official — the United Nations Attorney-General — to be appointed pursuant to Part D of Annex III." [48] So, you see, the global prosecutor post established by the ICC Statute of Rome in 1998 was actually the implementation of the Insider-directed Clark/Sohn plan issued 40 years earlier.

And supposing some "individuals, organizations and nations" decide they don't like the emerging tyranny of the globalists and determine to defy the "authority" of the new behemoth? For precisely these contingencies the *World Peace Through World Law* plan provides that "the United Nations Peace Force shall be regularly provided with the most modern weapons and equipment," with special provision being made "for the use of nuclear weapons in extreme circumstances." [49]

We needn't worry about abuse of such awesome power because the UN "shall in no event employ nuclear weapons except when the General Assembly ... has declared that nothing less ... will suffice to prevent or suppress a serious *breach of the peace* or a violent and serious *defiance of the authority* of the United Nations." [50] (Emphasis added.) Who could ask for better assurance than that? No need for concrete checks and balances when we have the promises of the one-worlders and the sound judgment and moral rectitude of the UN General Assembly to protect us!

The Plot Continues

Grenville Clark passed on to his eternal destination in 1967 but Professor Sohn has remained actively involved in the "new world order" business, writing legal treatises and training new generations of one-world lawyers, legislators, judges, and propagandists. The current UN drive for civilian disarmament is unmistakably a continuation of the scheme so methodically scripted by Clark and Sohn, adopted as official policy under *Freedom From War*, and developed in subsequent treaties under successive administrations.

In language very similar to that used by Clark and Sohn, the August 19, 1999 UN "Report of the Group of Governmental Experts on Small Arms" lists, as weapons to be banned, and ultimately confiscated, "revolvers and self-loading pistols, rifles and carbines, submachine guns, assault rifles and light machineguns."[51]

Furthermore, the 1999 "Experts" document is listed as part of the UN's provisional agenda for "general and complete disarmament"[52] — a phrase that figures prominently in the texts of *World Peace Through World Law*, *Freedom From War*, and subsequent policies. Suffice it to say the UN has a very literal understanding of the phrase "general and complete disarmament."

And what if you fail to turn in or register, say, your .22 rifle, your .38 pistol, or your gunpowder and reloading equipment, and you are charged with unlawful possession of "military equipment" under the UN General Assembly's ever-changing regulations? The UN Attorney-General (or his subordinates) will bring charges and a UN tribunal will be your judge and jury, Clark and Sohn say. And since they anticipate far more "business" than can be handled by a single court, a whole new global judiciary system must be put in place:

> In order to provide means for the trial of individuals accused of violating the disarmament provisions of the revised Charter or of other offenses against the Charter or laws enacted by the General Assembly ... provision is also made for regional United Nations

courts, inferior to the International Court of Justice, and for the review by the International Court of decisions of these regional courts. [53]

Our Global Neighborhood

The UN is proceeding according to the Clark and Sohn pre-scription — with help from the usual suspects. In 1995, the UN's 50th anniversary year, the UN-funded Commission on Global Governance (CGG) released *Our Global Neighborhood*, its much-heralded report for UN reform. [54] But the CGG's recipe for "reform" is in reality a regurgitation of Clark and Sohn's deadly brew. Targeting America's heritage of gun ownership, the CGG warned, "Widespread criminalization can threaten the very functioning of a state. In the United States, the easy avail-ability of weapons goes with a startling level of daily killings." "What is needed," according to the CGG's globo-savants, "is demilitarization of international society." [55] The report explained:

Militarization today not only involves governments spending more than necessary to build up their military arsenals. It has increasingly become a global societal phenomenon, as witnessed by the rampant acquisition and use of increasingly lethal weapons by civilians — whether individuals seeking a means of self-defence, street gangs, criminals, political opposition groups, or terrorist organizations. [56]

Yes, in the view of these globalists, the man defending his fam-ily and his home against robbers and gangsters, or the woman defending her person and her virtue against a rapist, have no more right to a firearm than do the rapists, robbers, gang bangers, and other vicious predators causing the "widespread criminalization" the CGG is decrying. Accordingly, the CGG sta-tists "strongly endorse community initiatives ... to encourage the disarming of civilians." [57]

The CGG report, remember, was a collaborative effort of top

members of the CFR, the UN plutocracy, the European Union, the Socialist International and various Communist Parties (see Chapter 2). It prefigured the 1999 UN "Report of the Group of Governmental Experts on Small Arms," which complained bitterly that "there are wide differences among States [nations] as regards which types of arms are permitted for civilian possession, and as regards the circumstances under which they can legitimately be owned, carried and used. Such wide variation in national laws raises difficulties for effective regional or international coordination."[58]

Among the proposals adopted by the panel and enthusiastically endorsed by UN Secretary-General Kofi Annan in his foreword to the report are measures aimed at increasing "control over the legal possession of small arms and light weapons and over their transfer," expanding prohibitions on "trade and private ownership of small arms and light weapons," and tightening efforts to "control ammunition."[59]

The UN Charter bars UN intervention in "matters which are essentially within the domestic jurisdiction of any state,"[60] but the UN, in typical fashion, has been defining "domestic jurisdiction" out of existence. Kofi Annan explained in a September 20, 1999 address before the UN General Assembly that "state sovereignty, in its most basic sense, is being redefined." What is needed, Annan continued, is "a new, more broadly defined, more widely conceived definition of national interest in the new century [where] the collective interest is the national interest."[61] Four days later, Annan emphasized that "controlling the easy availability of small arms was a prerequisite for a successful peace-building process," which is why the United Nations "had played a leading role in putting the issue of small arms firmly on the international agenda."[62]

All of this could, of course, be dismissed as meaningless UN blather — except for the fact that it is fully supported by the U.S. Insiders, including elected officials whom American citizens are naively counting on to protect us against any encroachments from the UN. Kofi Annan emphasizes in his foreword to the

"Report of the Group of Governmental Experts on Small Arms" that it was "prepared, and adopted by consensus" and was the product of "unanimity" among the "expert" members of the group. [63]

If we accept Annan's assertion at face value, we can presume that none of the "experts" objected to this full-tilt assault on the right to keep and bear arms. Yet among the "experts" who drafted the report was U.S. State Department Senior Foreign Affairs Specialist Herbert L. Calhoun. And none other than Secretary of State Madeleine Albright (CFR) told the first-ever UN Security Council Small Arms Ministerial, on September 24, 1999, that "the United States strongly supports these steps," that we "welcome the important precedent which the UN has set," and that the U.S. would work to "commit to finishing negotiations on a firearms protocol to the UN Transnational Organized Crime Convention by the end of 2000." [64]

The Orchestrated Disarmament Choir

The orchestrated "pressure from below" was already building steam by that time. In November 1998, the *UNESCO Courier* noted that "the political tides may be changing. An international campaign is now underway with non-governmental organizations of all stripes and colours — disarmament and gun control groups along with development and human rights associations in the North and South — building common ground with the active support of governments like Mali, Canada, Norway and Japan." [65] As in every other case we have seen, this "international campaign" of NGOs is entirely a front for the one-world internationalists, who pay the bills via foundations and government (i.e., taxpayer-funded) grants.

On September 24, 1999 Kofi Annan reported to a ministerial-level meeting of the Security Council on small arms: "The momentum for combating small arms proliferation has also come from civil society, which has been increasingly active on this issue. The establishment early this year of the International Action Network on Small Arms [IANSA] has helped to sharpen public focus on small arms, which has helped us gain the public support necessary for success." [66] IANSA is intended to "provide a transnational framework" for the mobilization of a broad citizen movement in favor of gun control, according to the organizational goals posted on its website. [67] The services IANSA intends to provide the UN-led global gun control movement include "campaigning and advocacy strategies," "developing culturally appropriate 'message' strategies," "information sharing" among NGOs, and "constituency building." [68]

And where will the funding for this propaganda campaign come from? IANSA notes on its website that its eight most significant financial donors include five government agencies: the Belgian Ministry for Development Cooperation; the Swedish Ministry of Foreign Affairs; the Netherlands Ministry of Foreign Affairs; the United Kingdom Department for International Development; and the Finnish Ministry of Foreign Affairs. In other words, this "non-governmental" organization is purely a front for the disarmament-obsessed totalitarians in the increasingly militant socialist regimes of the European Union.

The UN is putting our tax dollars to effective use in this campaign as well. Among other things, it is aggressively pushing its recent video, *Armed to the Teeth*. [69] This UN "shockumentary" is a brutal, hour-long diatribe aimed at convincing the viewer that "small arms" are the cause of all violence, crime, and bloodshed in the world. Replete with gruesome film footage of victims of crime and genocide, it relentlessly demonizes firearms and pounds home the message that this carnage will not stop until civilian populations are disarmed.

Armed to the Teeth invests firearms with human-like qualities, so as to more easily and effectively vilify these targeted instruments. "A killer is on the loose," we are told in the video's opening scenes. The "killer," of course, is "small arms," i.e., *guns*, which are shown over and over in the most menacing ways that the video's creators could come up with. We are told that "small arms are not fussy about the company they keep.... They can murder indiscriminately. Men and women, young and old, rich and poor." Amidst Hollywood-style edits of sound effects and images of gore and violence, comes the message: "Humankind is beginning a new millennium under the sign of the gun, and small arms are like uninvited guests who won't leave. Once they take over a country they are virtually impossible to get rid of."

Yes, according to this UN propaganda, a horde of "small arms" are "taking over" countries. Utilizing dramatic footage from Mozambique, Rwanda, South Africa, Brazil, Kosovo, Albania, Afghanistan, and elsewhere, the video repetitiously hammers this theme. At the same time, it conspicuously refrains from pointing any fingers at the *real* criminals responsible for the carnage it depicts: the *human* agents who are using the firearms for criminal purposes. This would be like fomenting a worldwide campaign against matches and gasoline because of the death and destruction caused by arson — and completely ignoring the need to apprehend the arsonists! The UN filmmakers know this, of course. They have focused on the matches and gasoline and ignored the arsonists for some very important reasons.

One reason is that they intend to so vilify "small arms" and associate them with everything evil that people will have an automatic emotional aversion to firearms and agree to civilian disarmament. Another reason for the conscious failure of the UN videographers to mention the responsibility of *human* agency is to divert attention from the *UN's* role in the very crimes it is denouncing. In virtually all of the examples shown in *Armed to the Teeth*, the UN and its institutions (particularly the IMF and World Bank) played major roles in creating chaos and revolution that produced the bloody scenes.

Rwandan Genocide

The UN's video treatment of Rwanda is especially noteworthy. Rwanda's 1994 genocide is one of the strongest examples imaginable proving the case *against* civilian disarmament. The slaughter of some 800,000 Rwandans in just 103 days makes it the most *concentrated* genocide in the bloody 20th century. This horrible mass-murder was possible because the killers — in this case, the government forces and government-organized mobs — were armed and the victims were not. Rwanda's draconian 1979 gun control legislation made it almost impossible for civilians to possess firearms. The government was thus given a monopoly on lethal force. Ultimately it used that force, and its victims were helpless before it.

Most of the Rwandan victims were not shot; they were brutally hacked to death with machetes or speared and clubbed to death. According to survivors and eyewitnesses, many of the victims did not meekly submit to slaughter; they tried to defend themselves with stones, sticks, and their bare hands. In the few instances where the victims were able to obtain firearms they succeeded in delaying or limiting the carnage and saving lives. The most detailed and enlightening analysis of the Rwandan genocide we have seen is published by Jews for the Preservation of Firearm Ownership (JPFO). Their heavily documented 1997 study, *Rwanda's Genocide, 1994*, authoritatively states: "The careful planning of this genocide — and the near-total disarmed state of its victims — explains the speed and intensity of the murder process." [70]

The JPFO study cites abundant evidence to support the claim "that 'gun control' was a critical element in this genocide." [71] "Had the citizens … not been disarmed," it notes, "they might have deterred the genocide entirely, or at very least reduced its extent. Those who place their faith in any other form of prevention — especially in the UN or other supranational organizations — seem blind to some hard realities." [72] After surveying the facts compiled by JPFO researchers, it is difficult to dispute that assertion. *Rwanda's Genocide, 1994* concludes with this sobering assessment:

> The hard lesson of Rwanda is that the only potential saviors for the intended targets of a genocidal government are the intended victims themselves. No one else is likely to care enough to do anything beyond protest, or to be able to provide direct help fast

enough. The intended victims of a genocidal government can save themselves only if they have ready access to firearms, particularly military-type. For them to have access to firearms, 'gun control' must be destroyed. How many more mountains of corpses need to be piled-up before this lesson is learned? [73]

This bitter truth learned from the horrors of Rwanda comports completely with what we know of the other major genocides of the 20th century. Again, we can thank the JPFO for document-ing the critical role of civilian disarmament, i.e., "gun control," for the slaughters in all of these cases. In their important 1994 study, *Lethal Laws: "Gun Control" is the Key to Genocide*, the JPFO provides a valuable examination of the massive genocides in Ottoman Turkey, Soviet Russia, Nazi Germany, Red China, Guatemala, Uganda, and Cambodia. [74] The report also photo-graphically reproduces the gun control laws (along with English translations) that disarmed the victims and made the genocides possible in each of those countries. It is a *devastating* indictment of the program for civilian disarmament that the UN is pushing for the entire world!

UN "Peacemaking": Drenched in Blood

The one-worlders' totalitarian scheme for personal disarma-ment and subjugation of all to an omnipotent UN is no longer idle theory; it has already received several recent trial runs, albeit on a limited scale. In Somalia, Haiti, and Kosovo the UN's "peacekeepers" have disarmed the civilian populations and left them at the mercy of UN-supported totalitarian thugs. (In Rwanda too, it should be noted, it was the UN-supported totali-tarian regime of General Habyarimana that carried out the hor-rendous slaughter.)

To get a picture of what the UN program for "peace" through disarmament is really all about, we need to take a brief look at one of the UN's most vicious crimes: its brutal 1961 invasion of peaceful Katanga, in the Congo. In that murderous assault on the people of the Congo, the UN's sainted "Blue Helmets" were

177

tasked with supporting Soviet-trained Communist terrorist Patrice Lumumba against the democratically elected, Christian, pro-Western president of Katanga, Moise Tshombe.

Since the incredible story of the UN's atrocities in Katanga has been consigned to the Orwellian "memory hole" by the CFR's "ruling class journalists" and "court historians," it is important that we make at least a modest attempt to recount what happened there. In *The Blue Helmets: A Review of United Nations Peace-keeping*, a self-serving encomium published by the UN, we read: "The United Nations Operation in the Congo ... July 1960 until June 1964, is by far the largest peacekeeping operation ever established by the United Nations in terms of the responsibilities it had to assume, the size of its area of operation and the manpower involved. It included ... a peace-keeping force which comprised at its peak strength nearly 20,000 officers and men...." [75]

What were all of these "peacekeepers" doing in the Congo? Supporting Congolese "self-determination" and "independence" says the UN. In reality, they were propping up a succession of Soviet stooges who were conducting a grisly reign of terror. For many years the Soviets had been supporting and establishing "independence" and "anti-colonialist" movements throughout the world — always with the aim of converting European colonies into new colonies in the global Communist empire. The United Nations proved over and over again that it supported this new Soviet colonialism by materially supporting the Kremlin-backed terrorists through its various agencies and by bestowing political legitimacy on them from the rostrum of the General Assembly.

In the Congo, Moscow had hedged its bets, as usual, by backing several thugs. As soon as Belgium's King Baudouin announced that the Congo was to be given its independence, however, the Soviets made clear that their top choice for viceroy in the area was Patrice Lumumba.

Lumumba, a thoroughly corrupt dope addict, ex-convict, and murderer, was lionized by the CFR media machine as the George Washington of Africa. Emboldened by his international acclaim and the financial and military backing of the U.S.S.R. and Red China, Lumumba dropped all pretenses of "democratic rule" and began an orgy of rape, pillage, torture, and terror.

On September 15, 1960, he issued a lengthy and detailed directive to the heads of the various provinces of the Congo which left no doubt as to his brutal intentions. Dictators frequently disguise their brutal decrees in genteel-sounding prose or bureaucratic legalese, but Lumumba, intoxicated with his new power, and brimming with the Marxist drivel he had learned from his Soviet masters, did not bother with such camouflage. In his directive, entitled, "Measures To Be Applied During the First Stages of the Dictatorship," he let it be known that he had assumed "full powers" and then listed the following points as the "most effective and direct means of succeeding rapidly in our task":

> Establish an absolute dictatorship and apply it in all its forms.
>
> Terrorism, essential to subdue the population.
>
> Proceed systematically, using the army, to arrest all members of the opposition.... I sent the National Army to arrest Tshombe and Kalonji and even to kill them if possible....
>
> Imprison the ministers, deputies and senators.... Arrest them all without pity and treat them with ten times more severity than ordinary individuals.
>
> Revive the system of flogging....
>
> Inflict profound humiliations on the people thus arrested.... [S]trip them in public, if possible in the presence of their wives and children.
>
> ...If some of them succumb as a result of certain atrocities, which is possible and desirable, the truth should not be divulged but it should be announced, for instance, that Mr. X has escaped and cannot be found....[76]

That was just the *first* stage of Lumumba's Communist revolution. He ended his directive with the promise that "the second stage will be to destroy anyone who criticizes us."[77] He ended a subsequent memorandum with this finale: "Long live the Soviet Union! Long live Khrushchev!"[78]

Long before this, however, Lumumba had left no doubt as to his brutal nature and totalitarian orientation. He had actually put his dictatorship of terrorism into practice before announcing it to his provincial officials in the directive cited above. Nevertheless, President Eisenhower (CFR) joined Soviet dictator Nikita Khrushchev in supporting a resolution authorizing the UN to send troops to assist Lumumba! He then dispatched U.S. Air Force planes to transport UN troops and supplies for that "peacekeeping" mission. He welcomed Lumumba to the U.S. with a royal reception and showered Lumumba's new regime with millions of dollars.

However, there was widespread opposition to Lumumba's Soviet brand of "independence" throughout the Congo. The stoutest opposition arose in Katanga Province, a multi-racial area about the size of France, under the able leadership of the educated and pro-Western Moise Tshombe. Declaring, "I am seceding from chaos," President Tshombe announced Katanga's independence from Lumumba's murderous central Congo government. Amidst the sea of carnage and terror that was then the Congo, the province of Katanga remained, by comparison, an island of peace, order, and stability.

Did the UN peacekeepers try to put an end to Lumumba's reign of terror — which included the systematic slaughter of civilian men, women, and children? No, they instead used UN power to squash the fledgling republic of Katanga and force it back under Lumumba's control.

"From the outset of the hostilities," say the UN disinformation specialists in *The Blue Helmets*, "United Nations military and civilian officers did their best, in cooperation with the International Committee of the Red Cross, to relieve the distress caused to innocent civilians."[79] That lie, as well as hundreds of others in the book's treatment of the Congo operation, could have been written by propagandists from the Kremlin (or Pratt House) — and, in fact, probably was. In truth, the UN's blue helmets engaged in the very war crimes that the UN now demands global jurisdiction to protect the world from. UN planes knowingly and intentionally bombed hospitals, churches, and schools. Its troops attacked the same targets, as well as ambulances, and slaughtered noncombatant men, women, and children.*

After Lumumba's mysterious death, UN support swung to the militantly pro-Communist Cyrille Adoula, and then to Communist Antoine Gizenga. In September 1961, U.S. newspapers carried this account of the UN invasion of Elisabethville, the capital of Katanga:

> The UN declared martial law and ... Michel Tombelaine of France, deputy UN civilian commander, announced over the UN controlled radio that *any civilians found in illegal possession of arms will be summarily executed.* [80] [Emphasis added.]

Yes, here was the UN imposing Communist-style disarmament — which is always a prelude to Communist-style terror. What the CFR-run U.S. media didn't tell the American people was that Mr. Tombelaine had been identified as a member of the French

---

*More details of this important and incredibly vicious chapter of UN history can be found in the following: *The Fearful Master* by G. Edward Griffin; [81] *Who Killed the Congo?* by Philippa Schuyler; [82] *Rebels, Mercenaries, and Dividends* by Smith Hempstone; [83] and *46 Angry Men* by the 46 doctors of Elisabethville. [84] In 1962, a private group of Americans, outraged at our government's actions against the freedom-seeking Katangese, attempted to capture on film the truth about what was happening in the Congo. They produced *Katanga: The Untold Story*, an hour-long documentary narrated by Congressman Donald L. Jackson. [85] With newsreel footage and testimony from eyewitnesses, including a compelling interview with Tshombe himself, the program exposed the criminal activities and brutal betrayal perpetrated on a peaceful people by the Eisenhower and then Kennedy administrations, other Western leaders, and top UN officials. It documents the fact that UN (including U.S.) planes deliberately bombed Katanga's schools, hospitals, and churches, while UN troops machine-gunned and bayoneted civilians, school children, and Red Cross workers who tried to help the wounded. This film is now available on videotape, and is "must-viewing" for Americans who are determined that this land or any other land shall never experience similar UN atrocities. (For ordering information, please see above-referenced endnote.)

Communist Party by a subcommittee of the U.S. Senate Judiciary Committee.[86] What they also failed to report (with a few brave exceptions) was that the UN forces were carrying out vicious atrocities against unarmed Katangese men, women, and children. Nevertheless, the CFR-dominated Kennedy administration, like the Eisenhower CFR gang before it, backed the Lumumba-Adoula-Gizenga lineup and opposed the pro-U.S. Tshombe.

More CFR-UN Treachery and Butchery

This sickening, treacherous pattern has been repeatedly reenacted in more recent times. In Somalia, for instance, the U.S.-led UN misadventure, Operation Restore Hope, was launched under "humanitarian" pretenses to suppress the forces that had ousted the brutal, Soviet-installed Communist dictatorship of Mohammed Siad Barre. During his reign of over two decades, Siad Barre had been the recipient of hundreds of millions of dollars from the U.S. and the UN.

After U.S. troops were sent to provide humanitarian assistance, their orders mutated into disarming the "civilian militias." The CFR team in the Bush administration and the CFR team in the succeeding Clinton administration — together with their CFR media allies — aimed all of their vitriol at the forces of General Mohammed Aidid, the leader most responsible for the overthrow of Communist dictator Barre, and the leader with the broadest national support.

General Aidid became the *villain du jour*. He and his civilian "militias" had to be disarmed, we were told. The disarmament program escalated into an illegal UN order for the *arrest* of General Aidid, with U.S. Army Rangers and Delta Force commandos assigned the job of effecting the arrest warrant. The result: a bloody U.S. defeat, with 19 American soldiers dead, 75 wounded, and ugly video footage — agonizingly reminiscent of Vietnam — of an American pilot being dragged through the streets of Mogadishu by an angry Somali mob.

What very few Americans ever learned was that the basis for

the illegal warrant issued by the UN Security Council was a deceptive report written by a CFR operative. The document cited by the UN as justification for the warrant was *The Report of an Inquiry, Conducted Pursuant to Security Council Resolution 837, Into the 5 June 1993 Attack on UN Forces in Somalia* written by Tom Farer (CFR), a professor of international law at American University in Washington, D.C.[87] This "Farer Report" was claimed to "prove" General Aidid's guilt in various crimes, most particularly the June 5, 1993 attack of Somalis upon UN Pakistani troops that resulted in the deaths of a number of the "Blue Helmets."

The Farer Report, however, proved to be a tissue of lies and deception. *It also proved to be an unintended indictment of the UN, rather than Aidid.* For the report showed that the deadly attack of June 5th had been precipitated not by General Aidid, but by a *UN provocation*. Specifically, it was the UN's blatantly *illegal* seizure of Radio Mogadishu, an organ of the free press of Somalia, that caused a spontaneous attack by the Somali people on the *UN criminals*.[88] Moreover, the Farer Report inadvertently shows that the UN-CFR cabal knowingly used this provocation as a pretext for grabbing more power — *and for using American troops to do its dirty work!*[89]

Obviously, the UN had to suppress its own self-indicting report. Which is precisely what it did. It refused to release the report to the U.S. Congress and the American people — even though we were paying for almost the entire operation and our soldiers were dying because of the UN's illegal and deceitful orders.

The New American magazine obtained a copy of the forbidden Farer Report and published a major exposé revealing the conspiracy and deception involved.[90] To date, this remains the only significant press exposure given to this incredibly explosive report. The CFR media cartel did not touch it, naturally; they were busy, instead, diverting the public's attention with the O.J. Simpson and Menendez brothers murder trials and other similarly bizarre scandals. And the CFR's Republican managers in

Congress, such as Newt Gingrich (CFR) and Bob Dole (who might as well be CFR), made sure that GOP members wouldn't raise a fuss over this UN outrage — even after the Republicans took control of Congress in 1994.

As a result, soon after the Somalia debacle, American troops were sent into Haiti on another UN assignment. Their job: restore to power the murderous, Communist, psychopath Jean-Bertrand Aristide,[91] so beloved by the CFR clerisy. Our troops had another job, as well: Disarm Aristide's opposition. Thanks to the mandatory gun registration program in effect for many years in Haiti, the soldiers knew exactly where to go to confiscate the weapons. U.S. soldiers interviewed by this writer said they did not like this job because they could see that it was leaving many obviously law-abiding citizens and their families open to slaughter by Aristide's Communist mobs and common thugs. Some soldiers admitted that they frequently disobeyed the orders to confiscate weapons and left them in the hands of those they believed needed protection. Several of these soldiers couldn't help commenting that they feared the Haiti exercise might prove to be a rehearsal for similar house-to-house searches for arms at some not-too-distant point in America's future.

More recently, U.S. forces were sent into Kosovo — again, initially, with the task of restoring order and providing support for "humanitarian assistance." Soon, however, they were ordered to disarm the Serbs, while concomitantly helping to arm the narco-terrorist Kosovo Liberation Army (KLA). The KLA is a vicious Albanian Communist mafia that is flooding heroin and other drugs into Europe and the U.S.[92] It is also closely allied with the terror regime in Iran and Osama bin Laden, the notorious financier of anti-American terrorism.[93] The KLA's well-documented, sordid record, however, did not sour the CFR coterie in the State Department or in the Establishment media on the terrorist group's "potential."

Subversive Marine Survey
On May 10, 1994, several hundred Marines stationed at the

Twenty-nine Palms, California Marine base were given a survey with potentially frightening ramifications. The "Combat Arms Survey" asked the Marines to respond along a scale running from "strongly disagree" to "strongly agree" to a series of questions and statements, including the following:

- "Do you feel that U.S. combat troops should be used within the United States for any of the following missions? Drug enforcement; Disaster relief...; Federal and state prison guards; National emergency police force; Advisors to S.W.A.T. units, the FBI, or the Bureau of Alcohol, Tobacco, and Firearms (B.A.T.F.)...."
- "U.S. combat troops should be commanded by U.N. officers and non-commissioned officers (NCOs) at battalion and company levels while performing U.N. missions."
- "I feel there is no conflict between my oath of office and serving as a U.N. soldier."
- "I feel a designated unit of U.S. combat soldiers should be permanently assigned to the command and control of the United Nations."
- "I would like U.N. member countries, including the U.S., to give the U.N. all the soldiers necessary to maintain world peace."
- "I would swear to the following code: 'I am a United Nations fighting person. I serve in the forces which maintain world peace and every nation's way of life. I am prepared to give my life in their defense.'" [94]

The final statement of the "Combat Arms Survey" posed this shocking scenario:

> The U.S. government declares a ban on the possession, sale, transportation, and transfer of all non-sporting firearms. A thirty (30) day amnesty period is permitted for these firearms to be turned over to the local authorities. At the end of this period, a number of citizen groups refuse to turn over their firearms.

Consider the following statement: I would fire upon U.S. citizens who refuse or resist confiscation of firearms banned by the U.S. government. [95]

The "Combat Arms Survey" was first brought to public attention when a Marine sent a copy to *The New American* magazine. [96] Disclosure of the survey by *The New American* touched off a firestorm of public and congressional outrage. According to a press release from the Marine Corps public affairs office at Twenty-nine Palms, the survey originated from Presidential Review [Decision] Directives 13 and 25, under which President Clinton (CFR) "directed DOD [Department of Defense] to create a U.S. military force structure whose command and control would include the United Nations." [97]

But most of those things happened during the nasty old Clinton regime; now that we have George W. Bush in the Oval Office, we can breathe a lot easier. Right?

Don't believe that for a moment. Yes, George W. received the endorsement of the NRA. But so did his father before him. As a Texas congressman in 1968, the senior Bush (CFR) voted for that year's draconian Gun Control Act. Twenty years later, he wrote to the NRA during his victorious presidential campaign, pledging to oppose "federal licensing, gun registration, background checks or a ban on firearms." [98]

Once in office, however, George the senior promptly issued an executive order banning the importation of 43 "military-style" semi-automatic rifles and endorsed a crime bill that called for the registration of rifle and pistol magazines capable of holding more than 15 rounds. [99] He also endorsed a five-day version of the Brady (waiting-period) bill, which caused Sarah Brady, chairman of Handgun Control, Inc., to exclaim that she was "very pleased." [100]

Perhaps even more important than those actions was George Bush's ambush of the NRA — and all gun owners, for that matter — in May 1995, shortly after the Oklahoma City bombing. It was a very crucial time, when all the country was reeling from shock over that deadly terrorist act, and the CFR media mavens were fastening blame for that vile deed on the NRA, "gun fanatics," "right-wing extremists," and "anti-government" Republicans. George Bush, as the immediate past president of the United States and the most prominent and well-known Republican, greatly aided that vicious smear campaign of the whole Political Right by very dramatically resigning from the NRA and denouncing the organization with the false claim that an NRA fund-raising letter harshly critical of ATF excesses was a slander against law enforcement.[101]

Is it fair to judge junior by daddy's record? No, unless he indicates that he is following in daddy's footsteps. George W. has done that. His top campaign and policy advisers were taken wholesale from his dad's CFR-Trilateralist cabinet: Dick Cheney, Brent Scowcroft, Colin Powell, Paul Wolfowitz, Robert Zoellick, Stephen Hadley, Robert Blackwill. To these he added Pratt House venerables Henry Kissinger and George Shultz and fast-rising CFR star Condoleezza Rice.[102]

Cheney, of course, then came on board as vice president, Powell as Secretary of State, Wolfowitz as Deputy Secretary of Defense, Zoellick as U.S. Trade Representative, and Rice as National Security Adviser. They were soon joined by other Pratt House regulars who were tapped for high Cabinet posts: Donald Rumsfeld, Elaine Chao, Christine Todd Whitman, Kenneth Juster, Faryar Shirzad, John Negroponte, and George Tenet — to name a few.

One of the first persons Colin Powell officially received as Secretary of State was Frank Carlucci, who recently chaired the CFR's panel on restructuring the State Department.[103] Powell then traipsed off to the UN for a meeting with Kofi Annan, where he announced that the new Bush administration would be putting an end to the Republican Party's traditional antagonism to the world body.[104]

Writing in the CFR's *Foreign Affairs* for September/October 2000, James M. Lindsay of the Brookings Institution noted that "Both Al Gore and George W. Bush are internationalists by inclination...." [105] In the CFR's globalese, that can be taken as meaning that, rhetoric notwithstanding, George W. will reliably continue to advance the one-world agenda of empowering the United Nations, including its attack on the right of private American citizens to own firearms. And because of the widespread misperception that Bush is a genuine "conservative" (thanks to the CFR's "ruling class journalists"), he is well-positioned to make strategic cave-ins on the gun issue that a Clinton or Gore could not pull off.

Chapter 10
Regionalism

*We cannot leap into world government in one quick step....
[T]he precondition for eventual globalization — genuine globalization — is progressive regionalization, because thereby we
move toward larger, more stable, more cooperative units.* [1]
— Zbigniew Brzezinski (CFR, TC),
former National Security Advisor, 1995

*Within and outside the United Nations, world federalists
should strongly support the growth of regional organizations
such as the European Community and the Organization of
African Unity and development of them into regional federations with governmental power in some policy areas.* [2]
— John Logue, Vice President,
World Federalist Association

*One of the most striking governance features of globalization is that it has a strong regional flavor. Deep integration
has proceeded fastest on a regional basis, notably within the
EU [European Union].* [3]
— The Commission on Global Governance

*A day would come when governments would be forced to
admit that an integrated Europe was an accomplished fact,
without their having had a say in the establishment of its
underlying principles. All they would have to do was to
merge all these autonomous institutions into a single federal
administration and then proclaim a United States of
Europe....* [4]
— Merry and Serge Bromberger in their sympathetic
biography, *Jean Monnet and the United States of Europe*

189

"How do you eat an elephant?" asks an old riddle. The answer: "One bite at a time." It is the same with any large task; successful accomplishment requires dividing the project into logical constituent parts and then systematically, incrementally, proceeding step by step, bite by bite. In the case of our elephant metaphor, that would mean skinning, dressing, and quartering or sectioning the animal, cutting it into smaller and smaller parts, until the desired consumable size is reached.

The globalist Insiders and their Communist partners have done precisely this throughout the course of the 20th century. From one corner of the globe to the other, the Communists have sponsored revolutions and "wars of national liberation," pitting tribe against tribe, or exploiting some other division based upon race, creed, class, nationality, or past grievances. The Insiders, operating from their positions of power in the business, financial, political, and media worlds, have repeatedly supported these ruinous tumults. They have provided financial and propaganda assistance as well as undermined the targeted governments through direct political pressure or diplomatic intrigue from Washington, D.C. and London.*

Through this convulsive process of controlled chaos, nations, kingdoms, and empires have been toppled, borders erased and redrawn, stable social and political systems uprooted, and whole peoples annihilated or driven as refugees into foreign lands. The maps of Europe, Africa, and Asia, especially, have been repeatedly redrawn in this fashion, with the result that the number of nation states in the world has increased from 72 at the end of World War II to 195 today. Some of these nations were artificially created by, and had their borders drawn by, the United Nations. Others, though not officially spawned by the UN, are the illegitimate offspring of the Insiders and the Communists who created the UN. In virtually every case where these new nations have been created or reformulated, the one-worlders have assured that corrupt, socialist regimes would be placed in power — either the totalitarian, revolutionary, socialist (Communist) variety, or the evolutionary, big-business, socialist (Fascist) variety.

These newly created entities have been manipulated, with relative ease, into joining various regional organizations established, ostensibly, for the mutual benefit of the countries involved. Thus, the Organization of American States (OAS), the Organization of African Unity (OAU), the North Atlantic Treaty Organization (NATO), the Asia Pacific Economic Cooperation (APEC), the European Union (EU), the European Monetary Union (EMU), the North American Free Trade Association (NAFTA), the Middle East-North Africa economic area (MENA), and other regional organizations have sprouted and grown into sizable establishments wielding increasing power.** Originally concerned primarily with a very narrow range of military and economic matters, these regional entities have, like the UN, gradually assumed more and more authority to deal with matters concerning the environment, labor policy, human rights,

---

*The prototype for these operations was first put into operation by the secret Rhodes network in South Africa in the late 19th Century. Carroll Quigley, in *The Anglo-American Establishment* (pp. 44-47 and 107-112) and *Tragedy and Hope* (pp. 136-144), provides an important inside look at the high-level conspiracy involved in the Jameson Raid (1895) and the instigation of the Boer War (1899-1902). James Perloff, in *The Shadows of Power*, shows the CFR-RIIA machinations in bringing about U.S. entry into World War I and II. That story is also powerfully told, in far greater detail, in *America's Second Crusade*, by William Henry Chamberlain (Chicago: Henry Regnery, 1950). The Insider-Communist collaboration in turning Poland into a Soviet satellite is told in: *I Saw Poland Betrayed*, by Ambassador Arthur Bliss Lane, *The Rape of Poland*, by Stanislaw Mikolajczyk, and *Allied Wartime Diplomacy*, by Edward J. Rozek. David Martin tells the brutal story of the one-worlders' betrayal of Yugoslavia into Communist hands in *Ally Betrayed*. Hilaire du Berrier's *Background to Betrayal: The Tragedy of Vietnam* is essential reading for an understanding of Insider treachery in undermining America's allies and supporting our Communist enemies in Southeast Asia. Nicaraguan President Anastasio Somoza tells the story of Insider perfidy and support for Communist revolution in Latin American in *Nicaragua Betrayed*. *The Betrayal of Southern Africa: The Tragic Story of Rhodesia and South Africa* by Warren McFerran details the Insider treachery in the repeated betrayal of America's allies in southern Africa and the handing over of that region to Communist terrorists and corrupt thugs.

immigration, commerce, education, transportation, etc.

It is no accident that these regional Intergovernmental Organizations (or IGOs, in globospeak) have been grasping for more power — at the expense of their nation-state members. Most of them were planned from the beginning to do that very thing. They were designed eventually to become — through gradual accretions of legislative, executive, and judicial powers — regional supra-state governments which could, ultimately, be merged with other regional entities to form a world government under the United Nations. What is now known as the European Union is a case in point. It was a colossal "bait and switch," presented as a trade pact, but intended from the start to become a nation-destroying super government.

In this, as in so many other areas we have already examined, we see an amazing parallelism between the plans of the Pratt House one-worlders and those of the Communist strategists. Joseph Stalin, for instance, recognized that populations will more readily merge their national loyalties with a vague regional loyalty — with which they may be able to find some sense of connection or identity — than they will for a world authority. In his 1912 essay, "Marxism and the National Question," the aspiring dictator insisted that *regional autonomy is an essential element* in the solution of the national problem."[5] (Emphasis in original.) Again and again over the decades, the Communists emphasized the necessity of creating "regional organs" to facilitate the "eradication" of nationalism. In 1936, the official program of the Communist International declared:

**We cannot examine all of these groups here, but we especially direct the readers to the following articles from *The New American* for important exposés on the more recently launched APEC and MENA regional organizations. "The Free Trade Charade" (December 27, 1993) reveals the CFR-TC hands and machinations in the formation and control of APEC. "Play It Again, Uncle Sam" (December 12, 1994) tells the amazing story of the overt controlling role of the CFR in sponsoring (together with the World Economic Forum and the Socialist International!) the 1994 Casablanca conference that launched MENA. Both articles are available at www.thenewamerican.com.

This world dictatorship can be established only when the victory of socialism has been achieved in certain countries or groups of countries, when the newly established proletarian republics enter into a federative union with the already existing proletarian republics ... [and] when these federations of republics have finally grown into a World Union of Soviet Socialist Republics uniting the whole of mankind under the hegemony of the international proletariat organized as a state.[6]

The Communists and the Insiders were (and still are) working from the same page: They are building regional blocs with structures that override national sovereignty and can later be merged into a global superstructure.

Two of the main regional IGOs that currently present a real and increasing danger to the United States are NAFTA and NATO, the former being a fairly recent creation formed for economic pretexts (trade, principally), and the latter of considerably older vintage established as a military alliance under a pretext of "collective security." Each of these IGOs is serving, in the words of a top globalist operative, as an "end run around national sovereignty, eroding it bit by bit."[7]

The North American Free Trade Agreement (NAFTA) and the campaign to secure its passage in Congress were closely modeled after the Insiders' game plan four decades earlier to establish the Common Market, later known as the European Community (EC) and (most recently) the European Union. And it is very clear that the Pratt House one-worlders intend to "evolve" NAFTA into a full-fledged, supra-national, regional government like the EU, but on an accelerated timeline, accomplishing in one decade what it has taken them four to do in Europe. We are not speculating on this; the CFR world planners have told us this repeatedly, as we will show.

NAFTA, which was originally promoted as a tripartite "free trade" agreement that would open markets and expand trade between Canada, the U.S., and Mexico, is now being transformed into a Western Hemisphere Free Trade Association (WHFTA), with a single currency (the U.S. dollar is being proposed, for now), a hemispheric central bank, and an entire hemispheric regime of regulations to "harmonize" business, industry, labor, agriculture, transportation, immigration, environment, health, trade, and other policies "from Alaska to Tierra del Fuego." NAFTA is not, and never was, about "free trade." Free trade — real free trade — is a voluntary exchange between two parties, unhampered by government intervention.

But NAFTA, like the European Union, seeks to regulate and control virtually every industrial, agricultural, environmental, and labor matter. Rather than creating or permitting economic freedom by eliminating government intervention, NAFTA seeks to homogenize the plethora of socialist interventions that now hamstring the U.S., Mexican, and Canadian economies.

Insider Jacques Delors, the socialist president of the European Community Commission in 1992, when the NAFTA debate was raging, clearly saw the parallels between the two regional organizations. Delors gloated that "NAFTA is a form of flattery for us Europeans. In many ways, we have shown what positive, liberating effect these regional arrangements can have."[8] Naturally, what a thorough socialist and internationalist like Delors considers "positive" and "liberating" tends to jarringly conflict with "negative" and "retrograde" concepts such as independence, sovereignty, free enterprise, property rights, and constitutional limitations on power.

The CFR journal *Foreign Affairs* led the way, with a continuous fusillade of pro-NAFTA articles. Some even conceded, in essence, a key point made by this author and other NAFTA opponents at the time, to wit, that NAFTA was, in reality, a stealth plan to foist an EU-type regional government scheme upon Americans. "The creation of trinational dispute-resolution mechanisms and rule-making bodies on border and environmental issues may also be *embryonic forms of more comprehensive structures*"[9] (emphasis added), M. Delal Baer approvingly wrote in the Fall 1991 *Foreign Affairs*. "After all, international organizations and agreements like GATT and NAFTA by definition mini-

194

mize assertions of sovereignty in favor of a joint rule-making authority." [10] Dr. Baer went on to draw a direct analogy to the EC, suggesting:

> It may be useful to revisit the spirit of the Monnet Commission, which provided a blueprint for Europe at a moment of extraordinary opportunity. The three nations of North America, in more modest fashion, have also arrived at a defining moment. They may want to create a wiseman's North American commission to operate in the post-ratification period.... The commission might also adopt a forward-looking agenda on themes such as North American competitiveness, links between scientific institutions, borderland integration, the continental ecological system and educational and cultural exchanges. [11]

Dr. Baer was not telling anything new to the CFR's top political operatives; they were already lined up behind the internationalist program. Republican President George Bush (the elder) (CFR), Democrat House Majority Leader Richard Gephardt (CFR), and Republican House Minority Leader Newt Gingrich (CFR)* played the pivotal political roles in pushing "fast track" authority for NAFTA through Congress — with massive help from their CFR confreres in the worlds of business, banking, media, and academia. And the same players campaigned furiously and continuously for final approval of the deceitful agreement.

The CFR internationalists intend to use NAFTA (and their proposed WHFTA) to foster, first, economic *interdependence* between the United States and other nations and then economic *integration* as a means, ultimately, to achieving *political* interdependence *and* integration. Which is precisely the path the Insiders trod in foisting the EU upon the unsuspecting peoples of Western Europe.

European Union
Because it is the internationalists' template for NAFTA/WHFTA,

a rudimentary understanding of the EU — how it was launched and by whom, what it has become, and what it is becoming — is absolutely essential for American patriots, in order to be successful in stopping this insidious attack on our sovereignty and independence. Our treatment here must necessarily be brief.**
The following points are key to an understanding of the Common Market/United Europe movement and its counterpart, NAFTA, in this hemisphere:

- While posing as a "bottom-up" popular movement, it was completely a "top-down" enterprise, conceived and run entirely by an elite coterie of one-worlders.

- While posing as a native European movement, it was largely

---

*As House Speaker, the CFR's Newt Gingrich — posing as the nation's premier Conservative — also played a decisive role in pushing the Insiders' World Trade Organization. During the 1994 hearings on the WTO, Gingrich disarmed WTO opponents by feigning concern over the WTO threat to our sovereignty. Gingrich noted that "yes, we could in theory take the power back. Yes, we, de jure, as [Judge Bork] points out, can take the power back. But the fact is we are not likely to disrupt the entire world trading system [by pulling out]. And, therefore, we ought to be very careful, because we are not likely to take it back."

Gingrich expressed concern about the transfer of U.S. authority to GATT, declaring that "we need to be honest about the fact that we are transferring from the United States, at a practical level, significant authority to a new organization. This is a transformational moment. I would feel better if the people who favor this would just be honest about the scale of change." He declared that GATT was very similar to the 1991 Maastricht Treaty, by which the European Union's member nations had ceded a good deal of their economic and political sovereignty, "and twenty years from now we will look back on this as a very important defining moment. This is not just another trade agreement. This is adopting something which twice, once in the 1940s and once in the 1950s, the U.S. Congress rejected. I am not even saying we should reject it; I, in fact, lean toward it. But I think we have to be very careful, because it is a very big transfer of power."

Nevertheless, Gingrich subsequently joined then-Senate Minority Leader Bob Dole (R-Kan.) in not only promoting and voting for the GATT pact, but urging that it be considered during a lame-duck session of Congress when its prospects for passage would be enhanced.

directed by U.S. Insiders and almost totally financed by U.S. taxpayers.

- Presented to Americans as a way to defend Western Europe from Communism, it has instead been used to drive Europe into socialism.
- Warnings that the Common Market would erode national sovereignty were shouted down as paranoid ravings, but they have proven true.
- The national and local governments of the EU countries are being swallowed up and increasingly overruled by unaccountable Eurocrats and Eurojudges.
- The EU currency, the euro, and the Eurobank are destroying the value of the individual national currencies and the economic sovereignty of the member states.
- The EU governing institutions, acting in coordination with their fellow one-worlders in national governments, are becoming increasingly socialistic and oppressive.

All of this was foreseen by astute observers many years ago, when the foundations for this diabolical scheme were being laid. One of the most knowledgeable historians of the Common Market/EU, and an indefatigable critic of it, is Hilaire du Berrier, a contributing editor to *The New American* (and its predecessors *American Opinion* and *The Review of the News*). For more than four decades he has published his authoritative *HduB Reports* from Monte Carlo, Monaco and has repeatedly exposed the machinations and plans of the European and American Insiders for Europe and the world.

"The CFR," wrote du Berrier in January 1973, "saw the Common Market from the first as a regional government to

---

**For a more detailed examination of the history of the Common Market/EC, please see this author's book *Global Tyranny*[12] and the following articles from *The New American*, available online at www.thenewamerican.com: "United States of Europe," April 10, 1989 ; "A European Suprastate," May 7, 1991; "From the Atlantic to the Urals (and Beyond)," January 27, 1992; "Forcing a United Europe," November 16, 1992; "European Nightmare," March 1, 1999.

which more and more nations would be added until the world government which the UN had failed to bring about would be realized. At a favorable point in the Common Market's development, America would be brought in. But the American public had to be softened first and leaders groomed for the change-over." [13]

Mr. du Berrier chronicled in his reports the "secret history" of the Common Market, utilizing published statements from the European and American press, official documents of European governments, the diaries and memoirs of European Insiders, and his own unparalleled intelligence sources developed over a lifetime of direct participation in some of the most momentous events of the 20th century. Step by step, he detailed the Insider-orchestrated program, from the pre-World War II era, through the war years, and then the post-WWII era.

As du Berrier notes, the first concrete step toward the abolition of the European nation-states was taken in 1951 with the signing of the seemingly innocuous treaty creating the European Coal and Steel Community (ECSC). The ostensible purpose of this move was to so integrate the basic industries of coal and steel that a future war between France and Germany would be "physically impossible."

The next nail in the coffin of European national sovereignty came on March 25, 1957 with the signing by the six ECSC nations (France, West Germany, Italy, Belgium, Netherlands, and Luxembourg) of the two Treaties of Rome. These created the European Economic Community (EEC or Common Market) and the European Atomic Energy Community (Euratom), which greatly furthered the process of merging the economic and energy sectors of the member states. (As the ECSC, Euratom, and EEC gradually assumed more and more economic and political powers, the name of this regional collective changed to the European Community.)

The next stage involved bringing the rest of Western Europe into the fold. In 1973 the United Kingdom, after more than two decades of resisting, came in, as did Ireland and Denmark. Greece joined in 1981, bringing the number of member states to ten. Spain and Portugal became the 11th and 12th members in 1986. The year 1986 also marked passage of the Single European Act, which mandated the establishment of "an area without internal frontiers, in which the free movement of goods, persons, services, and capital is ensured."

The 1991 Treaty of Maastricht committed the EU signatories to a single currency and a European central bank.[14] The European Monetary Institute (EMI), the embryonic European central bank created by the treaty, was officially launched on January 1, 1994. Frankfurt was chosen as the site for the new entity and Alexander Lamfalussy, former head of the Bank for International Settlements (BIS) in Basel, Switzerland, was tapped to be president.*

Work in the Shadows

Now let's drop back for a moment and briefly examine the nuts-and-bolts process and the main actors involved in putting this amazing scheme together, beginning with the European Coal and Steel Commission, or ECSC. "This was a truly revolutionary organization," wrote Georgetown University Professor Carroll Quigley, the Insiders' own inside historian, "since it had sovereign powers, including the authority to raise funds outside any existing state's power."[15] The ECSC merged the coal and steel industries of six countries under a single High Authority. It was, Quigley pointed out, "a rudimentary government." In his 1966 history of the world, *Tragedy and Hope*, Quigley wrote:

> This "supranational" body had the right to control prices, channel investment, raise funds, allocate coal and steel.... Its powers

---

*Significantly, the establishment of the EMI in Frankfurt coincided with that city's March celebration of the founding of the Rothschild banking dynasty. About 80 members of the famous first family of international banking Insiders gathered in Frankfurt during the first week of March to commemorate the birth of dynasty founder Meyer Amschel Rothschild, who was born there 250 years ago. The Lamfalussy-BIS connection is also significant, inasmuch as the BIS has long been recognized by all observers of banking as the central bank of international banking.

to raise funds for its own use by taxing each ton produced made it independent of governments. Moreover, its decisions were binding, and could be reached by majority vote without the unanimity required in most international organizations of sovereign states.[16]

The proposal for the ECSC was introduced, amidst great fanfare, in May 1950 as the "Schuman Plan." Although Jean Monnet, a consummate Insider and at that time head of France's General Planning Commission, was the real author of the plan, he thought it expedient to name it for his comrade, Robert Schuman, the Socialist French Foreign Minister who later became Prime Minister.

The American Insiders leapt to praise the Schuman Plan. John Foster Dulles, a CFR founder, called it "brilliantly creative."[17] Dulles had become close pals with Monnet decades earlier, when both labored at Versailles following World War I to establish the League of Nations. Later, as Secretary of State, he would use U.S. power to help Monnet quash European opposition to a United Europe. Secretary of State Dean Acheson (CFR) termed it a "major contribution toward the resolution of the pressing political and economic problems of Europe."[18] The CFR dominated Carnegie Foundation awarded Monnet its Wateler Peace Prize of two million francs "in recognition of the international spirit which he had shown in conceiving the Coal and Steel Community...."[19]

Insider Jean Monnet, a life-long, self-avowed, multi-millionaire socialist, whom columnist Joseph Alsop (CFR) admiringly dubbed the "good, gray wizard of Western European union,"[20] was appointed the first president of the powerful new ECSC. Monnet knew full well just how subversive and revolutionary his new creation was. Merry and Serge Bromberger record in their biography *Jean Monnet and the United States of Europe* that when Monnet and his "brain trust" had outlined the basics of the ECSC proposal, they called in legal expert Maurice Lagrange to take care of the detail work. The Brombergers wrote:

Lagrange was stunned. An idea of revolutionary daring had been launched and was being acclaimed by the Six and the United States — a minerals and metals superstate.... "I hope the structure will stand up," Monnet said dubiously.[21]

In other words, Monnet recognized that his scheme was so audaciously subversive it was doubtful that the governments of sovereign nations would ever agree to such a radical proposal. Unless, of course, the proponents just as audaciously employed deception, duplicity, bribery, extortion, and coercion. Which is precisely what they did.

The Brombergers, who are ardent admirers of Monnet, admit the conspiratorial and totalitarian mind-set of their hero:

Gradually, it was thought, the supranational authorities, supervised by the European Council of Ministers at Brussels and the Assembly in Strasbourg, would administer all the activities of the Continent. A day would come when governments would be forced to admit that an integrated Europe was an accomplished fact, without their having had a say in the establishment of its underlying principles. All they would have to do was to merge all these autonomous institutions into a single federal administration and then proclaim a United States of Europe....

Actually, the founders of the Coal and Steel Community would have to obtain from the various national governments — justifiably reputed to be incapable of making sacrifices for the sake of a federation — a whole series of concessions in regard to their sovereign rights until, having been finally stripped, they committed hara-kiri by accepting the merger.[22]

Again, a bald admission that the Insider founders of the ECSC/EU knew from the start that they were slipping a noose around the neck of an unsuspecting Europe and that they planned to gradually tighten it until it strangled their hapless victim — to death.

Another very important source on this "hara-kiri" phenomenon is Insider Ernst H. van der Beugel, honorary secretary-general of the Bilderberger Group, vice-chairman of the Netherlands Institute for Foreign Affairs (a CFR affiliate), member of the Trilateral Commission, Harvard lecturer, etc. In his book *From Marshall Aid to Atlantic Partnership* — which contains a foreword by "my friend Henry Kissinger" — van der Beugel explained the workings of the Monnet-CFR symbiosis and cited examples of the diplomatic bludgeoning of those officials who balked at administering national "hara-kiri." For instance, he reported how Monnet's Action Committee, which was "supported by funds from United States foundations," ramrodded the negotiations for the Rome Treaties:

> Monnet and his Action Committee were unofficially supervising the negotiations and as soon as obstacles appeared, the United States diplomatic machinery was alerted, mostly through Ambassador Bruce ... who had immediate access to the top echelon of the State Department....
>
> At that time, it was usual that if Monnet thought that a particular country made difficulties in the negotiations, the American diplomatic representative in that country approached the Foreign Ministry in order to communicate the opinion of the American Government which, in practically all cases, coincided with Monnet's point of view. [23]

Monnet's high-level friends, who assisted him in these strong-arm tactics, included President Eisenhower, John Foster Dulles, John J. McCloy, David Bruce, Averell Harriman, George Ball, and C. Douglas Dillon — all CFR one-worlders. All of this was occurring, remember, in the immediate post-WWII years, when war-ravaged Europe had become very dependent on U.S. aid and looked to the U.S. for protection from the growing (Insider-backed) Soviet threat.

Hilaire du Berrier relates a story from the diary of Joseph Retinger that illustrates how the CFR's agents built the movement for European merger. Retinger, a Polish one-worlder and inveterate socialist, was a longtime associate of CFR heavyweights John Foster Dulles, Averell Harriman, John J. McCloy, and Nelson and David Rockefeller. Retinger was seeking more funds for the European Movement headed at the time by Belgian Prime Minister Paul Henri Spaak, who was affectionately known in Europe as "Mr. Socialist." Du Berrier wrote:

> Retinger and Duncan Sandys, the British Eurocrat, went to see John J. McCloy, who in 1947 was American High Commissioner to Germany. McCloy, we learn from Retinger's diary, embraced the idea at once. Sheppard Stone, who was on McCloy's staff, and Robert Murphy, the U.S. ambassador to Belgium, whom Retinger called one of the European Movement's best supporters, joined McCloy in raiding the huge reserve of European currencies called 'counterpart funds' which had piled up as a result of Marshall Plan aid.... McCloy, Stone and Murphy "promptly and unhesitatingly put ample funds at the disposal of Paul Henri Spaak [to lobby for the European merger]," Retinger recorded. [24]

Michael J. Hogan, professor of history at Ohio State University and editor of *Diplomatic History*, is another authority who confirms this Insider use of Marshall Plan "counterpart funds." In fact, Dr. Hogan shows that the whole push for the European Recovery Plan (ERP, better known as the Marshall Plan) was a CFR-run affair to establish interventionist (socialist) policies for post-war Europe.

The Establishment effort was led, Hogan notes, by "the Committee for the Marshall Plan to Aid European Recovery, a private, nonpartisan organization composed of labor, farm, and business leaders who worked closely with government officials to mobilize support behind the ERP. The result was something like a coordinated campaign mounted by an interlocking directorate of public and private figures." [25]

"The leadership of this group," says Hogan "came largely from academic circles, from the major American trade unions, and from such business organizations as the Council on Foreign Relations (CFR), the Business Advisory Council (BAC), the

Committee for Economic Development (CED), and the National Planning Association (NPA)." [26] But the top leadership, he makes clear, were CFR cognoscenti.

The CFR corporate fascists were ever close at hand to assist Euro-socialist Insiders like Monnet, Retinger, Schuman, Spaak, Sandys and their ilk, and to sabotage all European opposition. Europeans representing anti-Communist, anti-socialist, anti-Soviet, pro-American, free market, Christian, monarchist, nationalist parties and viewpoints were undermined, co-opted, vilified, bribed, blackmailed, or otherwise eliminated from effective leadership positions.

Startling new evidence concerning this cabal was reported in September 2000 by Ambrose Evans-Pritchard, the EU reporter in Brussels for *The Telegraph* of London. The story bore the headline, "Euro-federalists financed by US spy chiefs," and reported on recently declassified American government documents showing "that the US intelligence community ran a campaign in the Fifties and Sixties to build momentum for a united Europe. It funded and directed the European federalist movement." [27] The U.S. effort was headed by "William J Donovan, head of the American wartime Office of Strategic Services, precursor of the CIA." [28]

Mr. Evans-Pritchard reported:

Washington's main tool for shaping the European agenda was the American Committee for a United Europe [ACUE], created in 1948. The chairman was Donovan, ostensibly a private lawyer by then.

The vice-chairman was Allen Dulles, the CIA director in the Fifties. The board included Walter Bedell Smith, the CIA's first director, and a roster of ex-OSS figures and officials who moved in and out of the CIA. The documents show that ACUE financed the European Movement, the most important federalist organisation in the post-war years. In 1958, for example, it provided 53.5 per cent of the movement's funds.

The European Youth Campaign, an arm of the European

Movement, was wholly funded and controlled by Washington. The Belgian director, Baron Boel, received monthly payments into a special account. When the head of the European Movement, Polish-born Joseph Retinger, bridled at this degree of American control and tried to raise money in Europe, he was quickly reprimanded. [29]

What the *Telegraph* article didn't mention (and perhaps Evans-Pritchard didn't know) was that all of the OSS-CIA-ACUE principals involved in the "European federalist movement" — Donovan, Smith, and Dulles — were CFR members and key Pratt House operatives.

With the media stranglehold exercised by the ruling elite of the Milner Group-Royal Institute of International Affairs-CFR thought cartel, few Europeans or Americans — even those who were politically sophisticated — could put all of the pieces together. Lone voices — even influential ones — could not break through the media blackout. In 1959, for example, few British citizens heard (and fewer still understood the importance of) the warning of Reginald Maulding, Chancellor of the Exchequer, concerning the real nature of the Common Market. Said Maulding: "We must recognize that for us to sign the Treaty of Rome would be to accept the ultimate goal — political federation in Europe including ourselves." [30]

"Twenty years ago, when the process began, there was no question of losing sovereignty," Sir Peregrine Worsthorne wrote in London's *Sunday Telegraph* in 1991. "That was a lie, or at any rate, a dishonest obfuscation." Further, said Worsthorne, "For the past twenty years or so anybody wanting to have a career in the public service, in the higher reaches of the city, or the media has had to be pro-European. In the privacy of the closet or among close friends, even many federalists would admit as much. But such is the momentum behind the European movement that none of these individual doubts, expressed separately, will be remotely sufficient to stop the juggernaut." [31]

Lord Bruce of Donington, a Member of Parliament from the Labour Party who has been a stalwart opponent of Euro-convergence schemes for four decades, was likewise given the media blackout treatment. In a 1962 speech he cited Maulding's warning that the Common Market was really aimed at eventual political unification. "This, of course, is not how the issue has been presented by the government to the people of this country," Lord Bruce cautioned. "The matter has been put forward in terms of the economic advantages which would accrue to Britain if we joined 'the Six' in a Customs Union ... allowing our industries to thrive in what appears to be a lush 'home' market of 214 million people." [32]

No "right-wing isolationist," Lord Bruce served in the European Parliament as a representative of the European Socialist Group. In a 1996 interview, Lord Bruce noted that much of the impetus for European convergence comes from the ruling elite of "the United States, which disguises its intent for public consumption but has consistently assisted the merging of Britain and the other European nations into a regional bloc." "The Americans," he said, "have subsidized and promoted this aberration almost since its inception, and they are very active today." [33]

Western Hemisphere EU

With this knowledge in mind, the first thing an observant onlooker should have noticed when proposals for NAFTA and WHFTA began floating about was the Pratt House imprint. It wasn't difficult to spot; the CFR logo was all over these schemes, as we have already seen in the case of NAFTA. [34]

The Insiders have stepped up their political, economic and propaganda efforts for the next step, an EU for the Western Hemisphere. Following the pattern of the ECSC-EU, most of the important early activity for the WHFTA was taking place "below the surface of public attention." In 1999, after years of preparation, the business pages of newspapers began buzzing over the startling proposal by Argentine President Carlos Menem to abandon his country's peso for the dollar. Similar proposals soon started flowing in from the leaders of Canada, Brazil, Mexico, and Venezuela. All of a sudden, "dollarization" became the sexy economic issue of the day, with Republicans and Democrats alike lining up with euphoric praise for the ultra-radical scheme.

What we were witnessing, in reality, was another CFR ventriloquism show; like the European leaders a generation earlier, the Western hemispheric choir hymning the dollarization theme were merely mouthpieces for the CFR puppet masters. In April 1974, the CFR telegraphed much of what was to come when *Foreign Affairs* published a remarkably frank attack on U.S. sovereignty. Authored by Columbia University law professor and veteran State Department official Richard N. Gardner (Clinton's Ambassador to Spain), the article was entitled "The Hard Road to World Order." It began with CFR member Gardner's lamentation that like-minded internationalists had failed to achieve what he termed "instant world government." He proposed a new and more effective route to the creation of an all-powerful, global superstate, asserting:

> In short, the "house of world order" will have to be built from the bottom up rather than from the top down. It will look like a great "booming, buzzing confusion," to use William James' famous description of reality, but an end run around national sovereignty, eroding it piece by piece, will accomplish much more than the old-fashioned frontal assault. [35]

Gardner's piecemeal scheme for world government proposed, among other things, luring all nations into a variety of economic and political entanglements, including trade traps like NAFTA and WHFTA.

The Dollarization Bandwagon
In 1984, 10 years after Gardner's "Hard Road" manifesto, *Foreign Affairs* brought forth another audacious piece entitled "A Monetary System for the Future," by Richard N. Cooper (CFR, TC). Cooper, a professor of international economics at Harvard, boldly stated: "I suggest a radical alternative scheme for the next

century: the creation of a common currency for all of the indus-trial democracies, with a common monetary policy and a joint Bank of Issue to determine that monetary policy." [36]

The main problem with this scheme, Cooper realized, is that "a single currency is possible only if there is in effect a single mon-etary policy, and a single authority issuing the currency and directing the monetary policy." "How can independent states accomplish that?" he asked rhetorically. Naturally, he had the answer: "They need to turn over the determination of monetary policy to a supranational body." [37]

More recently, in its July/August 1999 issue, *Foreign Affairs* explicitly took up the campaign for such a supranational power and dollarization, with an essay by Zanny Minton Beddoes of *The Economist*, one of Britain's leading Fabian Socialist periodi-cals. In the opening paragraph of his globalist propaganda tract, "From EMU to AMU?: The Case for Regional Currencies," Beddoes declared with oracular certainty: "By 2030 the world will have two major currency zones — one European, the other American. The euro will be used from Brest to Bucharest, and the dollar from Alaska to Argentina — perhaps even Asia." [38]

Mr. Beddoes paid specific tribute to Richard Cooper's 1984 *Foreign Affairs* article, and threw bouquets to other "farsighted academics" who share his one-world view and chided skeptics who "argue that a national currency is a basic symbol of sover-eignty that countries choose to forfeit only under extraordinary circumstances." [39] Mr. Beddoes and his devious allies would sure-ly like all of us to believe that a national currency is only a "sym-bol of sovereignty," but it is much more than that, of course. It is an essential ingredient of sovereignty, and a nation is at the fear-ful mercy of any entity to whom it may be foolish enough to for-feit so important a power. The Federal Reserve System and the International Monetary Fund have already vindicated that claim a thousand times over, and yet here we are about to be enticed into an even deeper abyss.

An even more extraordinary propaganda and disinformation salvo, this one aimed at a broader audience, was provided by the

Time magazine cover story for February 15, 1999. Along with the headline, "The Committee to Save the World," the cover featured the beaming visages of Federal Reserve Chairman Alan Greenspan (CFR), then-Treasury Secretary Robert Rubin (CFR), and Deputy Treasury Secretary Lawrence Summers (CFR), who followed Rubin in the top Treasury post. The article bore this riveting subtitle: "The inside story of how the Three Marketeers have prevented a global economic meltdown — so far." [40]

The adulatory piece, written by *Time's* Joshua Cooper Ramo (CFR), reverently refers to the CFR triumvirate as "the Trinity" and suggests that they are uniquely possessed of near-divine virtues and insights, and, thus, deserve our trust in establishing new monetary authority over the hemisphere. [41]

The "conservative," CFR-run *Wall Street Journal* assured its readers that "Dollarization has arisen as a spontaneous movement within our hemisphere," [42] and urged U.S. political leaders to embrace this opportunity to "score a powerful victory for free trade and free markets." But the dollarization bandwagon is about as spontaneous as the Normandy invasion, and it has nothing to do with free markets.

The current dollarization-NAFTA/WHFTA drive we are now witnessing is the culmination of a massive, long-range effort that began many years ago as an intermediate stepping stone to world government. Myriad documents, publications, statements, speeches, conferences, meetings, and events from the past several decades copiously document that effort. One such document is *Western Hemisphere Economic Integration*, a study by Gary Clyde Hufbauer (CFR and former CFR vice president) and Jeffrey J. Schott, published in 1994 by the Institute for International Economics (IIE). While hardly a household name in America, the IIE, according to Martin Walker of the *London Observer*, "may be the most influential think-tank on the planet," with "an extraordinary record in turning ideas into effective policy." [43]

The dedication at the beginning of this IIE book reads: "TO DAVID ROCKEFELLER, For his lifelong devotion to promoting economic development in Latin America and to improving relations among the countries of the Western Hemisphere. His wisdom has been an enormous source of encouragement to the work of the Institute and inspired us to explore the important ties that unite the Americas." [44]

Mr. Rockefeller, of course, was chairman of the CFR from 1970–85 and, as we will see, has played an especially key role in the dollarization and Western hemispheric economic convergence scheme. Likewise the IIE, which is virtually joined at the hip to the CFR.*

So what did the Hufbauer-Schott study published by the IIE advocate? Very simply, "a Western Hemisphere Free Trade Area (WHFTA)" following the sovereignty-destroying, mega-state pattern of the European Union (EU). "After four decades of dedicated effort," said the report, "Western Europe has just arrived at the threshold of ... monetary union, and fiscal coordination. It seems likely that trade and investment integration will proceed at a faster pace within the Western Hemisphere...." [45]

"Finally," the study stated, "the more countries that participate in integration and the wider its scope, the greater the need for some institutional mechanism to administer the arrangements and to resolve the inevitable disputes, and the stronger the case for a common legal framework." (Which means supra-

---

*The executive director of the IIE is former U.S. Assistant Secretary of the Treasury for International Affairs C. Fred Bergsten (CFR, TC), who appeared on May 21, 1999 before the House Banking and Financial Services Committee to argue for the dollarization power scam. The complete interlock between the CFR and the IIE is further demonstrated by the list of IIE officers and directors provided in the Hufbauer-Schott study. IIE's chairman is listed as Peter G. Peterson, who is also chairman of the board of the CFR, a position he has held since 1985, when he succeeded David Rockefeller in that position. Chairman of the IIE Executive Committee is Anthony M. Solomon (CFR). The study also lists the IIE board of directors, which includes such CFR luminaries as W. Michael Blumenthal, Carla A. Hills, Donald F. McHenry, Paul A. Volcker, Marina Whitman, and Andrew Young. Chairman of the Advisory Committee is (surprise!) Richard N. Cooper (CFR). One of the members of that same Advisory Committee for the Schott study was Lawrence H. Summers. Listed as an Honorary Director was Alan Greenspan.

national legislative, executive, and judicial institutions, naturally.) "The European Commission, Council, Parliament, and Court of Justice have many of the powers of comparable institutions in federal states," the report noted approvingly before commenting, "On this subject, we score Europe with a 5 [on a scale of 0 to 5]." [46]

Not satisfied with the EU model, the authors proposed going far beyond it. They asserted that "integration between NAFTA and Latin America should be legally open-ended; potentially the WHFTA should include countries outside the hemisphere." Indeed, presaging Beddoes, they asserted: "Economic logic suggests that the expansion of NAFTA in an Asian direction is just as desirable as its expansion in a Latin American direction." [47]

In countless similar studies, speeches, lectures, and programs over the years, the CFR elitists have prepped the upper echelon of the U.S. and Western intelligentsia and business communities so that they would enthusiastically embrace this deadly nostrum — long before it appeared "spontaneously" for general public consumption. But how did they succeed in drawing Latin American leaders into this snare and overcoming the long-standing fear of Yankee "dollar imperialism"? One obvious answer is that through the lending programs of the International Monetary Fund, World Bank, and Wall Street banks, they have saddled Latin American countries with hopeless debt burdens that have left them desperate and willing to try radical measures. But a more complete answer is to be found in the long-term activities of groups like the IIE and the Council of the Americas (COA), which have for two generations been assiduously grooming and tutoring the business, academic, and political leaders of Latin America.

The COA describes its origins thusly: "In 1965, David Rockefeller and a group of like-minded business people founded the Council of the Americas based on the fundamental belief that free markets and private enterprise offer the most effective means to achieve regional economic growth and prosperity." [48] (Those so naïve as to believe in the COA's professed embrace of "free markets and private enterprise" probably also believe that the Social Security Administration has set up a bank account with their name on it, awaiting their retirement!) Among the CFR brotherhood joining Mr. Rockefeller in the COA's leadership are COA chairman Robert A. Mosbacher, Sr., vice-chairman Robert E. Wilhelm, treasurer Richard de J. Osborne, and general counsel Sergio J. Galvis.

Some 240 COA corporate members with interests in Latin America — ranging from AT&T, Bank of America, Coca Cola, Citibank, and Dow Jones & Company to Exxon, Ford, General Electric, IBM, Microsoft, *Newsweek*, Turner Broadcasting System, Wal-Mart, and Xerox — provide impressive muscle (and financial support) for the COA's agenda.[49] Most of these companies, with a heavy CFR presence at their executive and directorate levels, have proven to be reliable supporters of the one-world corporatist line.

Working hand-in-glove with the COA-CFR corporate socialists are the pampered princelings of the U.S.-tax-dollar-subsidized multilateral lending institutions like the IMF and the Inter-American Development Bank (IDB), many of whose officers are also CFR members. The preface to the aforementioned Hufbauer-Schott study, for instance, notes that "… the Inter-American Development Bank provided support for the research underlying this project and the bank sponsored seminars for the discussion of its preliminary results."[50]

Indeed, a brief survey of the daily faxes sent out by the IDB, IMF, and their sister institutions makes very plain the completely corrupt process by which the Insiders form their convergence "consensus." Each day brings announcements of tens of millions (sometimes hundreds of millions) of dollars in IDB "loans" for natural gas pipelines in Mexico, electric power plants in Argentina, highways in Bolivia, coffee plantations in El Salvador, etc. IDB cooperation can lift a Latin American politician by financing the programs that make him look good, or help his opposition by pulling funds and destroying confidence in his economic program.

Thus, when President Carlos Menem of Argentina and Hugo Chavez, the Castroite, Marxist president of Venezuela, delivered their CFR-scripted speeches at June 1999 COA luncheons in New York, they knew they were addressing sympathetic movers and shakers of the COA-CFR-IIE-IDB axis who would parlay their proposals into the new "working consensus" that would become official U.S. policy.

Of course, what the new world order architects have in mind for the Americas is exactly what they are foisting on Europe in the form of the European Union and the new euro currency. That evolving supranational monstrosity was also presented to unwary Europeans as a "spontaneous" movement aimed at "free trade" and "free markets." But Europeans are belatedly waking up to the fact that it is no accident that the centralized, socialist bureaucracy of the EU is strangling their freedoms and national sovereignty. As we have seen, it was planned to develop into exactly that from the start.

Like the slime trail that leads to a slug, virtually every trail of American policy disasters leads back to the Council on Foreign Relations. There is no longer reason for any sensible American to doubt that the CFR coterie intends to take us down the same suicidal path that Europe is now traveling. The one-world architects of the European Monetary Union (EMU) are openly advocating an American Monetary Union (AMU), as we have already seen from the pages of *Foreign Affairs*.

Words fail to convey the enormity and audacity of this colossal, dangerous fraud we are witnessing in the current "spontaneous movement" to transform the Western Hemisphere into a carbon copy of the increasingly tyrannical European Union. But even that grim prospect of an America under an EU-style, centrally controlled economic bloc does not begin to convey the seriousness of the peril we face if we allow these plans to succeed. Regional "integration" is but a stepping stone to the real objective sought by the Insiders of this one-world conspiracy: Total, unrestrained power on a planetary scale is the real objective.

213

Chapter 11

The UN World Money System

What the Trilaterals truly intend is the creation of a world-wide economic power superior to the political governments of the nation-states involved.... As managers and creators of the system they will rule the future. [1]

— Senator Barry Goldwater

The only viable way, it seems to me, to structure the international economic order for the future is to install collective leadership among the Trilateral partners — to view the three regions not as the dictators or the dominators, but as a steering committee, which must work out its own differences first in order to lead a stable and prosperous world economy. [2]

— C. Fred Bergsten (CFR, TC), former U.S. Assistant
Secretary of the Treasury

In a globalized economy, everyone needs the IMF [International Monetary Fund]. Without the IMF, the world economy would not become an idealized fantasy.... [T]he IMF is the sovereign nations' credit union.... [3]

— David Rockefeller, Trilateral Commission Founder,
longtime former chairman of both the TC and CFR

[The IMF is] in essence a socialist conception. [4]

— Hilary Marquand of the Socialist International,
circa 1962–63

[A] single currency is possible only if there is in effect a single monetary policy.... How can independent states accomplish that? They need to turn over the determination of monetary policy to a supranational body.... The key point is that

monetary control ... would be in the hands of a new Bank of Issue, not in the hands of any national government....[5]
— Professor Richard N. Cooper (CFR, TC), Harvard University, former U.S. Under Secretary of State

The emerging multi-polar world ... presents a better opportunity to create a world central bank with a stable international currency than at any previous time in history.[6]
— Nobel Prize-winning economist Robert Mundell in the Trilateral-CFR-dominated *Wall Street Journal*, October 14, 1999

For a generation now these columns have preached economics from the gospel by Robert Mundell.[7]
— Lead editorial in the *Wall Street Journal*, October 14, 1999

The fifth plank of the *Communist Manifesto* calls for "Centralization of credit in the hands of the State, by means of a national bank with State capital and an exclusive monopoly."[8] It stands to reason: You can't establish the total state, the "dictatorship of the proletariat," if people are allowed the freedom to produce their own goods and services, buy and sell what they need and desire, and travel where they please when and how they please. Communism is about rationed scarcity and *total* regimentation. Under Communism, "the State" (i.e., the ruling oligarchy that rules in the name of "the people") controls and rations food, clothing, housing, transportation, fuel, health care, education, communications, publishing, entertainment — everything.

Monopoly control by "the State" of all money, savings, and credit is as essential to the totalitarian Communist system as its secret police, torture chambers, firing squads, and gulags. We have seen throughout the 20th century that everywhere the Communists have taken over they have religiously followed Marx's dictate in this matter. The reason is simple: power, control. Power to exercise total control over all human activity. Any private, independent initiative is seen as a threat to this monopoly control and, therefore, cannot be allowed.

Most people find it amazing, then, to learn that the world's premier "capitalist" bankers and financiers subscribe to the same Marxist program. For decades, led by the Rhodes-Milner-Morgan-Rockefeller-RIIA-CFR-TC cabal, in one country after another, the Insider bankers have successfully pushed for the establishment of central banks. These central banks are patterned after our own Federal Reserve System, a completely Marxist operation that was foisted upon the American people by the banking trust in 1913, in one of the most gigantic deceptions in world history.* While having all the appearances of being run by national governments, these central banks are, in reality, run by the private RIIA-CFR-TC banking fraternity.

Why do these "capitalists" support Marx's program? Again, the reason is simple: power, control. Recall that arch-conspirator

---

*An understanding of the incredible deception involved in the creation of the Federal Reserve System will greatly help us in our current battle against the same diabolic forces that are now so hellbent on establishing an all-powerful planetary central bank. The campaign for the Federal Reserve was completely a creature of the Insider banking cartel, but the proposal was presented to the American people by the cartel's front men as the only way to protect the country against the power of the "money trust." One of the central players in this scheme was Insider Frank Vanderlip of National City Bank of New York, who later divulged his role in the conspiracy to create the Fed. Two-and-a-half decades after the event, Vanderlip explained his role as a "conspirator" (his word) at a supersecret 1910 meeting at Jekyll Island, Georgia, where the Federal Reserve plot was conceived.[9] This very elaborate scheme, in which the Insiders financed and controlled both sides of the issue, is brilliantly revealed in G. Edward Griffin's masterful and detailed exposé, *The Creature from Jekyll Island: A Second Look at the Federal Reserve* (Appleton, Wis.: American Opinion Publishing, Inc., 1994). For a briefer treatment of the same subject, see also: *None Dare Call It Conspiracy* by Gary Allen (Seal Beach, Cal.: Concord Press, 1971); "The Federal Reserve System: The creature of a triumphant international banking establishment" (*The New American*, October 27, 1986); and "The Secret Science: How the Federal Reserve creates money out of debt" (*The New American*, December 19, 1988).

Cecil Rhodes' "simple desire" was nothing less than "the government of the world." The one-world *banksters*, like their Bolsheviki brethren, want to control the world. And these supposed "mortal enemies" have worked hand in hand throughout much of the past century to bring about this totalitarian, global control. As Ford Foundation President H. Rowan Gaither (CFR) put it (see Chapter 4), he and his one-world associates were making "every effort to so alter life in the United States as to make possible a comfortable merger with the Soviet Union." [10]

Spearheading the Merger

Spearheading this capitalist-Communist "merger" scheme for much of the past century has been one of America's wealthiest and most famous dynasties: the Rockefeller family. Microsoft mogul Bill Gates, investment wizard Warren Buffet, and dot.com upstarts have grabbed headlines in recent years as the "world's richest" tycoons, but their economic and political influence doesn't begin to compare with the global reach and power of the Rockefellers.

David Rockefeller, the current *pater familias* of the super-rich clan, was for many years chairman of the CFR (1970–85), chairman of the Trilateral Commission, and chairman of Chase Manhattan Bank (formerly the Chase National Bank). Although now officially retired, he has remained actively engaged as *chairman emeritus* of all three institutions. [11]

During the entire "Cold War" (and for decades before), the Rockefellers served as the primary banker for the Reds. As Congressman Louis McFadden, chairman of the House Banking Committee, noted in 1933:

> Open up the books of Amtorg, the trading organization of the Soviet Government in New York, and of Gostorg, the general office of the Soviet trade organization, and of the State Bank of the Union of Soviet Socialist Republics, and you will be staggered to see how much American money has been taken from the United States Treasury for the benefit of Russia. Find out what business has been

transacted for the State bank of Soviet Russia by its correspondent, the Chase Bank of New York....[12]

"Arch-capitalist" David Rockefeller has always enjoyed immediate, privileged access to Communist countries and received the royal "red carpet" welcome from them. His Chase Manhattan Bank's Moscow branch enjoys the distinctive *cache* of being located at "1 Karl Marx Square." In 1974, the bank even saw fit to boast of this supposed trophy address in full-page newspaper advertisements that read, in part: "From 1 Chase Manhattan Plaza to 1 Karl Marx Square, we're international money experts with a knack for making good sense out of confusing East-West trade talk."[13] David Rockefeller also expressed pride in the fact that Chase Manhattan was the first Western bank to open for business in Communist China.

A world central bank controlling all national monetary policies and currencies — until such time as a single global currency may be established — is essential to the one-worlders' East-West merger scheme. Much of their scheming, naturally, goes on secretly, behind closed doors, at the continuous and mysterious meetings of such Insider circles of high-level finance as the G-7, G-22, IMF, World Bank, Bank for International Settlements, the Paris Club, the Bilderberg Group, and the World Economic Forum, as well as many smaller, informal conclaves.

However, in order to advance their conspiratorial agenda, they must telegraph many of their plans to their lower-level operatives — in sanitized language, of course. By studying the documents, reports, speeches, and published utterances of these Insiders over the past several decades it is possible to determine their game plan and their ultimate goal. As we have seen in the preceding chapter, the Insiders' penultimate goal is to create regional blocs in which the nation-states will become so economically and politically interdependent and integrated that the nations are subsumed into regional supergoverments (the EU, WHFTA, APEC, etc.) with regional central banks and regional currencies. Once this is done, it is small work to merge the regional entities into a single global government.

Origins of Global Aid

The institutions of the current "international economic system" grew out of the 1944 Bretton Woods Conference. In addition to the original World Bank (WB) and International Monetary Fund (IMF), we now have an assortment of subsidiary institutions: International Development Association, International Finance Corporation, Asian Development Bank, Asian Development Fund, Inter-American Development Bank, African Development Bank, Multilateral Investment Guarantee Agency, and the Witeveen Facility. Over the past half century, this group of institutions has devastated our planet by stealing hundreds of billions of dollars from taxpayers in the West to fund socialism worldwide. No Communist butcher, socialist potentate, or Third World kleptocrat has escaped the largesse of these compassionate UN bankers.

The cumulative effect of their efforts has been to subsidize bankrupt Communist regimes while saddling the poor of the developing countries with an impossible debt load. Periodically, this has meant hitting up the taxpayers of Japan and the Western countries for additional tens of billions of dollars for the IMF and WB institutions so that they can issue new "loans" to the Communist and socialist kleptocracies to make payments on their loans from the global banksters. [14]

Although we have mentioned U.S. Assistant Secretary of the Treasury Harry Dexter White (CFR) previously, it is important to reemphasize his importance in the context of the Insiders' plan for a global monetary system. It was Soviet agent White who led the U.S. delegation and presided as the overall leader of the 45-nation Bretton Woods Conference. It was White — together with his inseparable "dear friend" John Maynard Keynes, the homosexual, Fabian Socialist, one-worlder — who designed the IMF. [15]*

On November 6, 1953, Attorney General Herbert Brownell

announced: "Harry Dexter White was a Russian spy. He smuggled secret documents to Russian agents for transmission to Moscow."[16] Brownell also reported that "Harry Dexter White was known to be a spy by the very people who appointed him to the most sensitive and important position he ever held in Government service. The FBI became aware of White's espionage activities at an early point in his government career and from the beginning made reports on these activities to the appropriate officials in authority. But these reports did not impede White's advancement in the Administration...."[17]

Attorney General Brownell made it clear that, in spite of his Red record, White had received Insider clearance from the very top: "White's spying activities for the Soviet Government were reported in detail by the FBI to the White House by means of a report delivered to President Truman through his military aide, Brig. Gen. Harry H. Vaughn."[18]

Comrade White was no ordinary "espionage" agent. As former Communist Whittaker Chambers observed, "Harry Dexter White's role as a Soviet agent was second in importance only to

---

*Lord Keynes, who was lionized by the Insider opinion cartel as a towering intellect and the "greatest economist of our age," was, in fact, a notorious pervert and pederast. He was a member of England's infamous "Bloomsbury Group," founded by Eleanor Marx (Karl Marx's lesbian, drug-addict daughter) to mix sexual depravity, drugs, and socialist thought. He also was a member of the infamous homosexual nest of "Apostles" at Cambridge University that produced the notorious British traitors Guy Burgess, Donald Maclean, and Anthony Blunt, all of whom spied for Stalin.[21] It is quite likely that Keynes was himself a conscious Soviet agent. Besides his "intimate" association with many Reds, he was married to Russian ballerina Lydia Lopokova (a common ploy among the Bloomsbury set to provide respectable "cover"). The unconventional couple were among the protected few allowed to travel freely throughout Soviet Russia even during the Red Terror. Although Keynes' hagiographers and promoters rigorously censored any public mention of his sexual deviancy or his socialist-communist connections, these were well known to most of his associates. In 1967, 21 years after Keynes' death, his perverse life was laid bare with the publication of Michael Holroyd's detailed, two-volume biography of Lytton Strachey, one of Keynes' numerous homosexual paramours.[22] Keynes' political, moral, and economic subversion were thoroughly exposed in *Keynes At Harvard* by Zygmund Dobbs.[23]

that of Alger Hiss — if, indeed, it was second."[19] It was Chambers who recruited White and introduced him to Col. Boris Bykov, of Soviet military intelligence, *in 1937*.[20]

In his capacity as U.S. Assistant Secretary of the Treasury, Harry Dexter White deliberately held up congressionally approved gold shipments to bolster China's currency during World War II. His purpose in doing so was either to bring down the anti-Communist Chiang Kai-shek or to force a coalition government between Chiang's Nationalists and the Communists. As Assistant Secretary of State for Far Eastern Affairs, Walter S. Robertson candidly explained at the time: "In China, we withheld our funds at the only time, in my opinion, we had a chance to save the situation. To do what? To force the Communists in."[24]

Serving as technical secretary at Bretton Woods and White's right-hand man was fellow Treasury official Virginius Frank Coe, also a Soviet agent. With White's help, Coe became the first secretary of the newly created IMF, a powerful post he immediately put in the service of the world revolution.[25] What is most extraordinary in all of this is not that a few clever Communists managed to penetrate the top levels of the U.S. government by "outsmarting" the "wise men" of the American Establishment. That was not how it happened. Instead, it was top U.S. Insiders in our government — Dean Acheson, Robert Lovett, Averell Harriman, Nelson Rockefeller, Edward Stettinius, et al. — who repeatedly interceded to prevent exposure of the records of these Soviet agents, and to *promote these traitors to even higher offices* where they could increase their damage to our nation!

Fruits of Global Aid

Under the leadership of White's and Coe's successors, the IMF has been subsidizing the global socialist revolution for decades. Cato Institute researcher Doug Bandow pointed out in 1994:

> [S]ix nations, Chile, Egypt, India, Sudan, Turkey, and Yugoslavia, had been relying on IMF aid for more than 30 years; 24 countries had been borrowers for between 20 and 29 years. And 47,

almost one-third of all the states in the world, had been using IMF credit for between 10 and 19 years.... Since 1947, Egypt has never left the IMF dole. Yugoslavia took its first loan in 1949 and was a borrower in all but three of the succeeding 41 years....

Bangladesh, Barbados, Gambia, Guinea-Bissau, Pakistan, Uganda, Zaire, and Zambia all started borrowing in the early 1970s and have yet to stop two decades later.[26]

Like domestic welfare drones, once these parasites attach themselves to the taxpayers, they never let loose. With the admission in 1992 of virtually all of the "ex-Communist" countries into both the IMF and World Bank, UN officials and their international welfare lobbyists launched a sustained campaign for massive new infusions of capital, which have thus far siphoned billions into Russia and its "former" Warsaw Pact allies,[27] all of which boast socialist regimes run by lifelong Communists, who are now called "reformers."

None of the above should surprise us, since the IMF was designed, as we've shown, by Communists, socialists and one-worlders. The Socialist International has acknowledged that the IMF is "in essence a Socialist conception."[28] Free market economist Henry Hazlitt, who stood virtually alone in exposing and opposing the IMF at its inception in 1944, clearly recognized its socialist essence. Forty years later, in his book *From Bretton Woods to World Inflation*, he warned: "The world cannot get back to economic sanctity until the IMF is abolished.... We will not stop the growth of world inflation and world socialism until the institutions and policies adopted to promote them have been abolished."[29] The warnings of this wise economist were absolutely correct in 1944. They were just as correct in 1984. And they are still correct today.

The World Bank, of course, has also played a central role in the global socialist revolution. India, one of the most pathetic socialist examples, has been the WB's biggest recipient. From the bank's creation in 1946 until the late 1960s, the WB funneled billions of dollars into socialist regimes, but by today's standards, the amounts divvied out were relatively small. "Then, in 1968, Robert McNamara became bank president and dedicated himself to continually raising loan levels," writes James Bovard in *The World Bank and the Impoverishment of Nations*. "By 1981, when McNamara resigned, lending had increased more than 13-fold, from $883 million to $12 billion. Loan levels have continued soaring: now the bank exists largely to maximize the transfer of resources to Third World governments." [30]

Unfortunately, Bovard points out, "the bank has greatly promoted the nationalization of Third World economies and increased political and bureaucratic control over the lives of the poorest of the poor." Whenever the public, the press, or members of Congress raise a hue and cry over the bank's deplorable activities, he notes, WB officials go on a "rhetorical crusade in favor of the private sector." But their bankrolling of revolution continues unabated. "The bank, more than any other international institution," says Bovard, "is responsible for the Third World's rush to socialism and economic collapse." [31]

Mr. McNamara is a former Secretary of Defense, a founding member of the ultra-leftist Center for the Study of Democratic Institutions, an endorser of the UN's occult Temple of Understanding, and a big wheel in both the CFR and TC. [32] His campaign to raise the WB loan levels was not something he dreamed up on his own, but reflected the collective "wisdom" of the top CFR-TC leadership. The IMF and WB have worked in close tandem with the top CFR-TC braintrusters and bankers from the beginning.

An example of this can be seen in the 1996 *Annual Report* of the CFR by Council Chairman Peter G. Peterson, who writes that "one of our most important initiatives in the recent past has been to expand our outreach to international institutions and to individuals supportive of the Council's work around the world. I am quite literally writing this letter on an airplane en route to Asia, where I will meet with leaders of the Hong Kong forum and then continue on to Beijing, where our unique and quite unprecedented 'home and home' dialogue with the Chinese People's

Institute of Foreign Affairs moves into its next phase at a critical time in the U.S.-China relationship. This trip was immediately preceded by an all-day discussion with our distinguished International Advisory Board, chaired by David Rockefeller, and capped off with an intensive dinner discussion with James D. Wolfensohn, president of the World Bank." [33]

This account suggests a fascinating decision-making hierarchy in international affairs. The CFR's International Advisory Board, under the direction of David Rockefeller, set the policy guidelines for U.S.-Chinese affairs; CFR Chairman Peterson was dispatched to Beijing to confer with his counterparts in the Chinese equivalent of the CFR; a few months later, Secretary of State Warren Christopher (CFR) was sent to lay the groundwork for an eventual summit between heads of state Bill Clinton (CFR) and Jiang Zemin. And James Wolfensohn (CFR) gets new WB funds rolling for the joint Beijing-Insider projects.

Revolution Over Profits

In his 1979 book *With No Apologies*, Senator Barry Goldwater opined that "the Council on Foreign Relations and its ancillary elitist groups are indifferent to Communism. They have no ideological anchors. In their pursuit of a new world order they are prepared to deal without prejudice with a communist state, a socialist state, a democratic state, monarchy, oligarchy — it's all the same to them." [34]

Although this cynical observation may seem, to the casual observer, an adequate explanation for the Insider-Communist symbiosis of the past few decades, it is sorely misleading. The Insiders are not "indifferent to Communism." It is not "all the same to them." Yes, they have done business with and arranged loans for democratic states, monarchies, and "right-wing" dictatorships and oligarchies, as well as socialist and Communist dictatorships. But the pattern that emerges is striking: Virtually always, they have used the leverage they have gotten through loans to undermine the non-socialist, non-Communist governments and push them into the Communist-socialist camp.

225

David Rockefeller returned from a visit to Communist China in 1973 (in his capacity as chairman of the Chase Manhattan Bank) declaring that "the social experiment in China under Chairman Mao's leadership is one of the most important and successful in human history." [35] According to the most reliable estimates, Mao Tse-tung's "social experiment" had by that time involved the murder of as many as 64 million Chinese by the Communists. [36]

In April 1974, David Rockefeller's Chase Manhattan Bank loaned the USSR $150 million to build the world's largest truck factory near the Kama River. The first trucks out of that plant carried Soviet soldiers into Afghanistan in 1979. [37] In 1982 the chairman of the CFR, TC, and Chase Manhattan expanded on his business "philosophy" during a 10-nation swing through Africa, saying that "we have found we can deal with just about any kind of government, provided they are orderly and responsible." [38] By that standard, Rockefeller would have had no trouble dealing with the "orderly and responsible" Nazi regime of Adolf Hitler. He found the Communist dictator of Zimbabwe, Robert Mugabe, to be a "very reasonable and charming person" and said that the presence of 20,000 Cuban soldiers had no "direct bearing on American business operations in Angola. Clearly it has not interfered with our own banking relations." [39]

As head Illuminatus at Pratt House, Rockefeller has welcomed Fidel Castro, Nelson Mandela, Thabo Mbeki, and other assorted terrorists and tyrants to the CFR's prestigious headquarters. This is not just about "business" and "profit," as Senator Goldwater suggested, and as David Rockefeller's remarks above were intended to infer. This is about power.

Masterminding Economic Collapse

An interesting window into the mindset of these Insiders was provided in 1990 by Canadian journalist Daniel Wood, who journeyed to the sprawling southern Colorado estate of one of Canada's most renowned citizens, Maurice Strong. Mr. Strong is an engaging and controversial fellow: mega-millionaire industrialist, radical environmentalist, New Age spiritualist, United Nations plutocrat, fervent one-world socialist, economic savant, global gadfly, and close pal of David Rockefeller and Mikhail Gorbachev. Mr. Wood spent a week at Strong's Baca Grande ranch interviewing this illustrious "world citizen."

During the course of Wood's visit, Strong told him of a novel he had been planning to write. It was about a group of world leaders who decided the only way to save the world was to cause the economies of the industrialized countries to collapse. Strong explained how his fictional leaders had formed a secret society and engineered a worldwide financial panic and, ultimately, the economic crash they sought. Mr. Wood's account of that conversation appeared in the May 1990 issue of *West* magazine:

> Each year, he [Strong] explains as background to the telling of the novel's plot, the World Economic Forum convenes in Davos, Switzerland. Over a thousand CEO's, prime ministers, finance ministers, and leading academics gather in February to attend meetings and set economic agendas for the year ahead. With this as a setting, he then says: "What if a small group of these world leaders were to conclude that the principal risk to the earth comes from the actions of the rich countries? And if the world is to survive, those rich countries would have to sign an agreement reducing their impact on the environment. Will they do it?... The group's conclusion is 'no.' The rich countries won't do it. They won't change. So, in order to save the planet, the group decides: Isn't the *only* hope for the planet that the industrialized civilizations collapse? Isn't it our responsibility to bring that about?"...
>
> It's February. They're all at Davos. These aren't terrorists. They're *world leaders*. They have positioned themselves in the world's commodity and stock markets. They've engineered, using their access to stock exchanges and computers and gold supplies, a panic. Then, they prevent the world's stock markets from closing. They jam the gears. They hire mercenaries who hold the rest of the world leaders at Davos as hostages. The markets *can't close*. The rich countries....[40] [Emphasis in original.]

Wood wrote that at that point the tycoon cum novelist "makes a slight motion with his fingers as if he were flicking a cigarette butt out the window." [41] Pffffft! The fates of hundreds of millions, even billions, of people callously sealed with the flick of a finger — their livelihoods, life savings, jobs, businesses, homes, dreams — tossed out like a cigarette butt. All for a good cause ("to save the planet"), of course.

Wood wrote: "I sit there spellbound. This is not *any* storyteller talking. This is Maurice Strong. He knows these world leaders. He is, in fact, co-chairman of the Council of the World Economic Forum. He sits at the fulcrum of power. He is in a position to *do it.*" [42]

Perhaps more important — and what makes this amateur, would-be novelist's tale so alarming — is that, from everything we know about the eminent Mr. Strong, he is very likely inclined to do it! Maurice Strong is the archetypal global elitist — a super-wealthy collectivist of unbridled arrogance, who believes that he, and a select few others, have been chosen to run the world and refashion it according to their utopian designs.

As Secretary-General of UNCED, the UN Earth Summit in Rio, Strong ranted against the lifestyles of "the rich countries" much like the "hero" of his novel. He declared that "the United States is clearly the greatest risk" to the world's ecological health. "In effect," Strong charged, "the United States is committing environmental aggression against the rest of the world." [43]

In a 1991 UNCED report, Strong wrote: "It is clear that current lifestyles and consumption patterns of the affluent middle-class ... involving high meat intake, consumption of large amounts of frozen and 'convenience' foods, ownership of motor-vehicles, numerous electric household appliances, home and workplace air conditioning ... suburban housing ... are not sustainable." Moreover, he insisted, a shift is necessary "towards lifestyles ... less geared to ... environmentally damaging consumption patterns." [44]

Those are just a small sampling of Strong's eco-Stalinist

tirades. And remember, as Daniel Wood said, this man is in a position to carry out the "fictitious" plan he outlined. Wood was not exaggerating. Maurice Strong is an Insider's Insider. The oil and energy magnate is the former head of Dome Petroleum of Canada, Power Corporation of Canada, Ontario Hydro, and Petro Canada. In 1972, he made his debut on the world stage as Secretary-General of the first UN environmental conference, held in Stockholm, Sweden. He was at the time also a trustee of the Rockefeller Foundation, one of the premier, longtime promoters of world government. Following the Stockholm confab, he was named to head the newly created United Nations Environment Program (UNEP).*

In 1991, Strong teamed up with David Rockefeller, founder of the Trilateral Commission, to write the promotional introductions to the Trilateral Commission plan for radical global "reform" entitled *Beyond Interdependence: The Meshing of the World's Economy and the Earth's Ecology*. This eco-socialist paean to world government, Strong claimed, "provides the most compelling economic as well as environmental case for such reform that I have read." [45]

One of the Trilateral "reforms" that Strong, no doubt, fancied was the proposal for "a new global partnership expressed in a revitalized international system in which an Earth Council, perhaps the Security Council with a broader mandate, maintains the interlocked environmental and economic security of the planet." [46]

As "luck" would have it, one of the new global entities that came into being as a result of the Earth Summit was an Earth Council. One guess as to who was appointed to head it. Yes, Maurice Strong is the chairman.

---

*Strong is also a mover and shaker in such Insider circles of power as the Club of Rome, the Aspen Institute for Humanistic Studies, the World Federation of United Nations Associations, the World Economic Forum, the World Future Society, the Lindisfarne Association, Planetary Citizens, the World Wilderness Congress, the Business Council for Sustainable Development, the Trilateral Commission, the World Resources Institute, the Gorbachev Foundation, the World Bank, and the Commission on Global Governance.

Mr. Strong has remained very much in the thick of all things green and global. In 1995, he addressed the Royal Institute of International Affairs, Britain's premier one-world organization, on his progress in organizing National Councils for Sustainable Development throughout the world to lobby for Agenda 21, the UN's mammoth blueprint for global eco-socialism. He has joined the globalist glitterati at the Gorbachev Foundation's annual State of the World Forum. In 1997, he hosted the global Rio+5 Conference.

Together with Mikhail Gorbachev and other one-world luminaries, Maurice Strong has been promoting the environmental manifesto known as the "Earth Charter." This charter envisions a planetary socialist welfare state, which would, among other things, "promote the equitable distribution of wealth within nations and among nations."[47] And Messrs. Strong, Gorbachev, Rockefeller, et al., will be in charge of the distribution, of course. But before they can "distribute" the world's wealth, they must first take full control of it. Which means it's really about power. That's what all wealth redistribution schemes are always really about. And, clearly, power is what Mr. Strong and his one-world confreres are after.

The creation of a global central bank, a global currency, a global tax system, and a global trading authority have been key objectives of world government advocates for decades. Centralized monetary and economic institutions of this kind would make the orchestrated world financial collapse scenario Maurice Strong envisions mere child's play. They would also facilitate the grand redistribute-the-wealth schemes of the UN's bureaucrats. As was evident in the previous chapter with regard to the EU and WHFTA, the one-world Insiders recognize that economic control is their sure path to political control.

Pooling Monetary Sovereignty

One of the Insiders' leading technicians helping to design their envisioned "new world order" is Harvard University Professor Richard N. Cooper (CFR, TC). Writing in the Fall 1984 edition of the CFR journal *Foreign Affairs*, Cooper proposed "a radical alternative scheme" (his words) that would mean the end of America as we know it. In his article entitled "A Monetary System for the Future," the Harvard don wrote:

> A new Bretton Woods conference is wholly premature. But it is not premature to begin thinking about how we would like international monetary arrangements to evolve in the remainder of this century. With this in mind, I suggest a radical alternative scheme for the next century: the creation of a common currency for all of the industrial democracies, with a common monetary policy and a joint Bank of Issue to determine that monetary policy. [48]

"The currency of the Bank of Issue could be practically anything," the CFR economist continued. "The key point is that monetary control — the issuance of currency and of reserve credit — would be in the hands of the new Bank of Issue, not in the hands of any *national government*...." [49] (Emphasis added.) The problem, he noted, is that "a single currency is possible only if there is in effect a single monetary policy, and a single authority issuing the currency and directing the monetary policy. How can independent states accomplish that? *They need to turn over the determination of monetary policy to a supranational body*...." [50] (Emphasis added.)

As the *Washington Post* put it: "The real point is that *a common currency means one common country*, and all else is details to be filled in later." [51] (Emphasis in original.) Precisely! And the CFR-TC *ueberlords* are more than willing to provide those details. Mr. Cooper realized that selling this flagrantly totalitarian idea to the public would not be an easy, overnight job. "This one-currency regime is much too radical to envisage in the near future," he admitted. "But it is not too radical to envisage 25 years from now.... [I]t will require many years of consideration before people become accustomed to the idea." [52]

Overcoming objections to "a pooling of monetary sovereignty" — even with friendly nations — would be difficult under any circumstances. But how could Americans ever be expected to go along with a "radical scheme" to merge economically with Communist countries? It would be difficult, Cooper conceded, but doable, nonetheless. He wrote: "First, it is highly doubtful whether the American public, to take just one example, could ever accept that countries with oppressive autocratic regimes should vote on the monetary policy that would affect monetary conditions in the United States.... For such a bold step to work at all, it presupposes a certain convergence of political values...." [53]

Creating Convergence

Cooper and his confreres in the CFR-dominated media, think tanks, and academia went to work to create that "convergence of political values" in the public mind. A flood of articles and op-eds in the *New York Times*, *Los Angeles Times*, *Washington Post*, *Wall Street Journal*, *Foreign Affairs*, *Foreign Policy*, *Christian Science Monitor*, *The Economist*, etc. soon began hammering home the theme that the United States and Western Europe must help Gorbachev's "perestroika" transform the Soviet Union in the direction of "democracy" and a market economy. After the purported "collapse of Communism" in 1989, they stepped up the convergence drum beat, asserting that the taxpayers of the West must provide Russia and all the nations of her "former" satellite empire more billions of dollars in credits and aid to help them make the transition to freedom and stability.

The essential point here should not be missed: The advocates of world government intend that their planned global superstate, although "initially limited," will, ultimately, exercise unlimited planetary power, a power far beyond that realized by Hitler, Stalin, or Mao. Surely, if we do not stop their megalomaniacal plans, we will see them use this power in much the same way as outlined by Maurice Strong — and in ways even more brutal and horrific.

Part III
Bringing It Home

Chapter 12

The UN's One-World Religion

The histories and symbols that served our fathers encumber and divide us. Sacraments and rituals harbor disputes and waste our scanty emotions.... The modernization of the religious impulse leads us straight to the effort for the establishment of the world state as a duty.... [1]
— H.G. Wells, author, historian, and one-world Fabian Socialist, *The Open Conspiracy*, 1928

The United Nations is the chosen instrument of God; to be a chosen instrument means to be a divine messenger carrying the banner of God's inner vision and outer manifestation. [2]
— Master Sri Chinmoy, head of the UN Meditation Room

The responsibility of each human being today is to choose between the force of darkness and the force of light. We must therefore transform our attitudes and values, and adopt a renewed respect for the superior law of Divine Nature. [3]
— Maurice Strong, UNCED Secretary-General, keynote address to the UN Earth Summit, 1992

We must now forge a new "Earth Ethic" which will inspire all peoples and nations to join in a new global partnership of North, South, East and West. [4]
— UN publication *In Our Hands: Earth Summit '92*

[T]he Antichrist and the Second Coming of women are synonymous. This Second Coming is not a return of Christ but a new arrival of female presence.... The Second Coming, then,

> *means that the prophetic dimension in the symbol of the*
> *Great Goddess ... is the key to salvation from servitude....*[5]
> [Emphasis in original.]
> — Mary Daly, radical feminist "theologian,"
> Boston College

> *Witches were freedom fighters for women because they*
> *taught contraception and abortion. The modern contribution*
> *is to elevate* reproductive freedom *to a universal human*
> *right....*[6] [Emphasis in original.]
> — Gloria Steinem, socialist, radical feminist,
> founder of *Ms.* magazine

Only a person totally deaf and blind could fail to notice the incredible occult, New Age, and neo-pagan explosion that has been rapidly transforming the Americas and Western Europe into what the advocates of global change gleefully refer to as "post-Christian civilizations." A majority of Americans still consider themselves Christian, but find they are increasingly in retreat before a steady onslaught of anti-Christian media assaults, court rulings, attacks from academia, and pop culture offerings. Meanwhile, hedonism, Satanism, witchcraft, astrology, vampirism, homosexuality, Eastern mystic cults, and "Indigenous Peoples" religions are exalted by the same media mandarins and Hollywood elites who control our "news" and "entertainment."

What very few of these Americans realize is that this hideous "spiritual transformation" is tied directly to the United Nations, where the one-world architects intend to enthrone their planned New World Religion. And as this Satanic enthronement progresses (yes, we mean, literally, Satanic), Christians — and Orthodox Jews and Muslims as well — will find themselves increasingly in the crosshairs of the new world order, singled out as "bigoted," "dogmatic," and "intolerant" for insisting on clinging to their "archaic" and "divisive" religious beliefs.

Religious leaders and adherents of all sects are being aggressively evangelized to adopt the UN's new "global ethic," a gooey mélange of religious syncretism, environmentalism, socialism, and militant secular humanism. People of all religious backgrounds are being enlisted to embrace this "global ethic" as a "core belief" of their religious faith.

As more and more people adopt this new "planetary consciousness," the one-world Insiders know that support will grow for:

- global disarmament, for both individuals and nations
- world government
- paganism
- environmental extremism
- socialism and Communism
- religious persecution, in the name of "tolerance" and combating "hate"

If the above statements are shocking and incredible to you, then you are unaware of easily verifiable facts concerning events and developments that are dramatically impacting our society. Many of the steps in this diabolic scheme are taking place before our very eyes, in the open, as British novelist and Fabian Socialist historian H.G. Wells proposed in 1928 in his *The Open Conspiracy: Blue Prints For a World Revolution.*

Wells, an ardent one-worlder and one of the most widely read authors and intellectuals of his day, conceded that human history has proven that religious ideals are essential to the sustaining of any society. However, having rejected Christianity and all other religions, he determined that only a new "modern" religion could sustain the socialist world government he was advocating. "The conspiracy of modern religion against the established institutions of the world must be an open conspiracy," he averred, and must reject "secret methods or tactical insincerities."[7]

This statement was itself a "tactical insincerity," of course, since Wells and his one-world, socialist comrades never planned to be completely open about their schemes. Thus the brazen symbol of deception on the Fabian Socialist coat-of-arms: a wolf in sheep's clothing!

"It seems unavoidable," said the Fabian strategist, "that if religion is to develop unifying and directive power in the present confusion of human affairs it must adapt itself ... ; it must divest itself of its sacred histories, its gross preoccupations, its posthumous prolongation of personal ends." "The time has come," said Wells, "to strip religion right down to" what he saw as the spiritual essentials: "the desire for service" and "subordination." [8]

But "service" and "subordination" to the deities created by Prophet Wells and his fellow high-priests. Never one to allow humility to dim the glory of his divine brilliance, Wells boldly proclaimed: "So I bear my witness and argue my design. This is, I declare, the truth and the way of salvation." [9] Moreover, he announced, "... it will be a world religion. This large loose assimilatory mass of groups and societies will be definitely and obviously attempting to swallow up the entire population of the world and become the new human community." [10]

Occult Connections

The global religion envisioned by Wells was a secular, socialist one, but some of his fellow Fabians had migrated from atheism to the occult. Two of the most important pilgrims of that variety were radical feminist Annie Besant and British journalist and newspaper publisher William Stead.

Besant became a fervent disciple of Madame Helena Blavatsky, the occultist, satanist founder of the modern Theosophical movement. Besant eventually became the international president of the Theosophical Society.

Alice and Foster Bailey, who succeeded Annie Besant, unabashedly revealed their demonic sympathies with the launching of Lucifer Publishing Company and its theosophical journal, *Lucifer*. Later, however, they realized that the Christian West was still too "unenlightened" to accept open Luciferian doctrine and changed the name of Lucifer Publishing Company to the more esoteric (and less likely to offend) Lucis Publishing Company. They also established the Lucis Trust to serve as the umbrella organization for a profusion of globalist/New Age/occult organizations and programs that are key catalysts of the emerging new world religion. These include the Arcane School, World Goodwill, Triangles, Lucis Publishing, Lucis Productions, Lucis Trust Libraries, and the New Group of World Servers. [11]

According to the Lucis Trust, "World Goodwill is recognised ... at the United Nations as a Non-governmental Organisation" and is "represented at regular briefing sessions at the United Nations in New York and Geneva." [12] The "regular weekly broadcasts of talks given at World Goodwill Forum meetings and programs produced by Lucis Productions" in London and New York are beamed by Radio For Peace International in English, Spanish, German, and French, on shortwave, to a "worldwide audience" from the UN University for Peace in Costa Rica. [13]

Lucis Trust also serves as custodian of the Meditation Room at the UN's New York headquarters. [14] This dark and ominous theosophical shrine contains no symbols of the world's major religions. A barren, metallic altar and a stark, Picassoesque mural of geometric shapes provide spiritual symbolism. Literature provided at the UN describes the symbols as "a rectangular six-ton block of iron ore lit by a single shaft of light and a muted abstract painting at the far end of the small room, similarly illuminated." [15]

And what does all this signify? Theosophist authors Eunice and Felix Layton connect the room's symbolism to "the story of the descent of the divine into every human life, its apparent death and burial in the material world and its inevitable final triumphant resurrection." [16] Keep in mind that it is Lucifer, the "light-bearer," who is the "divine" one in Blavatsky's twisted theosophist theology, and you'll understand why this bizarre temple is entirely apropos for the Tower of Babel on New York's East River.*

William Stead, publisher of the radical *Pall Mall Gazette*, was not only a socialist and theosophist — he was also an intimate associate of the super-rich, megalomaniacal, homosexual Cecil Rhodes, whom we discussed in Chapter 3.

Recall that Rhodes, William Stead, and a small group of high-born graduates of Oxford and Cambridge, all fervent apostles of the socialist Professor John Ruskin, formed a "secret society" (the words are Rhodes') called the "Society of the Elect." Rhodes admitted that his plan for dominion was "a scheme to take the government of the whole world." [17] In other words, a conspiracy.

Envisioning a UN-type world government vested with irresistible military force, Rhodes insisted that the scheme must entail "the foundation of so great a power as to hereafter render wars impossible." [18] It was in the furtherance of this conspiracy that Rhodes' secret society founded the Royal Institute of International Affairs and CFR. Both of these front groups, as we have seen, played key roles in establishing the UN, and are likewise involved in building the new global religion.

Indoctrination: Subordination to the State

Let us drop back for a moment to revisit H.G. Wells. We have

---

*Another principal conduit of UN spiritualism is the Temple of Understanding, operated with the support of the Lucis Trust. It is located near the UN at the historic Cathedral of St. John the Divine, a center of political and occult/New Age activism, which also houses the radical Interfaith Center of New York and the Luciferians of the Lindisfarne Center. Launched in the early 1960s as the "spiritual counterpart of the United Nations," The Temple of Understanding's founding sponsors included an odd assortment of Establishment Insiders, socialists, humanists, Communist fronters, religious figures, and entertainment celebrities: Senator John D. Rockefeller IV (CFR, TC); then-Secretary of Defense Robert S. McNamara (CFR, TC); Planned Parenthood founder Margaret Sanger; IBM president Thomas J. Watson (CFR); Socialist Party leader Norman Thomas; Eleanor Roosevelt; Time-Life president James A. Linen (CFR); homosexual author Christopher Isherwood; and Fabian Socialist professor and columnist Max Lerner. [19]

The Temple of Understanding works closely with the UN Secretariat, the World Council of Churches, the World Conference on Religion and Peace, the UN's Society for Enlightenment and Transformation, and other "spiritual leaders" to sponsor convocations for "global spirituality." These conferences, which have burgeoned in size and frequency over the past decade, invariably turn out to be workshops for religious syncretism, which aims at melding and blending the world's disparate faiths into one global, neo-pagan, occult religion or "Earth Ethic."

noted the continuing influence of his occult, socialist confreres Annie Besant and William Stead from early in the last century to the present day. But Wells himself is also very much alive in "world order" circles. Quotations from his works are scattered throughout New Age and new world order books and publications. The World Federalist Association (WFA), for instance, continues to publish some of his essays, including "How a Federal World Government May Come About," taken from his book *The Outline of History* (1920).[20]

According to Wells, in that one-world polemic:

> The essential task of men of goodwill in all states and countries remains the same, it is an educational task, and its very essence is to bring to the minds of all men everywhere, as a necessary basis for world co-operation, *a new telling and interpretation, a common interpretation, of history*.... The world perishes unless sovereignty is merged and nationality subordinated.[21] [Emphasis in original.]

Wells sets down what he sees as "the broad fundamentals of the coming world state." "It will be based," he says, "upon a common world religion, very much simplified and universalized.... This will not be Christianity nor Islam nor Buddhism nor any such specialized form of religion, but religion itself pure and undefiled; the Eightfold Way, the Kingdom of Heaven, brotherhood, creative service, and self-forgetfulness. *Throughout the world men's thoughts and motives will be turned by education.... And education, as the new age will conceive it, will go on throughout life.*"[22] (Emphasis added.)

Sound familiar? This is precisely what we have been experiencing in our schools and colleges, as well as the government-directed "lifelong learning" programs that gradually have become an integral part of so many corporate and governmental jobs. Which is not to imply that we are, or ought to be, opposed to "lifelong learning," as the term is commonly understood, in its most innocent and benign meaning. To the contrary, we accept it as a fact of life. Ours is not the first generation to realize that

learning does not (or should not) end with the completion of formal schooling; wise people (of all socio-economic and educational
backgrounds) throughout the ages have recognized the need for
(as well as the pleasure to be derived from) continuous lifelong
education. In today's fast-changing, technology-driven world, it
is more important than ever to be constantly updating skills and
learning new ones.

However, in using the same terms, we do not all mean the
same thing. We should be very familiar with this phenomenon by
now. "Tolerance" no longer means "live and let live" civility; it
means using the power of government to force majority acceptance of the perverse practices of a militant minority.
"Peacekeeping" means carpet-bombing and/or invading and militarily subjugating whomever the UN has designated as *villain
du jour*. "Multiculturalism" means demonizing Christian and
European civilization for genocide, exploitation, and raping
Mother Earth. "Investing" doesn't mean private individuals
freely deciding what to do with their own capital assets; it means
politicians and bureaucrats plundering your savings through
taxation, and then spending it on socialist boondoggles.

So we should not be surprised that the same coercive utopians
have also co-opted "lifelong learning." In their lexicon it no
longer is an elective; the individual cannot be allowed to determine if and when he will take any continued formal schooling.
Such important decisions must be made by superior "experts."
Or as Wells put it, "we should have the collective affairs of the
world managed by suitably equipped groups of the most interested, intelligent and devoted people" — such as himself and his
fellow Fabians. [23]

Subversive World Council of Churches

One of the early major attempts to co-opt religion in the service
of world government came in 1942. *Time* magazine devoted considerable space in its March 16, 1942 issue to a report on a gathering at Ohio Wesleyan University of hundreds of delegates representing the more than 30 denominations called together by the

notoriously pro-Communist Federal Council of Churches (FCC). The FCC (which later changed its name to the National Council of Churches, NCC) was the American branch of the Communist-controlled World Council of Churches, which still exists and has never ceased its subversive activities.

Chairing the 1942 FCC Wesleyan confab was Insider John Foster Dulles, a founder of the CFR and, together with his brother Allen Dulles (CFR), a member of the Woodrow Wilson-Colonel House team that tried to foist the League of Nations on the United States. John Dulles would later go on to promote the new world order as Secretary of State under President Eisenhower. However, at the 1942 FCC conference he was lining up church support for the United Nations that would be coming three years later.

As *Time* reported, the Dulles-led conference produced a political program of "extreme internationalism." Some of the "high spots" of that program were, said *Time*:

- Ultimately, "a world government of delegated powers."
- Strong immediate limitations on national sovereignty.
- International control of all armies and navies.
- "A universal system of money...."
- Progressive elimination of all tariff and quota restrictions on world trade. [24]

According to *Time*, the conference "held that 'a new order of economic life is both imminent and imperative' — a new order that is sure to come either 'through voluntary cooperation ... or through explosive political revolution.'" "'Collectivism is coming whether we like it or not,' the delegates were told by no less a churchman than England's Dr. William Paton, co-secretary of the World Council of Churches." [25] The problem is that Dr. Paton and his comrades *did* want collectivism, and they were doing everything in their power to fasten it upon the peoples of the world, through both patient gradualism and "explosive political revolution." The *Time* story finished on this note:

The ultimate goal: "a duly constituted world government ... an international court ... international administrative bodies with necessary powers, and adequate international police forces and provision for enforcing its worldwide economic authority." [26]

The Dulles-FCC propaganda parley no doubt greatly assisted the Insiders' globalist plans, both in building religious support for U.S. entry into the forthcoming United Nations, and in neutralizing opposition to the same organization. In the decades since that confab at Ohio Wesleyan University, UN religious summitry has played an increasingly important part in the one-world transformation scheme.

The World "Peace" Summit

The granddaddy of these convocations, the United Nations Millennium World Peace Summit of Religious and Spiritual Leaders, was held in New York City in late August 2000 (not to be confused with the gathering of Heads of State at the UN's Millennium Summit, which followed in September). The Peace Summit offered terrifying glimpses of the outrageous and demonic "global spirituality" the Insiders have planned for us.

The outrages began even before the Peace Summit began, when the UN organizers announced that the Dalai Lama would not be invited because his attendance would offend Communist China! [27] So, while more than a thousand religious leaders and gurus representing every conceivable "faith tradition" gathered in New York under banners of "tolerance," "peace," and "brotherhood," one of the world's best-known religious figures, the revered leader of millions of Buddhists, and a man who exemplifies those virtues the UN summit extolled, was barred from attendance — because the totalitarian, genocidal butchers who have been brutally occupying his tiny kingdom of Tibet for half a century would get upset!

The hypocrisy and outrage multiplied as the Summit got underway. Not only was the Dalai Lama excluded, but Red China was given a platform to denounce him and the many other victims of their brutal religious persecution. Representing the Butchers of Beijing at this UN spiritual confabulation was "Bishop" Michael Fu Tieshan of the PRC's "Patriotic Catholic Church."[28] Bishop Fu is not a genuine Roman Catholic bishop recognized by the Vatican; he is an agent of the Communist government who provides protective cover for his masters while they cruelly oppress *real* Catholic bishops, priests, and lay faithful. Real Chinese Catholics like the late Ignatius Cardinal Kung Pin-Mei, who spent more than 30 years in Red China's prisons.

Cardinal Kung was arrested in 1955, along with more than 200 other Catholic priests and Church leaders. They were abused, tortured, and publicly humiliated at show trials. Cardinal Kung was kept in solitary confinement during much of his heroic three decades of imprisonment. He died in exile, in the United States, at the age of 98, on March 12, 2000 — just a few months before the UN "Peace" Summit. He was the Catholic Church's oldest cardinal.[29] Other aged servants of God remain in prison. In February 2000, for example, shortly before Cardinal Kung's death, 80-year old Archbishop John Yang was arrested during a midnight raid at his home by the Communist authorities.[30]

The persecution continued after the Summit as well. On September 14, 2000, barely a week after the PRC butchers were welcomed to the Summit, Bishop Thomas Zeng Jingmu was arrested in his town of Hangpu, in the Southeastern province of Jiangxi. The frail, 80-year-old bishop was taken by force to the local prison of Linchuan. Bishop Zeng, who has been arrested many times for his faith, has suffered more than 30 years in prison since the 1950s. Also arrested at the same time as Bishop Zeng were Auxiliary Bishop Deng Hui and Father Liao Haiqing.[31]

Many other Christians in China share this same fate. A few days before the start of the Summit, three American evangelists were arrested in China in the tyrannical regime's crackdown on Evangelical Protestant "house churches." The Americans were among 130 Christians netted in the Communist sweep of worship services in private homes. [32] This was but the latest in an ongoing pattern of persecution that includes the execution by firing squad of Reverend Liu Jiaguo. [33] And the persecution of Christians has been *increasing and intensifying* — not mellowing — in recent years, with each new concession from the U.S. and the West. At the same time, the Beijing regime has also been engaged in an ongoing brutal suppression of the Falun Gong spiritual exercise and meditation sect, as well as a continuing persecution of Chinese Muslims. [34]

In his address to the UN's "spiritual" Peace Summit, Bishop Fu Tieshan, the puppet-stooge of these Red Chinese persecutors, said:

> Let us pray for the wisdom of the Holy Spirit, respect the purposes and principles of the U.N. Charter, and from now on, guard against and put an end to anything that taint and desecrate religious purity....
>
> Today in China, facts and other practice genuinely reflect the harmony between different religions. And under the protection of the Constitution and other laws, we enjoy comprehensive and full religious freedom. [35]

In an obvious attack on the Dalai Lama and the many brave religious believers suffering under the Communist regime, "Bishop" Fu said: "At present, there are still many violent and evil activities going on 'in the name of religion.' Some people have made use of religious differences to fuel ethnic feuds and provoke so-called conflicts of civilizations; some want to trample upon the sovereignty of other countries under the pretext of 'protecting religious human rights.'" [36]

Did any of the esteemed spiritual leaders attending the Peace Summit walk out in protest over this brazen display of hypocrisy? Did they announce their "solidarity" with their brothers who are suffering for their religious convictions? Did they demand that Red China stop its vicious persecution of all religions? Did they even timidly *ask* our Beijing "partners" to light-en up with the truncheons and thumbscrews? Hah! Not even close! Instead, they politely applauded (some enthusiastically cheered) this puppet of the Communist persecutors.

Most Americans, if they saw or heard any coverage of the Summit in the major CFR-dominated media, were not apprised of the cruel charade that was played out there. Few are aware that Bishop Fu Tieshan is a fraud or that religionists of all types are routinely persecuted in Red China.

CNN certainly wasn't going to expose this sham; CNN founder and current vice-chairman of CNN parent company Time Warner, Ted Turner, not only was a major financial sponsor of the Summit, but also honorary chairman of the event. Turner, who is infamous for his profanity, womanizing, and scathing verbal attacks on Christianity, Christian leaders, the Ten Commandments, and Biblical morality, couldn't resist using the Summit podium to criticize the "very intolerant" Christianity of his boyhood and to propose a more global, all-embracing spirituality for the "one human race." [37]

Global Ethic Kung Phooey
The "spirituality" that One-World Ted and his fellow Insiders have in mind is to be found in the UN's "Declaration of a Global Ethic," which UNESCO commissioned renegade "theologian" Hans Kung to draft. [38] Yes, while real Christian heroes like *Cardinal* Kung, who suffer torture for their faith, are completely ignored by the CFR "news" cartel, left-wing ideologues like Hans Kung are celebrated.

For those who like their theology dished up from the likes of Ted Turner and Bishop Fu Tieshan — which appears to be most of the globalist folk who populate the UN diplomatic corps and delegations to UN conferences — Hans Kung was a perfect choice. In his 1991 book *Global Responsibility: In Search of a New World Ethic*, Kung declared:

> Any form of ... church conservatism is to be rejected.... To put it bluntly: No regressive or repressive religion — whether Christian,

Islamic, Jewish or of whatever provenance — has a long-term future.[39]

Moreover, he said: "If ethics is to function for the well-being of all, it must be indivisible. The undivided world increasingly needs an undivided ethic. Postmodern men and women need common values, goals, ideals, visions."[40] That's right, UN "diversity" is broad enough to embrace every imaginable navel-gazing mystic, diapered swami, saffron-robed guru, befeathered sachem, spell-chanting shaman, New Age psycho-babbler, tree-worshiping pantheist, witch, warlock, druid, animist, or Marxian spiritualist — but *not* those terrible, monotheistic creeds. Mustn't tolerate any of those "dogmatic," "absolutist" faiths; of that the "tolerant" globalists are dogmatically, absolutely certain.

Another prominent "theologian" of the UN's "global ethic" is Dr. Robert Muller (whom we introduced in our Prologue). A former UN Assistant Secretary-General, Dr. Muller served 38 years as a United Nations "civil servant," and — following his retirement in 1985 — has served as chancellor of the UN's University for Peace in Costa Rica. He is the author of the World Core Curriculum now in use in schools worldwide. In his influential book *New Genesis: Shaping a Global Spirituality*, Muller opines: "If Christ came back to earth, his first visit would be to the United Nations to see if his dream of human oneness and brotherhood had come true. He would be happy to see representatives of all nations."[41]

We remind you, dear reader, that in the contorted theosophical sophistry of Muller and company, "Christ" is not Jesus Christ but Lucifer. According to Muller, the UN's wondrous endeavors are leading us on a "grand journey of humanity towards oneness, convergence and unprecedented happiness." What's more, "We were approaching Teilhard's point of convergence, Wells' last chapter of *The Outline of History* ... Sri Chinmoy's world oneness ... the apotheosis [deification] of human life on earth."[42]

The "Teilhard" Muller refers to is Pierre Teilhard de Chardin

— the renegade Jesuit priest, theologian-philosopher, and pale-ontologist who perpetrated the great "Piltdown Man" evolution-ist hoax. "Wells" is, of course, H.G. Wells, whom we introduced above. Sri Chinmoy is the one-world, New Age guru who runs the UN's Meditation Room and regularly leads the meditations. Chinmoy has offered his prophecy regarding the UN's divine mission:

> The United Nations is the chosen instrument of God; to be a cho-sen instrument means to be a divine messenger carrying the ban-ner of God's inner vision and outer manifestation. One day, the world will ... treasure and cherish the soul of the United Nations as its very own with pride, for this soul is all-loving, all-nourishing, and all-fulfilling. [43]

"Spiritual Leaders" for the New Millennium

It was Master Chinmoy, appropriately, who presented the UN's U Thant Peace Award to Maurice Strong, the globe-trotting bil-lionaire best known for his role as Secretary-General of the 1992 UN Earth Summit in Brazil. [44] Strong was receiving the honor, said Chinmoy, for "his lifelong commitment to the soaring ideals of the United Nations."

The award was named for U Thant, the Burmese Marxist who served as the UN's third Secretary-General and who, in 1970, brazenly declared: "Lenin was a man with a mind of great clari-ty and incisiveness." [45] Maurice Strong, who apparently shares Lenin's "great clarity and incisiveness," has been a driving force in bringing the most extreme enviro-Leninism and far-out reli-gio-Leninism into the social, political, economic, religious main-stream.

Other vaunted "spiritual leaders" who are guiding humanity into the developing "global ethic" of the new millennium include:

• Mohammed Ramadan, president of the UN's Society for Enlightenment and Transformation, which has offices in the basement of the UN building where every conceivable variety of "spiritual sage" — witch doctors, mystics, "channelers," UFO enthusiasts, reincarnated Masters — contribute their cosmic energies to the sacred mission of the UN.

- Apostate theologian Matthew Fox, whose radical New Age spirituality embraces Wicca, homosexuality, abortion, and one-world socialism. An apostle of the Gaia (Earth Goddess) Gospel, Fox says, "I believe the appropriate symbol of the Cosmic Christ ... is that of Jesus as Mother Earth crucified yet rising daily.... [T]he symbol of which I speak holds the capacity to launch a global spirituality of untold dimensions appropriate for the third millennium." [46]

- Gerald Barney, founder and executive director of the Millennium Institute and a co-chair of the 1993 Parliament of World Religions. In his keynote address at that summit, he said that "an internationally famous, highly influential author on sustainable development told me bluntly, 'Religion must die. It is the fundamental cause of virtually all social, economic, and ecological problems and much of the violence in the world.'" [47] The only alternative to the destruction of religion, Barney asserted, is the "reinterpretation and even rejection of ancient traditions and assumptions" and the creation of a "'sustainable' faith tradition on earth...." [48] "Every person," Barney said, "must learn to think like Earth, to act like Earth, to be Earth." [49] Barney was the lead author of the enviro-Leninist Global 2000 report for the Carter administration and was a national program director for the Rockefeller Brothers Fund.

- William Irwin Thompson, founder of the (Luciferian) Lindisfarne Association. "We have now a new spirituality, what has been called the New Age movement," Thompson says. "This is now beginning to influence concepts of politics and community in ecology.... This is the Gaia [Mother Earth] politique ... planetary culture." [50]

- Mikhail Gorbachev, former Soviet dictator, butcher of Afghanistan, and chairman of the Gorbachev Foundation and Green Cross International. In a *Los Angeles Times* interview of May 8, 1997, Gorbachev insisted humanity must embrace "a new environmental legal code rooted in an Earth Charter … a kind of Ten Commandments, a 'Sermon on the Mount,' that provides a guide for human behavior toward the environment in the next century and beyond." "The most important thing," he said, "is the shaping of a new value system" from a "new synthesis" of "democratic, Christian, and Buddhist values … which affirm such moral principles as social responsibility and the sense of oneness with nature and with each other."[51] Gorbachev's week-long State of the World Forum 2000 extravaganza in New York City was the bridging event between the Peace Summit and the Millennium Summit, with many of the heads of state, ambassadors, UN officials, and spiritual leaders from both events also participating in the Gorbachev Forum.

Earth Charter Subversion and Perversion

Comrade Gorbachev knows something about the Earth Charter, since he helped compose it. It was his good friend, Maurice Strong, as chief of the Earth Summit, who commissioned him to take up the important task. While much of the Charter sounds like harmless eco-babble, or even sensible earth stewardship that is compatible with Christian theology, it is larded with deceptive code words and traps aimed at destroying Judeo-Christian moral values and the non-socialist political-economic systems. Article 12 (a) of the Earth Charter commits signatory governments to:

> Eliminate discrimination in all its forms, such as that based on race, color, sex, *sexual orientation*, religion, language, and national, ethnic or social origin.[52] [Emphasis added.]

This is very clearly aimed at expanding the socialist state into all spheres of life and especially to undermine the legal codes of nations based upon the moral precepts of the monotheistic religions, all of which proscribe homosexuality. The Charter, like the many "human rights" conventions it promotes, seeks to give homosexual activists a pretext to claim legal footing to challenge in the courts and legislatures national, state, and local laws against sexual perversion.

This is already happening. The first case we are aware of was launched in 1992 when Nick Toonen, a homosexual rights activist in Australia, asked the UN Human Rights Committee to investigate the state of Tasmania's anti-homosexuality statute. The UN committee determined that Toonen could be classified as a "victim." [53]

Similarly, here in the United States, militant sodomites have charged that they are "victims" of human rights violations because of our laws against homosexual practices and have taken their cause to the United Nations. If we allow current trends to continue, we most certainly will see a federal court in the near future rule that U.S. state laws concerning sodomy must be struck down to comply with UN "human rights" law.

Christian-Marxist "Unity"

Following the conclusion of the State of the World Forum 2000 (September 4th–10th) in New York, Mr. Gorbachev was off on a multi-week evangelistic crusade that took him to some surprising venues. He was received with apparent enthusiasm at churches in Florida and Tennessee.

Then it was off to Salt Lake City, where Gorby addressed Franklin Covey's International Symposium at the Salt Palace.* At a Salt Lake City press conference, the Nobel Prize winner lamented to the assembled media corps that "we do not have a new world order, the kind of new world order that we need." [54]

Later, in California, he shared a stage with William "Star Trek" Shatner, before beaming his "global ethic" sermonette to a global television audience from the Reverend Robert Schuller's famous Crystal Cathedral. "I know that he calls himself an atheist," Rev. Schuller said, but Schuller believed, nonetheless, that

God had used Gorbachev "in a mighty way." And he hoped that one day the former Communist dictator would become "a man of faith." [55]

We join Rev. Schuller in that hope, as we hope that *all* atheists will become "men of faith" — as that term has been understood traditionally by believers. But, in the meantime, is there any justification for Christians to *turn over their pulpits* to atheists — to enemies of God — like Gorbachev? Comrade Gorbachev, after all, *is* a "man of faith": He believes in the gospels of Marx and Lenin. As we have already noted, Gorbachev declared in 1989: "I am a Communist, a convinced Communist. For some that may be a fantasy. But for me it is the main goal." [56] By both word and act, Gorbachev has confirmed many times since then his continued adherence to his *revolutionary* faith.

To anyone familiar with Communist *dialectical materialism* as it concerns religion, Gorbachev's fixation with religion over the past decade makes perfect sense. He is one of the leading global activists working to *transform* Christianity, to *unite* it with Marxism! As a master dialectician, he is expert in the use of words as weapons, particularly in using words that will appeal to and disarm Christians. According to one of Gorbachev's old friends, Natasha Rimashevskaya, he had one phrase he loved to say: " 'As to this question, one must approach it dialectically.' That meant he wanted to entertain a thesis and its contradiction at the same time." [57]

---

*Thanks to a celebrity status that has been bestowed on him by the Insiders, Gorbachev is received like a rock star by politicians, journalists, business and religious leaders, educators, and entertainers worldwide. He is, reportedly, the highest-paid name for hire in the world, commanding $100,000 for a half-hour talk. Gunter Kunkel, president of the Phoenix Club in Anaheim, California, felt his group had gotten a "bargain" because they only had to pay $75,000 for 50 minutes of the Gorbachev wisdom and charm. "Can you think of anybody bigger?" the awestruck Kunkel asked the *Los Angeles Times'* Mike Anton. "It will probably be the greatest night we have seen here." [58] Prior to the Millennium Summit, Gorbachev scored one of his biggest coups to date, when, on June 27, 2000, he was given a place of honor between Cardinals Sodano and Silvestrini at a Vatican press conference in Rome. [59]

Gorbachev's admiring biographer, Gail Sheehy, tells us: "Lenin is in his blood, say Gorbachev's friends. And Lenin's doctrine of 'two steps forward, one step back' — or complete tactical flexibility — appealed particularly strongly to him." [60] Gorbachev is following precisely the Leninist dialectical line that was spelled out by Li Wei Han of the Central Committee of the Chinese Communist Party in 1959, in instructions sent to Fidel Castro's new Communist regime. According to Comrade Li:

> The line of action to follow against the Church is to instruct, to educate, to persuade, to convince, and, gradually, to awaken and fully develop the political conscience of Catholics by getting them to take part in study circles and political activities. By means of these activities, we must undertake the dialectical struggle *within* religion. *Gradually, we will replace the religious element with the Marxist element.* [61] [Emphasis added.]

Have the Communists forgotten or abandoned this lesson? They have never been *more* active or aggressive in promoting it! In fact, Comrade Li's 1959 instructions have been reprinted in books currently available in Communist bookstores. More importantly, it is a simple matter to observe them in action. These same instructions form the basis of the "Liberation Theology" revolution that was launched from Cuba into Latin America and North America in the 1960s and is operating throughout the world today. These instructions form the basis of the Soviet push (under Gorbachev) for development of the new "global spirituality."

While Christian leaders naively praise the new "openness" to religion in Communist countries, Leninists like Gorbachev know this is only a temporary, tactical "one step back." There is no question that the Leninists — with the aid of foolish Christians, as well as agents posing as Christians — are "[replacing] *the religious element with the Marxist element.*" Thus we have seen a host of books and articles promoting the diabolic dialectic theme of "Christian-Marxist Unity." One example of this, *Christian-*

Marxist Unity: A Miraculous, Explosive Prescription, the influential text by Raimundo Garcia Franco, tells us: "Yes, Christian faith and Marxism-Leninism do share almost complete overlapping of common objectives in the building of socialism. We cannot look backward, since the path ahead is that of creative transformation to communism and to the Kingdom of God on this earth." [62]

This is the same subversive dialectic that permeates Gorbachev's annual State of the World Forums [63] as well as all of the UN's "spiritual" confabulations. When the leaders of these events aren't *directly* "replacing the religious element with the Marxist element," they are fast at work replacing the Christian element with various pagan and New Age elements, which they recognize as far more flexible and conducive to their Marxist one-world schemes than what they scornfully denounce as "dogmatic," "rigid," and "sectarian."

Christianity's Epitaph?

Where is this leading? It is worthwhile noting what the militant paganists themselves say about this. In the Fall 1995 issue of the occult journal *Gnosis* we find a very sobering report entitled "State of the Hidden Arts: An Overview of Esotericism Today," which offers analyses by a variety of pagan activists. [64] Christopher Bamford, head of Lindisfarne Press, exults that the last 10 years "have seen a fundamental revision in our understanding of Christianity, not in essence, but in application.... [A] dead monolith has been demolished, and in its place we can sense the presence of a living being...." [65] The creation of a "living" Christianity, according to Bamford, reflects the growing influence in "mainstream" Christianity of such thinkers as theosophist Rudolf Steiner, occultist/psychologist Carl Jung, and Pierre Teilhard de Chardin.

Gnosis also trumpeted the exultant reports of Diane Conn Darling regarding the rise of neo-paganism, which is busy "building interfaith relations with mainstream religious groups." One major achievement in this effort, the not-so-darling Ms. Darling reported, occurred when "several major Neopagan groups were represented at the 1993 World Parliament of Religions in Chicago. Our presentations were heavily attended, including a beautiful Full Moon Circle celebrated in a nearby park.... Pagan priestess Deborah Light and the Fellowship of Isis (the world's largest Pagan organization) are signatories on our behalf to the Declaration of [a] Global Ethic...." [66] Darling glowingly remarked that "polytheism is nearly universal in neopaganism." As is pantheism. According to Ms. Darling: "Neopagans see the God/dess in all things: in each other, in persons following different paths, in animals, plants, planets, rivers, rocks, and in ourselves.... The Neopagan mythos gives rise to an ethos grounded in the Earth. Indeed, for a great many Neopagans, the Great Goddess *is* the living Earth herself." [67] (Emphasis in original.)

These denizens of darkness, when speaking amongst themselves, are jubilant because they are positive that they are riding a cosmic neopagan wave that will soon overwhelm what they see as a crumbling, dying Christianity.

Darkness Clothed in Light

Having closely followed the UN for more than two decades as a journalist and researcher, and having attended UN Summits from Rio to San Francisco to Rome to New York, it is clear to this writer that the neo-pagan one-worlders at the UN Tower of Babel are accelerating the tempo of their program of spiritual subversion, even as they become more swollen with arrogance. The Rio Earth Summit was a watershed event, very powerfully and publicly wedding the UN to the New Age, one-world, neo-pagan "worldview."

In his opening address to the UNCED (Earth Summit) plenary session, Maurice Strong directed the world's attention to the Declaration of the Sacred Earth Gathering, which was part of the pre-Summit ceremonies. "[T]he changes in behavior and direction called for here," said Strong, "must be rooted in our deepest spiritual, moral and ethical values." [68] According to the declaration, the ecological crisis "transcends all national, religious, cultural, social, political, and economic boundaries.... The responsibility of each human being today is to choose between the force of darkness and the force of light. We must therefore transform our attitudes and values, and adopt a renewed respect for the superior law of Divine Nature." [69]

However, in the twisted theosophic theology of Maurice Strong, Robert Muller, Sri Chinmoy, and other occultists who dominate the United Nations, "light" is darkness and "darkness" is light. Their "light" comes not from Jesus Christ ("I am the Light of the world," John 8:12), but from Lucifer, "the Light bearer." The Earth Summit was a non-stop orgy of pagan, Gaia-worshiping ceremonies, rituals, sermons, eulogies, declarations, manifestos, and celebrations. It not only marked the introduction of the radical NGO legions as an emerging superpower, but brought the occult nature of the UN out in the open.

Not *entirely* into the open, however. The controlled U.S. media never gave the American *public at large* an accurate view of this clamorous chorus. Most frequently, the media presented them as noble, if sometimes eccentric, idealists. The viewing and reading public had no way of knowing the extent and depth of the specifically and rabidly anti-American, anti-Christian animus of the vast majority of the official delegates and NGO radicals. Nor were they made aware of the overtly pagan and communistic emphasis of the entire Earth Summit program and the conventions, declarations, and treaties that came out of it.

American television viewers did not see the ubiquitous Communist flags, posters, and graffiti that festooned the NGO's Global Forum at Rio's Flamengo Park. Nor did they see the even more plentiful pagan, occult, and Wicca symbols, exhibits, seminars, and programs that could not be avoided at the Summit. They did not see the incredibly gross homosexual pornography display that was allowed to daily assault the eyes of thousands of Brazilian families who visited Flamengo Park. This Ford Foundation-funded [70] exhibit of life-size photographs would have been illegal in most cities in America, but it was a welcome addition at the UN celebration.

Quite the opposite of the image of peace, brotherhood, and tolerance presented by the U.S. media, the Earth Summiteers were almost universally venomous, foul, blasphemous, and profane in their constant verbal attacks on the United States, the middle class, capitalism, technology, Christianity, and Christian leaders, viciously attacking Dr. James Dobson, Rev. Jerry Falwell, and most especially Pope John Paul II. When Fidel Castro arrived at the Summit, however, the NGOs and official delegates alike erupted in ecstasy.

Since Rio, the NGOs have become more emboldened, aggressive, sophisticated, professionally organized, and lavishly funded. But it hasn't tempered their fury and ranting; in fact, they have gotten worse. Having sat amongst the NGO leaders and cadres in their strategy sessions, and having interviewed, dined with, and mingled with top UN officials and delegates at UN venues around the world, I cannot help but arrive at the conclusion that these "peace people," these "civil servants" and self-appointed representatives of "global civil society," are the most pathetic and concentrated collection of pompous, privileged, pampered, hateful, tyrannical, hypocritical, morally revolting specimens of humanity one is likely ever to encounter.

Even more outrageous than the behavior of these miscreants, however, are the arguments of elected American officials that we must continue participating in and supporting this dangerous charade. The UN is elevating, legitimizing, and popularizing all of the demonic influences that are pushing our civilization into the dark abyss. The Pratt House one-worlders and their Communist allies have energetically embraced the H. G. Wells prescription for sustaining their desired society. In their vision, the human community must be suitably subservient to the UN. Religions advocating loyalty to a higher authority must give way to a "new" mandated orthodoxy demanding that all worship the one-world socialist state. In the emerging new world order, the UN superstate will tolerate no other god before it.

The average American has become so inured to the neo-pagan influences that are saturating our culture that he is apt to simply shrug his shoulders at each new offense, and figure there is nothing that can be done. It's all just part of our inevitable, downward moral spiral, he sadly reasons. But there *is* something that can be done about this. The American taxpayers and voters have it within their power to change that. We will explain that in detail in our final chapter.

Chapter 13

The UN Declares Total War on the Family

Abolition of the family!.... Do you charge us with wanting to stop the exploitation of children by their parents? To this crime we plead guilty.[1]
— Karl Marx, *The Communist Manifesto*, 1848

The kindergarten or infant school has a significant part to play in a child's education. Not only can it correct many of the errors of home training, but it can prepare the child for membership ... in the world society.... As long as the child breathes the poisoned air of nationalism, education in world-mindedness can produce only rather precarious results. As we have pointed out, it is frequently the family that infects the child with extreme nationalism. The school should therefore use the means described earlier to combat family attitudes that favor jingoism.[2]
— United Nations Educational, Social, and Cultural Organization (UNESCO), 1949

The people who have taught us to believe whatever they were told by their parents or their teachers are the people who are the menace to the world.[3]
— Dr. G. Brock Chisholm, Director General of the UN's World Health Organization, speech of September 11, 1954

If we want to talk about equality of opportunity for children, then the fact that children are raised in families means there's no equality.... In order to raise children with equality, we must take them away from families and communally raise them. [4]

> — Dr. Mary Jo Bane,
> U.S. Department of Health and Human Services,
> Clinton administration

Every child is our child. [5]
> — motto of the United Nations Children's Fund
> (UNICEF)

One of the most terrifying features of totalitarian society is the control and brainwashing of children and youth by the Omnipotent State. The 20th century's experiments with such "education" must never be forgotten, for they produced monstrosities of unimaginable evil: the Hitler Youth; Mao's Red Guard; the Young Pioneers of Vladimir Lenin, Joseph Stalin, and Fidel Castro; and the cold-blooded murderous youth of the Cambodian Khmer Rouge.

Children were "transformed" through a "reshaping of consciousness." They were taught to publicly denounce (and even execute) their parents, to reject all tradition, to renounce their religion and embrace atheism (or, in the case of Nazi Germany, to embrace Hitler's Teutonic paganism), and to betray their countries.

Matt Cvetic, who for nine years was an undercover agent in the Communist Party USA for the FBI, attended a secret meeting of top-level Communists in 1948, at which a Soviet agent relayed a speech that Stalin had given directing the American Communists to put new emphasis on the recruitment of youth. Here is part of Stalin's speech:

> Comrades, Hitler gained control of the Youth in Germany before he was able to wage a successful Nazi Revolution in Germany. We Communists gained control of the Youth in Russia before we were able to wage a successful Communist Revolution in Russia, and Comrades, we must gain control of the Youth in the United States

if we are to wage a successful Communist Revolution in that nation. For this purpose, we are ordering our Comrades to set up a new Communist Youth group in the United States.[6]

As Cvetic pointed out, "Within a few short months after this meeting, more than 6,000 American students were recruited into this new Communist Youth movement known as the Labor Youth League."[7] This youth apparatus has gone through various structural and name changes over the years, but its purpose has remained unchanged. In 1983, it was reorganized and renamed the Young Communist League (YCL), the name under which it still operates.

However, the *primary* danger to American children and youth at that time emanated not from the YCL or other groups overtly associated with the Communist Party. Those efforts that were openly Communist only reached tens of thousands of young people. Far more dangerous were the pro-Communist, pro-UN, internationalist programs in our schools that were reaching *tens of millions* of students. Thanks to generous funding from the Carnegie Endowment, the Rockefeller and Ford Foundations, and the other Insider foundations, subversive textbooks and curriculum materials were flooding our schools. Thousands of teachers were being programmed at college to serve as "change agents." Change agents like Lydia Shchevchenko. In his memoirs, former Soviet dictator Nikita Khrushchev told of the lasting influence of this childhood teacher on his life:

I suppose you could say my political education began during my boyhood in the little village of Kalinovka where I was born. My schoolteacher there was a woman named Lydia Shchevchenko. She was a revolutionary. She was also an atheist. She instilled in me my first political consciousness and began to counteract the effects of my strict religious upbringing. My mother was very religious, likewise her father — my grandfather.... When I think back to my childhood, I can remember vividly the saints on the icons against the wall of our wooden hut, their faces darkened by fumes from the oil lamps. I remember being taught to kneel and pray in front of the icons with the grown-ups in church. When we were taught to read, we read the scriptures. But Lydia Shchevchenko set me on a path which took me away from all that."[8]

Where did that path lead? Nikita Khrushchev's subsequent career was detailed in a seven-part study, *The Crimes of Khrushchev*, published by a congressional committee in 1959.[9] During Stalin's bloody purges, the report notes, Khrushchev, "as the Number 1 Communist official in the Moscow area ... sent thousands to their death, scores of thousands to hideous slave-labor camps."[10] When Stalin was ready to launch his planned genocide of the people of the Ukraine, Khrushchev "was sent in 1937 as Stalin's trusted killer.... When his two-year Ukrainian purge was over, an estimated 400,000 had been killed and terror gripped the whole population."[11] Later, he added to his infamy, gaining the title of "the Butcher of Budapest" for his ruthless subjugation of Hungary.[12]

State-of-Mind Marxists

How many would-be and wanna-be Khrushchevs have been cre-ated by Lydia Shchevchenko's myriad counterparts in America? The thought is frightening; the number is certainly far greater than most Americans would ever imagine. Khrushchev was born in 1894 and the time period of his revolutionary formation referred to above was probably around 1900–1910, before the Czar was overthrown and Lenin came to power. Khrushchev did not say whether Lydia was actually a member of one of the Communist organizations in Czarist Russia.

The important point is that it is not necessary for someone like Lydia to be an actual disciplined Party member in order to be an effective "change agent" in carrying forward the Communist rev-olution. As Lenin said, "We must build Communism with non-Communist hands."[13]

Lydia Shchevchenko was, at the very least, a "state-of-mind Marxist." She had consciously rejected God and country, embraced the "revolutionary faith," and dedicated herself to its propagation. Like Lydia, there are many thousands of American educators who have imbibed of the "revolutionary faith," and, to varying degrees, have adopted and propagated its tenets. Many are "state-of-mind Marxists" without even knowing it. Some of these consider themselves Democrats, Republicans, liberals, or even conservatives and libertarians, but they are transmitting the Marxist contagion nonetheless. They are greatly assisted in this subversion, as we shall see, by the major teachers unions, the CFR-dominated tax exempt foundations, and the various agencies of the United Nations.

Equally important to this subversion process is the massive disinformation and moral corrosion provided by the Insider-run mass media and pop culture, most especially the so-called "entertainment" aimed at youth. Over the past two generations, we have seen these educational and cultural elements carrying forward a massive, coordinated program of conquest through "a slow reshaping of consciousness," as prescribed by Italian Communist theorist Antonio Gramsci. [14]

"In a developed society, 'the passage to socialism' occurs neither by putsch nor by direct confrontation," Gramsci maintained, "but by the transformation of ideas, which is to say — a slow reshaping of consciousness." "And the stake of this war of positions is the culture, that is — the source of values and ideas," said Gramsci. *The seizure of political power is not possible until after the seizure of cultural power.*" [15] (Emphasis added.)*

Dumb Down, Bum Down, Numb Down, Scum Down
The Pratt House thought cartel has been doing all within its power to speed this "seizure of cultural power." Like their Fascist and Communist brethren, the CFR one-worlders realize full well that for their global totalitarian vision to succeed, they must

---

*For the most complete exposition of the Gramsci strategy for "the seizure of cultural power" in America, see the special "Gramsci issue" of *The New American*, "Prisoners of the Total State," July 5, 1999.

take control of the children and youth. For their New World Order to triumph they must have obedient, subservient masses — an unthinking, goose-stepping *lumpen proletariat*. In order to achieve this goal they know they must destroy, or "*de*construct," what they refer to as "mass thought patterns" and "consciousness" — most especially in children and youth — so they can "reconstruct" and "reshape" the thought patterns and consciousness according to their own designs.

Through their dominant influence in education, the mass media, and the centers and instruments that produce our popular culture, the Insiders' change agents are aggressively pursuing this destruction-deconstruction/reshaping-reconstruction process. This process contains several components, which we refer to as the dumbing down, bumming down, numbing down, and scumming down of American society and culture.

The dumbing down of America has been the subject of intense concern and great debate for several decades. The alarming 1983 report *A Nation At Risk*, by the National Commission on Excellence in Education, warned that "the educational foundations of our society are presently being eroded by a rising tide of mediocrity that threatens our very future as a nation and a people." [16] That report and dozens of others before and since have cataloged the grim results of this dumbing-down process: widespread illiteracy, high student dropout rates, continuous decline in scores in all areas of academic achievement, the plummeting of the U.S. to last or near-last place on test scores, etc.

These results should not surprise: Traditional academic core subjects have been replaced with "politically correct," multi-cultural programming; phonics instruction has been supplanted by various look-say, whole-word "reading" programs; and evolutionary dogma, sex education, and enviro-Leninist propaganda have replaced real science.*

The bumming down of America is proceeding on many fronts, but the attack through the schools is especially pernicious. The public (i.e., government) schools have trained several generations of children to look to Big Brother in Washington for the "solution" to every problem, whether real or contrived. Responsibility, initiative, pride of workmanship, self-sufficiency, and independence are being replaced by the irresponsibility, sloth, slovenliness, and dependence of the welfare state. The government schools are being transformed into socialist cradle-to-grave, womb-to-tomb "community centers" that also serve as daycare centers, medical clinics, senior citizen centers, and providers of "lifelong learning" for adult education.

The numbing down and scumming down of America, likewise, are proceeding on many fronts, the educational system working in tandem with the CFR-controlled mass media and the "entertainment" industry to destroy every vestige of decency, honor, and virtue. Since fomenting the social upheavals of the 1960s, these same forces have been accelerating their attack, promoting alienation, rebellion, cynicism, hedonism, promiscuity, paganism, and false idealism. They are pressing on to destroy the residual Christian culture of America and the values system it upholds in order to clear the way for their planned "reshaping" process.**

Attack From Within
The aforementioned study *A Nation At Risk* ominously noted: "If an unfriendly foreign power had attempted to impose on America the mediocre educational performance that exists today, we might well have viewed it as an act of war. As it stands we have allowed this to happen to ourselves.... We have, in effect, been

---

*For one of the most informative exposés of this scheme to intellectually cripple and subvert American children and youth, see: *The Deliberate Dumbing Down of America* by Charlotte Iserbyt (Ravenna, Ohio: Conscience Press, 1999). This 750-page, telephone book-size opus is a masterpiece of research and educational detective work by one of America's top education experts. Other important works along these lines are *Educating for the New World Order* by Beverly K. Eakman (Portland, Ore.: Halcyon House, 1991) and *America 2000 / Goals 2000 — Moving the Nation Educationally to a "New World Order,"* compiled and edited by James R. Patrick (Moline, Ill.: Citizens for Academic Excellence, 1994). *Deliberate Dumbing Down* is available from American Opinion Book Services, P.O. Box 8040, Appleton, WI 54912.

committing an act of unthinking, unilateral, educational disarmament." [17]

The statement is both true and false at the same time. While it is true that no foreign nation has "imposed" (in the military sense, that is) our educational disaster upon us, it is not altogether true that we have "done this to ourselves." A close examination of the subversive educational "reforms" of decades past that produced our present catastrophe shows that the individuals and organizations most responsible do indeed constitute a power "foreign" to — and militantly hostile to — our constitutional and spiritual heritage. And they have indeed been carrying out unrelenting, total warfare against American society.

Integral to this total war is the rooting out of individualism and all loyalties that compete with supreme loyalty to the omniscient, omnipotent, omni-beneficent state — in this case, the world state. Thus the traditional family is viewed by these aspiring global overlords not just as a competitor, but as a mortal enemy. Philosophers as varied as Aristotle, Cicero, John Locke, and G.K. Chesterton have noted that the family is ordained by God and Nature to raise and educate children. That truth is plainly obvious. But the one-worlders will have none of that. The parents and the family must be supplanted by agents of the global state: the school and other social agencies.

This is basic Tyranny 101; it follows the statist, textbook dogmas of Rousseau, Marx, Lenin, Hitler, Stalin, Mao, and others of their totalitarian ilk throughout history. The Hitlerian UNESCO

**Some of the most important works exposing this war on America's moral foundations are: Judith A. Reisman, *Kinsey: Crimes and Consequences* (Arlington, Va.: Institute for Media Education, 1998); Samuel Blumenfeld, *Is Public Education Necessary?* (Boise, Idaho: The Paradigm Co., 1991); Balint Vazsonyi, *America's Thirty Years War* (Washington, D.C.: Regnery Publishing, 1998); Berit Kjos, *Brave New Schools* (Eugene, Ore.: Harvest House Publishers, 1995); Barbara Morris, *The Great American Con Game* (Escondido, Cal.: Image FX, 1997); Paul C. Vitz, *Faith of the Fatherless: The Psychology of Atheism* (Dallas, Texas: Spence Publishing Company, 1999); Brenda Scott, *Children No More* (Lafayette, La.: Huntington House Publishers, 1995); and Claire Chambers, *The SIECUS Circle: A Humanist Revolution* (Belmont, Mass.: Western Islands, 1977).

screed quoted at the head of this chapter, charging the family with "infecting" the child with bad attitudes, is taken from a UNESCO program for teachers, published in 1949 under the heading *Towards World Understanding*. In this 10-part series, UNESCO (United Nations Educational, Scientific and Cultural Organization) complained that "before the child enters school his mind has already been profoundly marked, and often injuriously, by early influences" — most particularly by parents, of course, who are deemed hopelessly ignorant and insufficiently "world-minded." [18] Parents are seen by UNESCO as retrograde influences who tend to teach their children love for God and country, which UNESCO condemned as "infecting" the minds of children with "nationalism," "chauvinism," and "sclerosis of the mind." [19]

This pernicious one-world, anti-parent, anti-family, anti-patriotism sentiment was already being spread through the schools many years earlier by the radical National Education Association (NEA), the nation's largest teachers union. When the United Nations was created, the NEA became (and remains) one of its biggest promoters. [20]

For the NEA, the United Nations became the hope of the world. In January 1946, Joy Elmer Morgan wrote in the NEA *Journal*:

> In the struggle to establish an adequate world government, the teacher has many parts to play. He must begin with his own attitude and knowledge and purpose. He can do much to prepare the hearts and minds of children for global understanding and cooperation.... At the very top of all the agencies which will assure the coming of world government must stand the school, the teacher, and the organized profession. [21]

The NEA's ardor for the UN and a global school board has intensified over the years. In 1993, the militant teachers union took a major step in its push for one-worldism by launching Education International (EI), a worldwide federation of teachers unions. [22] Mary Hatwood Futrell, the NEA's radical-left former president, moved to Brussels, Belgium (headquarters for the European Union) to head EI's new global union operation.[23] Futrell, ever the darling of the CFR coterie, had proven her one-world bona fides by serving on many Carnegie panels and commissions and reliably promoting the big government, globalist line. The Insiders knew she could be entrusted with the task of spearheading this new global initiative.

Education International, which now claims 24 million members through its 304 affiliate organizations, serves as an important teachers auxiliary to the Socialist International, dependably supporting just about every socialist scheme imaginable. EI boasts of its "privileged" status with UNESCO: "At UNESCO, EI is one of 16 organisations worldwide holding the coveted status of *NGO in formal associate relations.*"[24] With Futrell holding the reins at EI, it is not surprising that the union behemoth follows the NEA lead, supporting every move to empower the UN, particularly in the area of education.

The NEA's 2000-2001 Resolutions include this paean to the UN:

> The National Education Association recognizes the interdependence of all people.... The Association urges all nations to develop treaties and disarmament agreements.... The Association further believes that the United Nations (UN) furthers world peace and promotes the rights of all people by preventing war, racism, and genocide.[25]

The NEA and EI support increased funding for the UN, increased authority for the World Court, creation of the International Criminal Court, ratification of most UN treaties, and expansion of UN power in virtually all areas.[26] The NEA-EI education mafia is tailor-made for the Insiders' one-world purposes. With tens of millions of dollars in dues forcibly taken from members' paychecks, the union is a cash cow for revolution. With tens of millions of teachers worldwide as members, it can exert enormous influence in classrooms, as well as local, state and national elections.[27]

The NEA one-world subversives also affect the classrooms and national and state education policy through think tanks like the National Training Laboratory (NTL) in Bethel, Maine. The NTL was set up by the NEA in the 1940s to reeducate teachers along politically correct lines. NTL says it works "to change teachers' inflexible patterns of thinking." [28] An NTL teachers manual says of children: "Although they appear to behave appropriately and seem normal by most cultural standards, they may actually be in need of mental health care in order to help them change, adapt, and conform to the planned society in which there will be no conflict of attitudes or beliefs." [29]

Another NEA-created and -supported think tank is the Association for Supervision and Curriculum Development (ASCD), one of the leading educational purveyors of "global think." At a 1985 international-curriculum symposium in Enschede, Netherlands, ASCD officials told participants of the need for a "world core curriculum" to meet the needs of our "increasingly global interdependency." [30] ASCD executive director Gordon Cawelti told symposium participants that the proposed world core curriculum would be based on UN guru Robert Muller's book *New Genesis: Shaping a Global Spirituality*.[31]

At the beginning of his *World Core Curriculum Manual* Muller states that "the underlying philosophy upon which [his] School is based will be found in the teaching set forth in the books of Alice A. Bailey by the Tibetan teacher Djwhal Khul..." and M. Morya.[32] This is quite an admission considering that Mrs. Bailey's exalted position in the occult theosophical firmament is second only to that of Theosophy founder and high priestess Madame Blavatsky. Bailey, who alleged that Khul and Morya communicated with her telepathically, was a rabid Luciferian and founded the Lucifer Publishing Company and the theosophical journal *Lucifer*.[33]

So we are not engaging in hyperbole at all when we refer to the Insiders' attack on families and children as devilish, demonic, diabolic, or satanic. The totalitarian threat to the family posed

271

by UNESCO, NEA, EI, NTL, ASCD, Carnegie, et al., is real and is thoroughly evil. The threat presents itself in three significant ways:

- **The Rule of Law.** The militant shock troops first lobby for ratification of UN treaties, such as the Convention on the Rights of the Child. Once ratified (or even before ratification), they fraudulently assign these treaties the exalted status of "international law," which, they assert, overrides all federal, state, and local authority. In order to show our respect for the "rule of law," they and their prostitute "legal scholars" say, we must "harmonize" our laws and policies with those of the "international community." They know that most local officials, school board members, state legislators, and congressmen are unfamiliar with, and unable to muster an effective defense against, the supposed authority of "international law." Thus the UN treaties provide the homegrown revolutionaries with the weapons to undermine our laws and transform our government and institutions into subservient instruments of the UN to enforce global political correctness.

- **The Global School Board.** Through UNESCO, NEA, EI, and hundreds of other organizations and think tanks, the global structure bureaucracy is already being established for a worldwide socialist system that is intended to provide school teachers with indoctrination and certification, schools with accreditation, and students with the subversive materials and programs they "need" for graduation.

- **The New Faith.** In our "interdependent" world, the UN provides the new focal point to teach children about our global "oneness." Loyalty will be transferred from the family to the state and from the nation to the UN. Children will be (or are already being) taught to be "citizens of the world." They are being programmed to reject "narrow," "divisive," "bigoted," "dogmatic" Christianity and to adopt pagan and occult beliefs.

UNESCO Subversion

In the early 1950s, as the UNESCO programs began working their way into school textbooks and curricula, and as the truly subversive nature of the programs became known, a significant number of parents and educators became alarmed. They prevailed upon elected officials, who began to challenge and condemn the UN's perfidious insinuation of collectivist propaganda into the schools.

In 1953, Senator William Jenner (R-Ind.), the courageous chairman of the Senate Internal Security Subcommittee, attacked the UNESCO subversion head-on, challenging his Senate colleagues in these words:

> How many of you Senators know what the UN is doing to change the teaching of the children in your own home town? The UN is at work there, every day and night, changing the teachers, changing the teaching materials, changing the very words and tones — changing all the essential ideas which we imagine our schools are teaching to our young folks.
>
> How in the name of Heaven are we to sit here, approve these programs, appropriate our own people's money — for such outrageous "orientation" of our own children, and of the men and women who teach our children, in this nation's schools?[34]

Some of the one-worlders were audacious and zealous enough candidly to admit the subversive agenda of UNESCO, though they praised it as a necessary and righteous subversion. Such, for instance, was the case at the *Saturday Review*, which, in 1952, published a wildly pro-UNESCO editorial which declared:

> If UNESCO is attacked on the grounds that it is helping to prepare the world's peoples for world government, then it is an error to burst forth with apologetic statements and denials. Let us face it: the job of UNESCO is to help create and promote the elements of world citizenship. When faced with such a "charge," let us by all means affirm it from the housetops.[35]

More astute Insiders realized, however, that the time was not yet ripe for open confrontation on such fundamental and emotionally charged issues. The wiser course was to ease up and drop back for awhile, and cloak their true aims in more noble-sounding and less threatening verbiage about "world peace," "collective security," "ending world hunger," etc. Which is what they did.

Now, however, after decades of softening up the American public with one-world propaganda, calculatedly undermining our morality and religious fervor with carnal and irreligious "entertainment," and destroying patriarchal authority and responsibility and family ties through welfare statism, the totalitarian internationalists are pressing forward with fresh audacity.

They are rapturously pushing on toward the dystopic vision of the developing cradle-to-grave socialist world state outlined years ago by UNESCO director-general Julian Huxley. In 1947, Huxley announced that UNESCO would be exploring "the application of psycho-analysis and other schools of 'deep' psychology to education." [36] The use of such techniques to cultivate a sense of world citizenship, said Huxley, "would mean an extension of education backwards from the nursery school to the nursery itself." [37]

This Huxleyite conception of lifelong, womb-to-tomb, UN-driven indoctrination (and re-indoctrination, repeated as often as the UN mandarins deem necessary) has been integral to the UNESCO drive over the decades. It has come frighteningly close to fruition in many current UN programs, declarations and proposals, such as the UN's Millennium Forum Declaration of May 2000, which states that "education will be universal and lifelong, and will nurture a sense of world citizenship." [38]

"The Rights of the Child"
In 1989, the UN General Assembly adopted the United Nations Convention on the Rights of the Child (CROC), which, shorn of its pretended concerns for the welfare of children, is a blatant statist attack on the family and parental authority and respon-

sibility. It proposes a massive intrusion of government into family matters. Implementation of the CROC would radically alter the parent-child relationship, interjecting government-appointed "child advocates" between parents and children. Ultimately, it aims at stripping parents of their traditionally recognized rights to control the upbringing and education of their children and to pass on to their children their religious values and beliefs. If the people of the United States allow the conspirators in our government to subject us to the supposed authority of the CROC, we will soon see UN-approved government child "experts" assuming complete control over our children and parental rights completely destroyed.*

In March 1990, representatives from more than 150 countries met in Jomtien, Thailand, for a five-day World Conference on Education for All (WCEFA).[39] Official sponsors of this Insider-run event included UNESCO, UNICEF, UNDP (United Nations Development Program), the World Bank, other UN agencies, and one-world NGOs. Out of this major agenda-setting palaver came two documents: The World Declaration on Education for All, and The Framework for Action to Meet Basic Learning Needs.[40] The Framework set forth six education goals, which just happened to be virtually identical to the controversial Outcome-Based Education (OBE) program set out by then-President George Bush (CFR) in his "America 2000" education plan.[41]

In order to facilitate coordination of U.S. OBE policies with those of the UN globocrats, a U.S. Coalition for Education for All (USCEFA) was launched at a meeting held on October 30-November 1, 1991 in Alexandria, Virginia.[42] Gathering under the banner of "Learning for All: Bridging Domestic and

---

*For a more detailed analysis of the dangers posed to families, parents, and children by the CROC and other related UN schemes, see: this author's book, *Global Tyranny*, Chapter 8; William Norman Grigg, *Freedom on the Altar: The UN's Crusade Against God and Family*; and the following articles posted on our Internet website: "Your Child, the Global Citizen," July 21, 1997; "A Higher Warfare," April 17, 1995; and "UN Takeover of the Child," August 8, 1994. For a complete text of the UNCROC, see www.unicef.org/crc/crc.htm.

International Education" were movers and shakers from the government and private sector. Conference cosponsors included Apple Computer, IBM, the National School Board Association, the American Federation of Teachers, the National Education Association, the U.S. Department of Education, the College Board, USAID — and the usual tax-exempt foundations.[43] Heading up the USCEFA as president was Janet Whitla, director of the Education Development Center, Inc., infamous for its pro-homosexual, pornographic, promiscuity-promoting sex education programs and globalist curricula.[44] The Coalition is pushing to make UNESCO the global school board which will dictate educational policy for the world.

For the past decade, unbeknownst to American parents, the Convention on the Rights of the Child has been in the process of implementation through the USCEFA programs. One indication of the frightening progress of this subversion is the increasing acceptance, especially in political and academic circles, of totalitarian sentiments. Among those promoting dangerous new state authority, we point to Professor Jack C. Westman of the University of Wisconsin-Madison, Professor David Lykken of the University of Minnesota, and Connecticut Superior Court Judge Charles D. Gill, a co-founder of the National Task Force for Children's Constitutional Rights (NTFCCR). Dr. Westman, Dr. Lykken, and Judge Gill are leaders in the despotic drive to mandate government licensing of all parents.

"The United Nations Convention [on the Rights of the Child] clearly declares that the state has a role in child-rearing," says Dr. Westman, approvingly. "Because the consent of children is not required for the exercise of parental power, it is in the privacy of their homes that their civil rights are least assured."[45]

In a 1991 law journal article, Judge Gill wrote: "The [UN] Convention makes a total break from previous approaches to children's rights. Previous 'rights' were paternalistic, whereas the Convention makes the state directly responsible to the child."[46] Westman, Lykken, Gill, et al., view the family and parents with outright hostility, while idolizing the state and its supposed capacity to raise better children.

These extreme, totalitarian sentiments have been made "respectable" in influential circles thanks to help from the Pratt House one-world elites. These statist nostrums have moved from the stage of advocacy by socialist fringe groups to acceptance by "mainstream" Democrat and Republican politicians. The forces pushing this agenda have enormous financial resources at their disposal, and they are geared up for major, continuous, offensive action. If they are not aggressively exposed and opposed by a significant, growing, and increasingly determined constituency of parents, grandparents, and concerned citizens, an American version of the Hitler Youth or Red Guard — under the rubric of national service, of course — will not be long in coming.

That is a terrifying prospect, but even that does not begin to depict the full extent of the anti-family agenda the Insiders and their UN lackeys envision for their global police state. Space permitting, we would detail the UN programs for global:

- Forced abortion;[47]
- Proliferation of chemical abortions (RU486);[48]
- Coercive population control and eugenics programs;[49]
- Forced mass population relocation;
- Mandatory school "sexual orientation" programs promoting homosexuality;
- Outlawing of independent home schooling and independent private and religious schools;
- Euthanasia and assisted suicide.

The piecemeal Marxist abolition of the family is a fact, and the UN is the instrument through which the one-world Insiders intend to carry out their abolition program worldwide.

Chapter 14

What Must Be Done

When bad men combine, the good must associate; else they will fall one by one, an unpitied sacrifice in a contemptible struggle. [1]

— Edmund Burke (April 23, 1770)

[I]t does not require a majority to prevail, but rather an irate, tireless minority keen to set brush fires in people's minds. [2]

— Samuel Adams

If we wish to be free ... we must fight! I repeat it, sir, we must fight!! [3]

— Patrick Henry (March 23, 1775)

In the preceding chapters, we have painted, we admit, a very alarming picture of reality. It was entirely our intent to do so. We believe, like Founding Father James Madison, that it is proper and prudent to sound the alarm, wake the town, and tell the people when danger is threatening. In fact, it would be immoral *not* to warn others about an imminent peril. Madison wisely advised, as we have noted previously:

[I]t is proper to take alarm at the first experiment on our liberties. We hold this prudent jealousy to be the first duty of citizens and one of [the] noblest characteristics of the late Revolution. The freemen of America did not wait till usurped power had strengthened itself by exercise and entangled the question in precedents. They saw all the consequences in the principle, and they avoided the consequences by denying the principle. We revere this lesson too much, soon to forget it. [4]

Tragically, most Americans *have* forgotten this important lesson. We are long past "the first experiment on our liberties." We are rushing headlong to destruction, tyranny, and slavery.

Some will say that our concerns are wildly exaggerated, that the UN, while often obnoxious and corrupt, is toothless and can present no real danger to the mighty United States. And besides, they will aver, it still represents mankind's noblest aspirations for peace. We can *reform* it and use it to good purpose. We can *trust* our president and Congress to watch out for our interests.

Others will react in the opposite direction, asserting that the Insiders' new world order and their plans to empower the UN have proceeded too far to be stopped now. The enemy is too rich and powerful, too well organized and deeply entrenched. Resistance is futile; we have already lost.

Both of these attitudes — blind, senseless optimism and hopeless defeatism — should be equally repugnant to free peoples. We assure you there is nothing exaggerated about the dire threat posed by the UN in anything we have written. But it is not necessary for anyone to rely on our word. We have quoted extensively from UN and U.S. documents and copiously cited the statements of many of the key players in this drama. We have gone to considerable lengths to make many documents available on our Internet website and to provide links to many other primary sources. Any person of ordinary intelligence, with an open, honest mind, can read the literature and compare it with readily verifiable facts concerning the rapidly growing "empowerment" of the UN in all of the areas we have discussed.

Let us take a lesson from the patriots who founded our nation. In the summer of 1775, these courageous souls faced a situation not dissimilar from our own. Some argued that, in spite of the Crown's tyrannical acts, things were not all that bad and that the prudent course was to continue entreating England for fairness and justice. Others warned that it would be futile and foolhardy to dare to challenge the British military might.

In his famous oration at St. John's Church, Patrick Henry addressed the faulty arguments of both the Panglossian optimists and the defeatists. He eloquently and forcefully expressed the position that full and complete information, even though unpleasant, was the necessary basis for a proper decision:

> [I]t is natural for a man to indulge in the illusions of hope. We are apt to shut our eyes against a painful truth — and listen to the song of that siren till she transforms us into beasts. Is this the part of wise men, engaged in a great and arduous struggle for liberty? Are we disposed to be of the number of those who, having eyes, see not, and having ears, hear not, the things which so nearly concern their temporal salvation? For my part, whatever anguish of spirit it might cost, I am willing to know the whole truth; to know the worst and to provide for it.[5]

Mr. Henry then spoke words that are as relevant today (if not more so) as they were in that desperate time:

> They tell us, sir, that we are weak — unable to cope with so formidable an adversary. But when shall we be stronger? Will it be the next week, or the next year? Will it be when we are totally disarmed, and when a British [or a UN] guard shall be stationed in every house? Shall we gather strength by irresolution and inaction? Shall we acquire the means of effectual resistance by lying supinely on our backs, and hugging the delusive phantom of hope, until our enemies shall have bound us hand and foot? Sir, we are not weak, if we make a proper use of those means which the God of nature hath placed in our power. Three millions of people, armed in the holy cause of liberty, and in such a country as that which we possess, are invincible by any force which our enemy can send against us. Besides, sir, we shall not fight our battles alone. There is a just God who presides over the destinies of nations, and who will raise up friends to fight our battles for us. The battle, sir, is not to the strong alone; it is to the vigilant, the active, the brave. Besides, sir, we have no election. If we were base enough to desire it, it is now too late to retire from the contest. There is no retreat, but in submission and slavery! Our chains are forged, their clanking may be heard on the plains of Boston!...

Is life so dear, or peace so sweet, as to be purchased at the price of chains and slavery? Forbid it, Almighty God! I know not what course others may take; but as for me, give me liberty or give me death![6]

The submission and slavery the American colonists faced was a very real and dire prospect, but was nothing compared to that which we will face under a fully empowered UN. The British government was autocratic, abusive, even tyrannical at times, but not outright *totalitarian*. The organized one-worlders, however, intend to transform the UN into the global governing instrument of their ruthless, totalitarian "New World Order."

Projecting the Lines

Let us summarize the case we have made and, from what is already known, project the lines concerning what we can expect in the future — if, that is, by "irresolution and inaction" we allow the Insiders' plans for the UN to come to fruition. Those plans include:

- Creating a United Nations Military, with army, navy, air force, and nuclear weapons.
- Dispatching U.S. military personnel on ever-increasing UN missions throughout the world.
- Gradually disarming all nation states, including the U.S., so that the UN military forces will be unchallengeable.
- Establishing the International Criminal Court and rapidly expanding its jurisdiction.
- Establishing a global UN police force and bringing all local police under its control.
- Outlawing private ownership of firearms and disarming citizens.
- Imposing global draconian regulations on all human activity under the pretext of protecting the environment.
- Drastically restricting and, ultimately, destroying property rights.

- Forcing vast relocations of human populations in order to create "Wildlands" for UN-designated animal species.
- Imposing global "carbon taxes" on all fuels, a "Tobin tax" on financial transactions, and myriad other tax proposals.
- Placing a vast regulatory regime on all labor, business, and employment policies.
- Imposing population controls, including mandatory abortion *à la* Red China's UN-approved-and-funded "one child policy."
- Accelerating UN subversion in our schools and bringing all education under the jurisdiction of UNESCO.
- Subjecting all parents to licensing and claiming UN "protective" authority over all children.
- Striking down all laws against homosexuality and pedophilia/pederasty.
- Greatly expanding the practice of euthanasia and assisted suicide.
- Promoting paganism, "New Age" spirituality, the occult, and Satanism under the guise of promoting peace, brotherhood, and a "Global Ethic."

The list above is far from exhaustive. Anyone willing to study the facts will be able to readily verify that the Pratt House mafia promoting the UN is pushing for all of these insidious programs and more. All of these incredible grabs for power are, in fact, already in various stages of implementation.

So what will be the consequences of inaction? What will an all-powerful UN government mean to life as Americans know it? Isn't it possible that our would-be slavemasters will be more benevolent than old-style Communist dictators? Surely *American* leaders would not want to preside over bloodletting, torture, and genocide.

That is a dangerous assumption. First of all, while many of the Insiders of this one-world cabal are American citizens, they are not *Americans*; they are internationalists, with loyalties to no country. Many of them hold, or have held, public office and have sworn to uphold and defend the Constitution — while doing everything in their power to subvert and destroy it. Secondly, while no one can predict with absolute certainty what others would do given the power and opportunity, nonetheless there are compelling principles we dare not ignore. Let's look first at the lessons of history regarding the consequences of power.

We have previously invoked Lord Acton's famous maxim, "Power tends to corrupt and absolute power corrupts absolutely." [7] This principle was accepted as an undisputed truism by the American Founding Fathers. They were so firmly convinced that the best of men, regardless of character and intentions, could not be trusted with unrestrained power that they designed our government to thwart the ambitions of men. Thomas Jefferson expressed it this way: "In questions of power, then, let no more be heard of confidence in man, but bind him down from mischief by the chains of the Constitution." [8]

The situation is even worse when the system encourages the worst of men to gravitate to the top as happened so often in so many nations in the last century. Then we are no longer talking about "mischief" with our liberties. Our lives, the lives of our families and neighbors, and the lives of billions of others are at stake.

John Locke warned centuries ago that "he that thinks absolute power purifies men's blood, and corrects the baseness of human nature, need read but the history of this, or any other age, to be convinced of the contrary." [9] The history of the spectacularly bloody 20th century offers a definitive rebuke to those who believe that a world government would be a blessing.

In his important book *Death by Government*, Professor R. J. Rummel documents that the case for global government rests entirely upon an essentially superstitious belief in the benevolence of government as an institution. [10]

Rummel, a professor of political science at the University of Hawaii, is perhaps the world's foremost authority on the phenomenon of "democide" — the systematic murder of human beings by governments. "Democide is committed by absolute Power; its agency is government," Rummel declares, and the death toll of democide is nearly incomprehensible: "In total, during the first eighty-eight years of this [20th] century, almost 170 million men, women, and children have been shot, beaten, tortured, knifed, burned, starved, frozen, crushed, or worked to death; buried alive, drowned, hung, bombed, or killed in any other of the myriad ways governments have inflicted death on unarmed, helpless citizens and foreigners. The dead could conceivably be nearly 360 million people." [11]

Although "the common and fundamental justification for government [is] that it exists to protect citizens against the anarchic jungle that would otherwise threaten their lives and property," in the era of the total state "government has been truly a cold-blooded mass murderer, a global plague of man's own making." The supposed "wisdom" of academic elites who depict government as a benign institution, says Rummel, ignores a "preeminent fact about government" — namely, "that some of them murder millions in cold blood. This is where absolute Power reigns." [12]

One of Professor Rummel's most important insights is that "peace" under a tyrannical government is actually more lethal than war. "Putting the human cost of war and democide together, Power has killed over 203 million people in this century," Rummel points out. [13] However, "even if all to be said about absolute and arbitrary Power was that it causes war and the attendant slaughter of the young and most capable ... this would be enough. But much worse [is the fact that] even without the excuse of combat, Power also massacres in cold blood those helpless people it controls — in fact, several times more of them." [14]

If this has been the record of death and desolation caused by the exercise of unrestrained power by totalitarian governments of nation-states, can we expect the horrors of unrestrained *world* government to be less? Remember, it is the same perpetrators of these unspeakable crimes (or their totalitarian successors) whom the one-world Insiders insist we must join in common cause for "peace." The "respectable" CFR elites have always been comfortable with mass-murdering thugs like Stalin, Mao, Tito, Castro, Sukarno, Nkrumah, Kenyatta, Lumumba, Ben Bella, Ceausescu, Aristide, Mandela, Arafat, et al.

As we have noted, David Rockefeller, one of the most powerful drivers of the Establishment agenda during the 20th century, has praised "the social experiment in China under Chairman Mao's leadership" as "one of the most important and successful in human history." [15] He made this incredible statement in spite of the well-known fact that Mao Tse-tung's "social experiment" had by that time (1973) cost the lives of as many as 64 million Chinese at the hands of their Communist masters!

Rockefeller and his fellow one-worlders share with "Mao the Master Butcher" the addictive lust for absolute power. Again, Patrick Henry has provided us the proper attitude toward a record of tyranny. He said, "I have but one lamp by which my feet are guided; and that is the lamp of experience. I know of no way of judging the future but by the past." "And judging by the past," he declared, "I wish to know what there has been in the conduct of the British ministry for the last ten years to justify those hopes with which gentlemen have been pleased to solace themselves ... ?" [16]

What has there been in the conduct of the CFR-UN cabal in the last *fifty* years to justify any hopes of benign intent on their part? Patrick Henry's exhortation is echoed today by the FBI's famous profiling pioneer John Douglas, who has written extensively on the criminal mind and obstacles to criminal rehabilitation. [17] From his extensive studies, Douglas maintains that the best predictor of human conduct is previous conduct. [18] While many violent criminals may perform well and give indications of rehabilitation under the restraints of prison, when they are released and confront the same opportunities and pressures that gave rise to their original offenses, they repeat their crimes. What would be the crimes of such men if they attained sufficient power that they did not have to fear being caught or brought to justice? That is the near reality we face today.

What could we expect from men with proven amoral character

who would gain unrestrained power and the opportunity to do evil? Moreover, can anyone imagine that a Hitler could, let alone would, turn his back on the evil forces that propelled him to power?

Some may seek comfort in the illusion that tyranny is strictly a foreign phenomenon — that domination and exploitation of one's fellow man are not in the heart of American leaders. After all, these men are cultured, genteel, and highly educated. They are some of the most famous political, business, and academic leaders. Some of them kiss babies, smile convincingly, and talk of God, patriotism, and family values. Some of them give millions of dollars to hospitals, schools, and charitable causes. They are courted and praised by the media and responsible, respectable members of society. *Surely* these eminent men are not capable of the criminal activities we suggest.

This naïveté and inability to judge by objective facts instead of deceptive appearances have always been the boon of criminals and the bane of their victims. Even the worst of criminals do not always openly display their wickedness. In fact, most of the time they disguise their evil beneath unctuous charm.

Adolf Hitler is universally recognized today as having been one of our planet's premier criminals. Yet, during his rise to power (and even after he attained power) prominent American and British "liberals" and Insiders were singing his praises.[19] They pointed to the schools, hospitals, roads, and social projects he had built, and they belittled or denied his well-known criminality and totalitarian aspirations. We all have seen innumerable documentaries in which Hitler is maniacally ranting to his Nazi hordes. However, he was very capable of presenting an entirely affable, congenial image as well, and was frequently filmed hugging children, petting dogs, visiting war veterans, or chatting amiably with foreign dignitaries.

Al Capone, perhaps America's most notorious criminal, likewise, knew how to turn on the charm at strategic moments and to posture as the champion of "the little guy." According to the *World Encyclopedia of Organized Crime*:

Capone was a murderous thug without remorse.... He was responsible for perhaps as many as one thousand or more murders, certainly hundreds. Worse, for a decade the city of Chicago embraced this bragging, boasting, strutting killer, its newspapers paying homage to him and quoting his every cretinous statement, its citizens — a goodly portion of the population — nodding tolerantly, if not approvingly, in his direction. [20]

With the fabulous wealth gained from his criminal enterprises, Capone bribed cops, judges, jurors, prosecutors, and reporters — and "gave generously to charity." Notes the *Encyclopedia*:

Capone spent money lavishly on himself and those about him, projecting the image of generosity, of a philanthropist to the common man. Old-timers in Chicago still pay his bloody memory offhand compliments about the so-called soup kitchens Capone established in Chicago during the Depression to feed the hungry, little realizing that the crime boss did this at the suggestion of attorneys attempting to improve his horrible reputation when he was being tried for income-tax evasion. [21]

Much of the public and many politicians were willfully blind, refusing to believe that Capone was in fact the evil crime lord his accusers made him out to be. Public officials, such as Chicago Mayor William Hale Thompson, Chicago Police Chief John Garrity, and Illinois Governor Len Small, who should have been protecting the public from the likes of Capone, were actually in league with the Capone mob. [22] So it was also with the crime bosses who followed after him.

Although now largely forgotten, during the 1970s and '80s Pablo Escobar Gaviria was one of the most feared organized crime bosses in the world. As head of Colombia's infamous Medellin drug cartel, he was also touted as one of the world's richest men. His thugs unleashed a reign of terror that included the assassination of dozens of judges, prosecutors, presidential candidates, governors, police officials, and journalists. Many more were bribed into complicity with his criminal operation. Yet he showered millions of dollars on churches, clinics, hospitals, and schools; provided college scholarships to many students; and funded many public works and charitable institutions.[23] Was this "bad guy" just misunderstood? Did he really have a heart of gold underneath a rough exterior? That's what his defenders claimed, including some members of the press. Of course that was a lie. Escobar was just doing what all smart bad guys do: buy protection in the form of public relations. He bought the loyalty of thousands of people, and was elected to the Colombian Congress, in spite of his murderous record.

The point is that hiding behind a patina of false respectability is standard modus operandi for "smart" criminals. If relatively uneducated street thugs like Capone, Escobar — and the infamous John Gotti, the "Teflon Don," as he was glamorized in the press — can figure this out, isn't it foolish to think that that lesson has escaped the notice of our fabulously wealthy Insiders with their Ivy League pedigrees and hordes of think-tank "experts" at their beck and call? Just because these "respectable" leaders do not pull the triggers does not absolve them from culpability anymore than a "respectable" Mafia boss is innocent of the killings perpetrated by his underlings.

With more space, we could credibly demonstrate that U.S. Insiders (direct forebears to the current new world order cabal) orchestrated the rise of Communism to a world power in the USSR and in China and supplied these criminal regimes with Western technology and the means for nuclear weapons.[24]

It is also true that they willingly sent U.S. sons to die in no-win wars to build their new world order. They betrayed friendly, anti-Communist allies into Communist tyranny. They used U.S. foreign aid to further communize and socialize nations under petty despots.[25] They supported brutal terrorist groups and Communist-directed wars of "national liberation."[26] They have facilitated the Communist drug offensive against the United States and frustrated all genuine efforts to expose and oppose it.[27] They have then turned around and offered dangerous, totalitarian proposals disguised as a "War on Drugs," but which, in reality, are aimed at making war on our freedoms. They have promoted the destruction of morality and the family. They have sought the destruction of private property and the middle class. They have worked to subvert the influence of monotheistic religions. They have encouraged teaching methods that promote illiteracy, conformity known as political correctness, and worship of the Almighty State as God.

These and a host of other crimes too numerous to mention should leave no doubt that top leaders of the Pratt House presidium are out to create the kind of absolutist, all-pervasive, mind- and soul-destroying, Big Brother dictatorship depicted with such horrifying force in George Orwell's *1984*.

In case your memory of that nightmarish world has dimmed since you read Orwell's classic in high school, it may help to recall commissar O'Brien's hideous colloquy with the tortured protagonist, Winston Smith. After delivering an excruciatingly painful electric shock to Smith, who is strapped to a bed, O'Brien casually explains:

> Obedience is not enough. Unless he is suffering, how can you be sure that he is obeying your will and not his own? Power is in inflicting pain and humiliation. Power is in tearing human minds to pieces and putting them together again in new shapes of your own choosing. Do you begin to see, then, what kind of world we are creating? It is the exact opposite of the stupid hedonistic Utopias that the old reformers imagined. A world of fear and treachery and torment, a world of trampling and being trampled upon, a world which will grow not less but *more* merciless as it refines itself. [Emphasis in original.] Progress in our world will be progress toward more pain. The old civilizations claimed that they were founded on love and justice. Ours is founded upon hatred. In our world there will be no emotions except fear, rage, triumph, and self-abasement. Everything else we shall destroy — everything. Already we are breaking down the habits of thought which have survived from before the Revolution. We have cut the links between child

and parent, and between man and man, and between man and woman. No one dares trust a wife or a child or a friend any longer. But in the future there will be no wives and no friends. Children will be taken from their mothers at birth, as one takes eggs from a hen.... There will be no loyalty, except loyalty toward the Party. There will be no love, except the love of Big Brother. There will be no laughter, except the laugh of triumph over a defeated enemy.[28]

The brutish O'Brien then matter-of-factly continued his explanation to the helpless and supine Winston Smith. "But always — do not forget this, Winston — always there will be the intoxication of power, constantly increasing and constantly growing subtler. Always, at every moment, there will be the thrill of victory, the sensation of trampling on an enemy who is helpless. If you want a picture of the future, imagine a boot stamping on a human face — forever."[29]

A Call to Action

A ruthless, tyrannical, Orwellian world state is *precisely* what the top Insiders plan to have. Like Orwell's O'Brien, they are intoxicated with power. They crave *absolute* power. And if they should ever attain it, we will experience a murderous "plague of power" such as this planet has not seen before. We will know democide on a scale not previously imagined.

The moral man who fully realizes the terrible consequences of allowing such a future to come to pass by default will be highly motivated to join the battle against the forces of evil and oppression. The moral person who understands what is at stake — for himself, his loved ones, and the incredible heritage of freedom with which we have been blessed — will be imbued with a high level of commitment to stopping these would-be tyrants.

But how does one go about such a daunting task? Those committed to this UN world-government goal enjoy, as we have shown, enormous influence and prominent positions throughout our institutions, especially in the media. They are able to create the appearance of universal support for their agenda. As the late

Admiral Chester Ward, a former longtime member of the Council on Foreign Relations, observed: "Once the ruling members of CFR have decided that the U.S. Government should adopt a particular policy, the very substantial research facilities of CFR are put to work to develop arguments, intellectual and emotional, to support the new policy, and to confound and discredit, intellectually and politically, any opposition." [30]

Clearly, anyone who dares to sound the alarm or question the globalist agenda invites well-orchestrated attacks and ridicule. In short, Americans face a very perilous situation: the major power centers and safeguards on which they depend to protect their interests have either been compromised or are secretly working to enslave us. With the major channels of communication in internationalist hands, alerting other Americans to this situation is a formidable challenge. Yet, as we shall see, the situation is not hopeless if a core of responsible Americans will organize and act in pursuit of a sound plan.

A Commensurate Response

What needs to be done commensurate with the seriousness of the danger? Our answer: *Enlist many more citizens to follow a sound program to get the United States out of the United Nations completely.*

With the UN as a foundation, the globalists are waging assaults on our sovereignty on an incredible number of fronts. And they have equally incredible resources at their disposal for doing so, including the support of now more than 1,000 NGOs lobbying for the UN agenda. We cannot expect to obtain the resources to defend against all of those attacks. Moreover, such a purely defensive strategy is always doomed to defeat. The only sensible strategy is to put the globalists' gains up for grabs by going after the *foundation* for their assaults — the United Nations itself.

"There are a thousand hacking at the branches of evil," said Henry David Thoreau, "to one who is striking at the root." [31] Rather than hacking at the ever-proliferating branches of the

UN program, we must concentrate our forces where it counts. We must wield a sharp axe to the root and trunk of the UN tree — by forcing the U.S. to withdraw from the UN. U.S. withdrawal before the UN acquires real, independent power would condemn the UN to the ash heap of history. Without U.S. support, the United Nations would share the same fate as its predecessor League of Nations. When the U.S. Senate wisely refused to have the U.S. join the League following World War I, the League soon faded into oblivion.

The UN is not the only program or assault on the U.S. system that has been mounted by the Establishment one-worlders. But it is a cornerstone of their plans — an investment of over five decades. As a mechanism to destroy our sovereignty, it threatens to take many other battles in resisting the collectivist assault out of the hands of Congress and the American people. Depriving the Conspiracy of its creation, the UN, is essential to the preservation of liberty and accomplishing this would be an incredible setback to the Insiders' plans.

Of course, we are not claiming that convincing Congress to take such a step will be easy. It will not be. We are not minimizing the difficulty in the least. But, with an effort commensurate to the danger, Congress *can* be persuaded. It will take enormous effort, planning, and organization by thousands of concerned citizens in order to overcome the momentum and influence that the many powerful proponents of the new world order have built through labor, subversion, and deceit. But just as America after Pearl Harbor had to work to catch up, we shouldn't expect to overcome a tough opponent who has the initiative with easy, half-way measures.

One very significant advantage we have on our side in this monumental effort is truth and the natural, God-given, human desire to be free. Another is the considerable freedoms and protections that still exist under what remains of our badly tattered constitutional system. There are many layers of strength not yet rotted and corrupted. One very important indication of that reality is the fact that the Insiders still must resort constantly to

293

massive lies and deception to sell their fraudulent, totalitarian programs. If the fight were already over, as the defeatists claim, our enemies would not be going to such lengths to deceive; they would be flying their colors openly.

But they *cannot* promote their agenda openly. As dumbed-down, numbed-down, bummed-down, and scummed-down as a growing segment of the American public is, there is still sufficient residual morality and intelligence to force the conspirators for world tyranny to cloak their schemes in noble-sounding rhetoric and extravagant charades. This means they must invest hundreds of times (even thousands of times) more in labor and resources to sell their lies than what it takes to offset their lies by promoting the truth.

The architects of the new world order have not yet been able to entirely erode the republican form of government that our Founding Fathers established and that has been passed on to us through the sacrifices of so many dedicated Americans who have gone before us. Concerned Americans just need to inform themselves and use the rights, freedoms, and blessings we enjoy in order to reverse our course.

Most Americans are not aware of what already has been accomplished in this struggle. In 1997, 54 representatives voted for the first measure ever to come before the full House calling for the termination of our membership in the United Nations. [32] Two years later, 74 representatives voted to kill all funding for the UN, which, if successful (218, a majority, would be required), would effectively stop our participation in this traitorous sham. [33] And blocking all funding is an easier legislative step than outright withdrawal, for the House alone can refuse to fund UN operations (whereas withdrawal would require Senate action, and the president would likely claim the constitutional power to veto such action).

Even though there is growing legislative support for withdrawal from the UN, at the moment there is not nearly enough support to accomplish the task. The involvement of concerned citizens who inform themselves and then inform others is the only route to generating sufficient political pressure that will force Congress to vote to terminate U.S. support for the UN. This informed pressure will be required to offset the enormous Establishment pressure that would be brought to bear to prevent Congress from taking such a step. Unfortunately, with so much at stake, it is not sufficient to sell politicians on the merits of our case. Instead, success will take clout. Realistically, most representatives will bow to pro-UN pressure until there is sufficient, well-informed outrage to force them to quit making excuses and act! The vast majority will not budge *until they see that they must* if they want to remain in office.

What we are talking about is a plan to rebuild a higher standard in Congress. The defense of freedom requires that principle must govern our affairs, else pragmatism, dictated by the Conspiracy for a global collectivist order, will destroy us. While we would like to see more statesmen gain office, this is only a small part of the solution. In today's climate even statesmen, who act on principle rather than political pragmatism, will require the support of an informed electorate if they hope to remain in office. And that same informed electorate is also the key to holding all politicians accountable for actions in defense of freedom. So the real challenge is building and leading that informed electorate.

Sound Organization Required
Building sufficient understanding in time will require organization under extremely tough, responsible, and knowledgeable leadership. Taking on the UN means taking on the power and influence of the Establishment, and in particular the Council on Foreign Relations (the UN's creator and sponsor) as well as all of the politicians and media moguls the CFR has in its pocket. This battle can't be carried through to success without leadership that understands the wiles of politicians and the pressures that the CFR can bring to bear.

For example, as public understanding grows that the UN is not our friend, inevitably new proposals to "reform" the UN will be offered — which politicians will be tempted to support. This is not only a bad idea, but also a dangerous trap. No reforms will change the nature of the beast. The UN was designed from the beginning to promote global tyranny. But politicians love to champion "compromise" because they see a chance to pacify uninformed constituents while not risking the wrath of the globalists. Which also means that freedom loses. These politicians love to posture with calls for "reform" in order to deflect mounting pressure that would force them to take real action with real political consequences. Unfortunately, many conservative groups that oppose *most* of the UN's agenda have already been co-opted to adopt the "reform the UN" agenda. That is a prescription for defeat.

To force serious political action (and keep politicians from wiggling, stalling, and doing nothing in the face of enormous pressure and deception from the Establishment) requires a well-informed, well-organized action group under sound leadership. And that's why we recommend The John Birch Society (JBS) as uniquely qualified to serve that role.

The JBS has a track record of over four decades of principled leadership, of taking tough stands including working to expose the influence of the Conspiracy we have been discussing in this book. For more than 40 years, it has been courageously fighting the good fight, blocking or slowing down many dangerous programs of that Conspiracy, and, most importantly, surviving the heat directed at anyone who takes the point in this fight.

And the Society has the plan and organization to get the job done. In countless battles great and small, in cities and rural areas, the challenge comes down to reaching enough Americans with the problem and a workable solution in time. This book is part of that plan. But success requires the wise and committed help of many more like yourself. We encourage readers to contact the Society for more information or the individual from whom the reader got this book.*

*The John Birch Society, P.O. Box 8040, Appleton, WI 54912. Phone: (800) JBS-USA1 [(800) 527-8721]. Or contact us through our website: www.jbs.org.

We also urge readers to get informed and to contact their congressman insisting that he support measures to *Get US out!* The name of the game is to be effective. Be firm, but don't insult or be strident. And most importantly, gain muscle by getting others to help. Membership in the Society helps enormously with that challenge.

The variety and extent of UN agencies and programs can be bewildering. When one first comes to understand the incredible organization the enemy has built to confuse, confound, and deceive Americans into giving up their inheritance of freedom, it is easy to become discouraged. But that reaction, if allowed to stand, only serves the enemy. One of the key strategies of this cabal is to create the "illusion" of overwhelming support — so that Americans see no leadership for sanity. The Establishment one-worlders want to demoralize good Americans so that they give up any idea of resistance. And so these conspirators fear — and try to capture, corrupt, discredit, or isolate — any leaders who would give Americans hope that there is resistance, that there is sound leadership to follow.

For more than four decades, members of The John Birch Society have been educating their fellow citizens concerning the dangers of the United Nations. Their work has been largely responsible for the disfavor that befell the UN for many years. It took major deception and planning by the new world order advocates, including new "threats" and the "collapse" of Communism, to dust off the UN and put their plans on a fast track. We now face the looming threat of world tyranny — a danger greater than our nation has faced at any previous time in its history. The danger is great because it is neither seen nor understood by most of our citizens. And so The John Birch Society has created a new drive to meet this challenge. We are all fueled by the urgency to capture the attention of our fellow citizens and finally put an end to the creature on the East River. We respectfully ask for your help. [34]

We are asking for your help in an epic educational battle. Thankfully, the primary challenge is not a military one. In fact, for today's problems a call to arms would only serve the cause of our enemy most powerfully and help him consolidate and acquire the unrestrained power he seeks.

Our enemy's success all stems from the ignorance, delusion, and lack of understanding of the American people. If good Americans gain a proper understanding of what is happening, our problems can be resolved within the institutions that George Washington and others fought to give us.

If the people don't gain the understanding to choose better leaders and hold their politicians accountable to the Constitution, they cannot expect to improve their government through revolution. In fact, just the opposite would happen. What is needed instead is to use the resources and the freedoms we have to inform our fellow citizens and put the government our Founding Fathers gave us back on track.

But for success in the educational battle ahead, we do need to find the same spirit of patriotism and determination that Patrick Henry captured so well in his previously mentioned "Give Me Liberty or Give Me Death" oration:

If we wish to be free — if we mean to preserve inviolate those inestimable privileges for which we have been so long contending — if we mean not basely to abandon the noble struggle in which we have been so long engaged, and which we have pledged ourselves never to abandon until the glorious object of our contest shall be obtained — we must fight! I repeat it, sir, we must fight!! An appeal to arms and to the God of Hosts is all that is left us!

...Is life so dear, or peace so sweet, as to be purchased at the price of chains and slavery? Forbid it, Almighty God! I know not what course others may take; but as for me, give me liberty or give me death! [35]

Notes

Prologue

1. Alfred Lord Tennyson, "Locksley Hall," *Poems* (Boston: W.D. Ticknor, 1842).
2. Thomas Molnar, *Utopia: The Perennial Heresy* (New York: Sheed and Ward, 1967), p. 215.
3. Attributed to George Washington by G. Edward Griffin, *The Fearful Master* (Appleton, Wis.: Western Islands, 1964), p. 196.
4. Robert Muller, *New Genesis: Shaping a Global Spirituality* (Garden City, N.Y.: Doubleday, 1984), pp. 27–28.
5. Ibid., pp. 28–29.
6. Ibid., pp. 29–30.
7. Ibid., p. 30.
8. Daniel Sitarz (ed.), *Agenda 21: The Earth Summit Strategy to Save Our Planet* (Boulder, Colo.: EarthPress, 1993), p. 6.
9. Robert Muller, *My Testament to the UN* (World Happiness and Cooperation, U.S.A., 1994), p. 172.
10. Muller, *New Genesis*, p. 30.
11. Molnar, p. 227.
12. Ibid.
13. Muller, *New Genesis*, p. 35.
14. Nesta H. Webster, *The French Revolution: A Study in Democracy*, Second Edition (Hawthorne, Calif.: Christian Book Club of America, 1969), p. 427. Note: Author used different translation for text.
15. R.J. Rummel, *Death by Government*, (New Brunswick, N.J.: Transaction Publishers, 1994), p. 5.
16. Ibid.
17. John Barron and Anthony Paul, *Murder of a Gentle Land*, (New York: Reader's Digest Press, Thomas Y. Crowell Co., 1977), p. 209.
18. Rummel, *Death by Government*, p. 3.
19. Ibid., p. 25.
20. Ibid., p. 27.
21. John Emerich Edward Dalberg-Acton (Lord Acton) (1834–1902), quoted in John Bartlett, *Familiar Quotations* 16th ed. (Boston: Little, Brown, and Company, 1992), p. 521.

Chapter 1 • The Threat

1. *The New Republic*, January 17, 2000.
2. Walter Cronkite's remarks in accepting the Norman Cousins Global Governance Award, October 19, 1999, as cited by John B. Anderson, "In Response to Senator Helms: Cronkite and Clinton make a strong case for recasting the United Nations as a world federation," The World Federalist Association advertisement in the *New York Times*, February 18, 2000. [Note: Source of quote in ad is ambiguous: Mr. Cronkite's acceptance remarks in 1999 or his 1996 autobiography, *A Reporter's Life*. We verified the former from a video of his remarks in 1999.]
3. *Cleveland Plain Dealer*, October 29, 1945, quoted in Frank Hughes, *Prejudice and the Press* (New York: Devin-Adair, 1950), p. 577.
4. Roy P. Basler (ed.), "Address Before Young Men's Lyceum of Springfield, Illinois, January 27, 1838," *The Collected Works of Abraham Lincoln*, Volume I, p. 109, per http//home.att.net/~rjnorton/Lincoln78.html on 3/29/01.
5. Kofi Annan, *We the Peoples: The Role of the United Nations in the 21st Century* (report from the September 2000 UN Millennium Summit).
6. World Federalist Association ad, *New York Times*, February 18, 2000.
7. Same as 2 above.
8. Bill Clinton, letter to World Federalist Association, June 22, 1993.
9. Strobe Talbott, "The Birth of the Global Nation," *Time*, July 20, 1992, p. 70.
10. Richard Falk and Andrew Strauss, "On the Creation of a Global Peoples Assembly," *Stanford Journal of*

International Law, Summer 2000, pp. 36:1, 36:3.

11. Richard Falk and Andrew Strauss, "Toward Global Parliament," *Foreign Affairs*, January/February 2001, pp. 212–220.

12. Robert Wright, "Continental Drift," *The New Republic*, January 17, 2000, p. 18.

13. Jim Leach, "A Republican Looks at Foreign Policy," *Foreign Affairs*, Summer 1992, pp. 11–31.

14. Henry Grunwald, "A World Without a Country?" *Wall Street Journal*, January 1, 1999, p. R44.

15. Lead editorial, "A Supply-Side Nobel," *Wall Street Journal*, October 14, 1999, p. A26.

16. Robert A. Mundell, "Mundell on Supply-Side Economics," *Wall Street Journal*, October 14, 1999, p. A26.

17. Rashmi Mayur, "World Government," *The War & Peace Digest*, March/April 2000, p. 1.

18. Sean Scully, "Armed Troops Sought for UN," *Washington Times*, June 1, 2000, as posted on Global Policy Forum – UN Security Council webpage: www.globalpolicy.org/security/peacekpg/reform/mcgovern.htm on 03/13/01.

19. Elizabeth Greathouse, "Justices See Joint Issues With the EU," *Washington Post*, July 9, 1998, p. A24.

20. Quoted by Paul Kurtz (International Academy of Humanism, USA) in "Humanist Manifesto 2000," *The War and Peace Digest*, March/April 2000, p. 4.

Chapter 2 • Disarmament and Submission

1. Lincoln P. Bloomfield, *A World Effectively Controlled By the United Nations* (Washington, D.C.: Institute for Defense Analyses, 1962), p. iv.

2. Ibid., pp. 23, 25.

3. *Freedom From War: The United States Program for General and Complete Disarmament in a Peaceful World*, (Washington, D.C.: Department of State Publication 7277, 1961), pp. 18–19.

4. Paul H. Nitze, op-ed: "A Threat Mostly to Ourselves," *New York Times*, October 28, 1999.

5. Charles P. Howland, *Survey of American Foreign Relations 1928*, (New Haven: For Council on Foreign Relations by Yale University Press, 1928), p. 237.

6. Bloomfield, p. iv.

7. Ibid.

8. Ibid., p. 1.

9. Ibid., p. 3.

10. Ibid., p. 23.

11. Ibid., p. 22.

12. *Freedom From War,* p. 18.

13. Ibid.

14. Ibid., pp. 18–19.

15. Lewis C. Henry (ed.), *Best Quotations for All Occasions* (Greenwich, Conn.: Fawcett Publications, 1964), p. 45.

16. U.S. Constitution, Article III, Section 3.

17. *Blueprint for the Peace Race: Outline of Basic Provisions of a Treaty on General and Complete Disarmament in a Peaceful World*, (United States Arms Control and Disarmament Agency Publication 4, General Series 3, Released May 1962), p. 33.

18. "Remarks by Mikhail Gorbachev on the Release of the Global Security Programme Findings on October 19, 1994 at the New York Council on Foreign Relations," *Global Security Programme: Final Report of the Global Security Project* (The Gorbachev Foundation/Moscow; The Gorbachev Foundation/USA; Rajiv Gandhi Foundation, October 1994), p. 3.

19. "Investigation of Un-American Activities in the United States," ("Hearings before a Special Committee on UN-American Activities, House of Representatives, Seventy-eighth Congress, First Session, on H. Res. 282") (Washington, D.C.: United States Government Printing Office, 1943), p. 3386; Frank A. Capell, "Alan M. Cranston," *The Review Of The News*, February 17, 1971; Gary Allen, "Alan Cranston: The Shadow In The Senate," *American Opinion*, June 1974, pp.

1–17.

20. *Global Security Programme*, p. 3.

21. Ibid., pp. 3, 15.

22. Ibid., pp. 17–20.

23. George Cothran, "One World, Under Gorby," *SF Weekly*, Vol. 14, No. 16, May 31–June 6, 1995, pp. 11–12.

24. *Our Global Neighborhood: The Report of the Commission on Global Governance* (Oxford: Oxford University Press, 1995).

25. Ibid., pp. 372, 374.

26. Frank L. Kluckhohn, *Lyndon's Legacy: A Candid Look at the President's Policymakers* (New York: Devin-Adair, 1964), pp. 194-195. See also: William J. Gill, *The Ordeal of Otto Otepka* (New Rochelle, N.Y.: Arlington House, 1969), especially Chapter XIV "Cleveland."

27. Francis X. Gannon, *Biographical Dictionary Of The Left, Consolidated Volume I* (Belmont, Mass.: Western Islands, 1969), p. 281.

28. "Institute of Pacific Relations," Report of the (Senate) Committee on the Judiciary, Eighty-Second Congress, Second Session, July 2 (legislative day June 27), 1952, p. 223.

29. Kluckhohn, pp. 197, 200–201; Gannon, p. 281. Regarding the "Operation Keelhaul" betrayal itself, see: Julius Epstein, *Operation Keelhaul: The Story of Forced Repatriation from 1944 to the Present* (Old Greenwich, Conn.: Devin-Adair, 1973); and Robert Welch, *The Politician* (Belmont, Mass.: Belmont Publishing Co., 1964).

30. Harlan Cleveland, *The Third Try at World Order: U.S. Policy for an Interdependent World* (New York: Aspen Institute for Humanistic Studies, 1976), p. 2.

31. Ibid., Chapter 2: "Nobody in Charge," pp. 5–9.

32. Harlan Cleveland, "The United Nations: Its Future is its Funding," *Futures*, March 1995, p. 109.

33. Ibid., p. 110.

34. Ibid., p. 111.

35. Ibid.

36. Ibid.

37. George H. W. Bush, "Presidential Address: Bush Announces War on Iraq, Assures 'We Will Not Fail,' " reported in *Congressional Quarterly*, January 19, 1991, p. 197.

38. "U.S. Participation in Military Operations, 1990-Present," a May 2000 report prepared for the Joint Chiefs of Staff by the General Accounting Office, quoted in William F. Jasper, "New World Army," *The New American*, July 3, 2000, p. 10.

39. Ibid.

40. Floyd Spence, "Chairman's Views...," *Military Readiness Review*, July 1999, p. 1.

41. Ibid., "The U.S. Air Force and Kosovo."

42. Ibid.

43. Sean Scully, "Armed Troops Sought for UN," *Washington Times*, June 1, 2000, as posted on Global Policy Forum – UN Security Council webpage: www.globalpolicy.org/security/peacekpg/reform/mcgovern.htm on 03/13/01.

44. Ibid.

45. Ibid.

Chapter 3 • The Secret Network of Power

1. Professor Arnold Toynbee in a June 1931 speech before the Institute for the Study of International Affairs in Copenhagen, quoted in Tony Pearce, "Is there really a New World Order?" posted on www.saltshakers.com/midnight/nwo.html.

2. "Revision of the United Nations Charter: Hearings before a Subcommittee of the Committee on Foreign Relatßions, United States Senate, Eighty-First Congress, Second Session, on Resolutions relative to revision of the United Nations Charter, Atlantic Union, World Federation, etc.," February 2, 3, 6, 8, 9, 13, 15, 17, and 20,1950, p. 494.

3. Carroll Quigley, *Tragedy and Hope: A History of the World in Our Time* (New York: Macmillan, 1966), p. 950.

4. George Cothran, "One World, Under Gorby," *SF Weekly*, Vol. 14, No. 16, May 31–June 6, 1995, pp. 11–12.

5. Lawrence Shoup and William Mintner, *Shaping a New World Order: The Council on Foreign Relations' Blueprint for World Hegemony*, excerpted from Holly Sklar (ed.), *Trilateralism* (South End Press, 1980), posted on www.thirdworldtraveler.com.

6. Robert W. Lee, *The United Nations Conspiracy* (Appleton, Wis.: Western Islands, 1981), p. 243.

7. William F. Jasper, *Global Tyranny ... Step By Step* (Appleton, Wis.: Western Islands, 1992), p. 68. (Reference: *Time* magazine, April 16, 1945).

8. Richard Rovere, "The American Establishment," *Esquire*, May 1962, p. 107.

9. Arthur M. Schlesinger, Jr., *A Thousand Days* (Boston: Houghton Mifflin, 1965), p. 128.

10. *Newsweek*, September 6, 1971, p. 74.

11. Lawrence Shoup and William Mintner, *Imperial Brain Trust: The Council on Foreign Relations and U.S. Foreign Policy* (New York: Monthly Review Press, 1977), p. 16.

12. Richard J. Barnet, *Roots of War* (New York: Atheneum, 1972), p. 46.

13. Barry M. Goldwater, *With No Apologies* (New York: William Morrow and Co., Inc., 1979), p. 279.

14. Richard Harwood, "Ruling Class Journalists," *Washington Post*, October 30, 1993, p. A21.

15. Ibid.

16. Ibid.

17. *Minute*, June 19, 1991 and *Lectures Francaises*, July/August 1991, quoted in *HduB Reports*, September 1991, p. 2.

18. Hilaire du Berrier, *HduB Reports*, September 1991, p. 2.

19. William F. Jasper, "Europe: Meeting Ground of East and West," *The New American*, February 24, 1992, pp. 19–25.

20. du Berrier, pp. 1–2.

21. Harwood, op. cit.

22. Quigley, p. 950.

23. Ibid., p. 324.

24. George J. A. O'Toole, *Honorable Treachery, A History of U.S. Intel-* *ligence, Espionage, and Covert Action from the American Revolution to the CIA* (New York: The Atlantic Monthly Press, 1991), p. 303.

25. Peter Grose, *Continuing the Inquiry: The Council on Foreign Relations from 1921 to 1996* (New York: Council on Foreign Relations Press, 1996); Quigley, *Tragedy and Hope*, pp. 950–952.

26. Quigley, p. 131.

27. Ibid., p. 324.

28. Ibid.

29. Ibid., p. 325.

30. Ibid.

31. Ibid., p. 326–27.

32. Sarah Gertrude Millin, *Cecil Rhodes* (New York: Harper & Brothers, 1933), p. 8.

33. Herbert Baker and W. T. Stead, *Cecil Rhodes: The Man and His Dream*, (Bulawayo, Rhodesia: Books of Rhodesia, 1977. Includes: W. T. Stead (ed.), *The Last Will and Testament of Cecil John Rhodes* (London: "Review of Reviews" Office, 1902)), pp. 39–40, 44, 52.

34. Ibid., pp. 39–40, 44.

35. William F. Jasper, "A 'Rhodie' In the White House," *The New American*, January 25, 1993, pp. 37–39.

36. Carroll Quigley, *The Anglo-American Establishment: From Rhodes to Cliveden* (New York: Books in Focus, 1981), p. 197.

37. Ibid.

38. Chester Ward, *Kissinger on the Couch*, (New Rochelle, N.Y.: Arlington House Publishers, 1975), p. 150.

39. Ibid, p. 146.

Chapter 4 • "Capitalists" and the Communist Dimension

1. Earl Browder, *Victory and After* (New York: International Publishers, 1942), p. 110.

2. V.I. Lenin, quoted in "Target: World Government," *The New American*, September 16, 1996, p. 23.

3. *Program of the Communist International* (New York: Workers Library

Publishers, 1936), p. 36.

4. Socialist International 1962 Conference, Oslo, Norway, quoted in Rose L. Martin, *The Selling of America* (Santa Monica, Calif.: Fidelis Publishers Inc., 1973), p. 17.

5. Mortimer J. Adler, *Haves Without Have-Nots* (New York: Macmillan Publishing Company, 1991), p. 251.

6. Browder, p. 110.

7. See *Global Tyranny ... Step By Step*, chapters 3 and 5 (Appleton, Wis.: Western Islands, 1992); *Shadows of Power* (Appleton, Wis.: Western Islands, 1992); *The Insiders*, 4th edition (Appleton, Wis.: The John Birch Society, 1996); *Financial Terrorism*, (Appleton, Wis.: The John Birch Society, 1993).

8. Robert W. Lee, *The United Nations Conspiracy* (Appleton, Wis.: Western Islands, 1981), p. 11.

9. Gary Allen with Larry Abraham, *None Dare Call It Conspiracy* (Rossmoor, Calif.: Concord Press, 1971), p. 138.

10. *Soviet World Outlook: A Handbook of Communist Statements*, U.S. Department of State Publication 6836 (Washington, D.C.: U.S. Government Printing Office, 1959), p. 171.

11. Browder, p. 110.

12. Ibid., pp. 160, 169.

13. William Z. Foster, *Toward Soviet America* (Balboa Island, Calif.: Elgin Publications, 1961), pp. 272, 326.

14. Official 1936 program of the Communist International, recorded in hearings before the Senate Committee on Foreign Relations, July 11, 1956, p. 196, quoted in G. Edward Griffin, *The Fearful Master: A Second Look at the United Nations* (Appleton, Wis.: Western Islands, 1964), pp. 69–70.

15. Bella V. Dodd, *School of Darkness* (New York: Devin-Adair, 1963), p. 179.

16. *Pravda*, March 23, 1946, quoted in Robert W. Lee, *The United Nations Conspiracy* (Appleton, Wis.: Western Islands, 1981), p 73.

17. "Organized Communism in the United States," U.S. House of Representatives, Committee on Un-American Activities, May 1958, p. 130.

18. Griffin, p. 88.

19. Regarding White's leadership role at the Bretton Woods Conference, see, for example: *The American Banker*, April 20, 1971, as cited in Gary Allen, *Say "No!" to the New World Order* (Seal Beach, Calif.: Concord Press, 1987), p. 241. Regarding White's efforts as a Soviet agent of influence, see: David Rees, *Harry Dexter White: A Study in Paradox* (New York: Coward, McCann & Geoghegan, 1973); Whittaker Chambers, *Witness* (New York: Random House, 1952); Allen Weinstein, *Perjury: The Hiss-Chambers Case* (New York: Vintage Books, 1978); James Burnham, *The Web of Subversion: Underground Networks in the U.S. Government* (New York: The John Day Co., 1954); Elizabeth Bentley, *Out of Bondage* (New York: Devin-Adair, 1951); and Christopher Andrew and Oleg Gordievsky, *KGB: The Inside Story Of Its Foreign Operations from Lenin to Gorbachev* (New York: HarperCollins Publishers, 1991). For more recent revelations, see also: Allen Weinstein and Alexander Vassiliev, *The Haunted Wood: Soviet Espionage in America — The Stalin Era* (New York: Random House, 1998); Herbert Romerstein and Eric Breindel, *The Venona Secrets: Exposing Soviet Espionage and America's Traitors* (Washington, D.C.: Regnery Publishing, Inc., 2000).

20. Griffin, p. 87.

21. Ibid., p. 120.

22. "Lenin Aims Like U.N.'s, Thant Says," *Los Angeles Times*, April 7, 1970.

23. This Kremlin influence at the United Nations extended even to American nationals employed by the UN, according to the United States Senate Judiciary Committee's 1953 report, "Activities of United States Citizens Employed by the United Nations." That report concluded American nationals employed by the UN as well as other "UN officials were involved in the Communist conspiracy."

For a more detailed background on the United Nations' support of communism abroad from the 1940s through the 1980s, see: *The Fearful Master* by G. Edward Griffin, *The United Nations Conspiracy* by Robert W. Lee, or the author's *Global Tyranny...Step by Step.*

24. Arthur Bliss Lane, *I Saw Poland Betrayed* (New York: Bobbs-Merrill Company, 1948), pp. 143, 214.

25. "Soviet Schedule for War: 1955," Executive Hearings Before the Committee on Un-American Activities, House of Representatives, May 13 and 14, 1953 (Washington, D.C.: U.S. Government Printing Office, 1953), p. 1727.

26. Eugene W. Castle, *Billions, Blunders, and Baloney* (New York: Devin-Adair, 1955), p. 47.

27. Robert Welch, *May God Forgive Us* (Chicago, Ill.: Henry Regnery Company, 1952), p. 87.

28. *Activities of United States Citizens Employed by the United Nations*, Hearings before the Senate Internal Security Subcommittee of the Committee on the Judiciary (1952), pp. 181–182.

29. Amity Shlaes, "Communism Becomes Cronyism at the U.N.," *Wall Street Journal*, October 24, 1991, p. 35A.

30. Carroll Quigley, *Tragedy and Hope: A History of the World in Our Time* (New York: Macmillan, 1966), p. 950.

31. Ibid., p. 954.

32. Ibid., p. 956.

33. Ibid., pp. 954–955.

34. Ibid., p. 955.

35. René A. Wormser, *Foundations: Their Power and Influence* (New York: Devin-Adair, 1958), p. 304.

36. Ibid., pp. 304–305.

37. Ibid., p. 305.

38. "Tax-Exempt Foundations, Report of the Special Committee to Investigate Tax-Exempt Foundations and Comparable Organizations," U.S. House of Representatives, Eighty-Third Congress, Second Session on H. Res. 217 (Washington, D.C.: U.S. Government Printing Office, 1954), pp. 176-77.

39. William H. McIlhany II, *The Tax-Exempt Foundations* (Westport, Conn.: Arlington House, 1980), p. 63. As recorded in note number 30 (p. 235) to Chapter 3, McIlhany interviewed Norman Dodd in 1976 and recorded that conversation as the "Dodd Interview Transcript." McIlhany also compared Mr. Dodd's memory of the conversation in 1976 "with his description of it years earlier in a letter he wrote to Howard E. Kershner on December 29, 1962." "Where there are any slight discrepancies between the two accounts [Mr. McIlhany] used the 1962 version." In later years, Mr. Dodd gave similar statements in other interviews.

40. See: Antony Sutton, *National Suicide: Military Aid to the Soviet Union* (New Rochelle, N.Y.: Arlington House, 1975); *The Best Enemy Money Can Buy* (Billings, Mont.: Liberty House Press, 1986); and *Western Technology and Soviet Economic Development, 1917–1930* (Stanford, Calif., Stanford University: Hoover Institution, 1968); James Perloff, *Shadows of Power* (Appleton, Wis.: Western Islands, 1988); Joseph Finder, *Red Carpet* (New York: Holt, Rinehart and Winston, 1983); Charles Levinson *Vodka Cola* (London: Gordon & Cremonesi, 1978); Gary Allen with Larry Abraham, *None Dare Call It Conspiracy* (Rossmoor, Calif.: Concord Press, 1971); John F. McManus, *The Insiders* (Appleton, Wis.: The John Birch Society, 1996); William F. Jasper, *Global Tyranny* (Appleton, Wis.: Western Islands, 1992).

41. Bloomfield, *A World Effectively Controlled by the United Nations*, February 24, 1961.)

42. Ibid., p. 12.

43. Ibid.

44. Ibid., p. 22.

Chapter 5 • Orchestrating the Globalist Concert

1. *Our Global Neighborhood: The Report of the Commission on Global Governance* (New York: Oxford University

Press, 1995), pp. 254, 255, 257.

2. Jessica T. Mathews, "Power Shift," *Foreign Affairs*, January-February 1997, pp. 50, 53.

3. Robert Hormats, "Non-Governmental Organizations at the Table," a presentation of Edelman Public Relations Worldwide at Atlanta, Singapore, and Sydney, October 2000, www.edelman.com/ceo_corner/ngo/NGO_files/slide00 01.htm on 3/10/01.

4. Kofi Annan, address to the (NGO) Millennium Forum, New York, May 22, 2000. (See: www.millenniumforum.org/html/docs/Speech_UNSG_openingplenary.htm)

5. Steven C. Rockefeller address, UN Millennium Forum, May 2000, as videotaped by The John Birch Society.

6. Sun Tzu, *The Art of War* (Ware, Hertfordshire: Wordsworth Editions, Ltd, Cumberland House, 1995), pp. 132–133.

7. Ibid., p. 133.

8. E. H. Cookridge, *The Net That Covers the World* (New York: Henry Holt & Co., 1955), pp. 15,16.

9. Ibid., p. 16.

10. Martin Malia, foreword to Stéphane Courtois et al., *The Black Book of Communism: Crimes, Terror, Repression* (Cambridge, Mass.: Harvard University Press, 1999), pp. xi, xvi.

11. "Interlocking Subversion in Government Departments," Senate Internal Security Subcommittee report (Washington, D.C.: U.S. Government Printing Office), July 30, 1953, p. 49.

12. J. Edgar Hoover, *The Elks Magazine*, August 1956, quoted by Jerreld L. Newquist in *Prophets Principles and National Survival* (Salt Lake City: Publishers Press, 1964), p. 273.

13. Interview with author.

14. Dennis L. Bark and Owen Harries (ed.), *The Red Orchestra, Volume 3: The Case of the Southwest Pacific* (Stanford University, Stanford, Calif., Hoover Institution Press, 1989), pp. xix, xx.

15. Anatoliy Golitsyn, *New Lies for Old* (New York: Dodd, Mead, and Company, 1984.)

16. Anatoliy Golitsyn, *The Perestroika Deception: Memoranda to the Central Intelligence Agency* (London & New York: Edward Harle, 1995).

17. Jan Kozak, *And Not A Shot Is Fired* (Appleton, Wis.: Robert Welch University Press, 1999).

18. Kofi Annan, address to the World Civil Society Conference, Montreal, December 8, 1999, www.un.org/MoreInfo/ngolink/sgmontre.htm on March 29, 2001.

19. *Freedom From War: The United States Program for General and Complete Disarmament in a Peaceful World* (Washington, D.C.: Department of State Publication 7277, 1961); Lincoln P. Bloomfield, *A World Effectively Controlled By the United Nations* (Washington, D.C.: Institute for Defense Analyses, 1962).

20. Kofi Annan, address to the Millennium Forum.

21. "The Hague Agenda for Peace and Justice for the 21st Century," UN Ref A/54/98 (Hague Appeal for Peace).

22. Cora Weiss remarks at Forum videotaped by JBS staff.

23. William Norman Grigg, "Building World Order," *The New American*, July 3, 2000, p. 6.

24. S. Steven Powell, *Covert Cadre: Inside the Institute for Policy Studies* (Ottawa, Ill.: Green Hill Publishers, 1987), pp. 38–39.

25. Grigg, pp. 6–7.

26. UN Charter, Chapter VII, Article 42.

27. "The Hague Agenda," p. 4.

28. Ibid., pp. 34, 44.

29. Ibid., p. 44.

30. *Peace Matters*, Newsletter of the Hague Appeal for Peace, May 2000.

31. James Kunen, *The Strawberry Statement: Notes of a College Revolutionary* (New York: Avon, 1969), pp. 130-131.

32. Gary Allen, "Who is Paying: For the Student Revolutionary Movement," *American Opinion* magazine, November 1970, p. 4. (Note: Kirk was also interviewed by House and Senate investigative committees. See: "Investigations of Students for a

Democratic Society, Part 5," Hearings Before the Committee on Internal Security, House of Representatives, August 6 and 7, 1969 (Washington, D.C.: U.S. Government Printing Office, 1969); "Testimony of Gerald Wayne Kirk, Part 1," Hearings before Senate Internal Security Subcommittee, March 9, 1970 (U.S. Government Printing Office, 1970); and "Testimony of Gerald Wayne Kirk, Part 2," Senate Internal Security Subcommittee Hearings on March 11, 1970 (U.S. Government Printing Office, 1970).

33. William Shawcross, *Deliver Us from Evil: Peacekeepers, Warlords, and a World of Endless Conflict* (New York: Simon and Schuster, 2000).

34. Jonathan Schell, "The Folly of Arms Control," *Foreign Affairs*, September/October 2000.

35. Ibid., p. 25.

36. Igor Ivanov, "The Missile-Defense Mistake," *Foreign Affairs*, September/October 2000, pp. 15–20.

37. Andrew J. Goodpaster, "Advice for the Next President," *Foreign Affairs*, September/October 2000, p. 159.

38. Chester Ward, *Kissinger on the Couch*, (New Rochelle, N.Y.: Arlington House Publishers, 1975), p. 151.

39. *UN 2000: The United Nations Millennium Summit, New York, 6-9 September 2000* (London: Agenda Publishing, 2000).

40. Robert D. Green, *Fast Track to Zero Nuclear Weapons: The Middle Powers Initiative*, Revised Edition (Cambridge, Mass.: Middle Powers Initiative, 1999), p. 6.

41. Ibid.

42. Ibid., pp. 37, 38.

43. Ibid., p. 37.

Chapter 6 • Enviromania

1. World Association of World Federalists, *The Humanist*, January-February 1972, quoted in *Global Tyranny ... Step By Step* (Appleton, Wis.: Western Islands, 1992), p. 123.

2. George F. Kennan, "The Wall Falls: This is No Time for Talk of German Reunification," *Washington Post*, November 12, 1989.

3. Michael Oppenheimer, "From Red Menace to Green Threat," *New York Times*, March 27, 1990, p. 19B.

4. Quoted in Robert James Bidinotto, "What is the Truth about Global Warming?," *Reader's Digest*, February 1990, page 97.

5. Alexander King and Bertrand Schneider, *The First Global Revolution*, A Report by the Council of the Club of Rome (New York: Pantheon Books, 1991), p. 115.

6. "The New World Army," *New York Times*, March 6, 1992, p. A14.

7. William Norman Grigg, "Insider Report," *The New American*, October 4, 1993, p. 12.

8. Dixy Lee Ray, *Environmental Overkill* (Washington, D.C.: Regnery Gateway, 1993), p. 205.

9. *Heidelberg Appeal to Heads of States and Governments*, publicly released at the 1992 Earth Summit in Rio de Janeiro. See: www.ceednet.org/ issues/ globalclimate/heidelberg_appeal.htm.

10. Ibid.

11. Ibid.

12. The UN's Intergovernmental Panel on Climate Change (IPCC) approved the IPCC WG III Third Assessment Report at the 6th session of WG III, held at Accra, Ghana, from February 28th through March 3rd, 2000.

13. 1991 Gallup Poll cited in Kelly Stewart, "Global Warming and the Kyoto Protocol," April 24, 1998, www.publicsectorconsultants.com/PSR /Periscop/1998/0402498.cfm on 3/19/01. Same poll also cited in "Myths of Global Warming Cited as Kyoto Approaches," *Environment News*, August 1997, www.heartland.org/envi-ronment/aug97/myths.htm on 3/19/01.

14. See the author's interview with Dr. Miranda, "The Amazing Amazon," in *The New American*, August 10, 1992, pp. 16–17.

15. Ibid.

16. William F. Jasper, "Earth Summit

Alternatives," *The New American*, July 27, 1992, p.16.

17. Ibid.

18. Ibid.

19. Lincoln P. Bloomfield, *A World Effectively Controlled by the United Nations, Institute for Defense Analyses*, March 10, 1962, p. 12. Prepared for IDA in support of a study submitted to the Department of State under contract No. SCC 28270, February 24, 1961.

20. Ibid., p. 12.

21. Herman Kahn and Anthony J. Wiener, "World Federal Government," essay in *Uniting the Peoples and Nations: Readings in World Federalism*, compiled by Barbara Walker (Washington, D.C.: World Federalist Association, 1993), p. 306.

22. Ibid.

23. Ibid.

24. Benjamin B. Ferencz and Ken Keyes, Jr., *Planethood: The Key to Your Future* (Coos Bay, Ore.: Love Line Books, 1991), pp. 90–91.

25. *Report From Iron Mountain on the Possibility and Desirability of Peace*, (New York: The Dial Press, 1967).

26. Ibid.

27. Ibid., p. 66.

28. Ibid., p. 71.

29. Ibid., p. 66.

30. Ibid., p. 70.

31. Bloomfield, p. 22.

32. *Iron Mountain*, p. 71.

33. Mikhail Gorbachev speech, "The River of Time and the Necessity of Action," delivered at Fulton, Missouri, May 6, 1992.

34. Jeremy Rifkin, *Entropy: Into the Greenhouse World* (New York: Bantam Books, 1989), p. 245.

35. Benjamin Ferencz, quoted by the author in "Courting Global Tyranny," *The New American*, August 31, 1998, p. 8.

36. Corinne McLaughlin and Gordon Davidson, *Spiritual Politics: Changing the World From the Inside Out* (New York: Ballantine Books, 1994).

37. Alvin Toffler, *The Third Wave* (New York: William Morrow and Company, Inc., 1980), p. 342.

38. Jessica Lipnack and Jeffrey Stamps, *Networking: The First Report and Directory* (New York: Doubleday, 1982), quoted in Kirk Kidwell, "Network Difficulty," *The New American*, October 12, 1987, p. 6.

39. "Foundations Pay the Way," *The New American* special report: "Conspiracy for Global Control," 1997 expanded edition, pp. 56, 57.

40. Alvin and Heidi Toffler, Foreword by Newt Gingrich, *Creating a New Civilization: The Politics of the Third Wave* (Atlanta: Turner Publishing, 1995).

41. McLaughlin and Davidson, p. 29.

42. Donnela H. and Dennis L. Meadows, et al., *The Limits to Growth: A Report for the Club of Rome's Project on the Predicament of Mankind* (New York: Universe Books, 1972), p. 196.

43. Ibid., p. 197.

44. Ibid.

45. Gus Hall, *Ecology*, quoted in Holly Swanson, *Set Up & Sold Out: Find Out What Green Really Means* (White City, Ore.: CIN, 1995), p. 30.

46. Ibid.

47. Ibid., p. 272.

48. See the author's report: "Socializing at Rio," *The New American*, August 10, 1992, p. 18.

49. Ibid.

50. Rene Dubos and Barbara Ward (Lady Jackson), *Only One Earth: The Care and Maintenance of a Small Planet* (New York: W.W. Norton, 1972).

51. Richard A. Falk, "Toward a New World Order: Modest Methods and Drastic Visions," in Saul H. Mendlovitz (ed.), *On the Creation of a Just World Order: Preferred Worlds for the 1990's* (New York: The Free Press, 1975).

52. Jeremy Rifkin, *Voting Green*, quoted in Swanson, op. cit., p. 40.

53. *The State of the World*, annual Worldwatch Institute report. See the Worldwatch Institute website (3/14/01): www.worldwatch.org.

54. Ibid., see: www.worldwatch.org/bios/brown.html.

55. Ibid.

56. From "Acknowledgements," *State of*

the World 1995 (the "flagship publication of the Worldwatch Institute").

57. Stephen Schmidheiny and the Business Council for Sustainable Development, *Changing Course* (Cambridge, Mass.: MIT Press Books, 1992).

58. Al Gore, *Earth In The Balance: Ecology and the Human Spirit* (New York: Plume, 1993), p. 269.

59. William Norman Grigg, "Al Gore's Red Connections," *The New American*, March 31, 1997, pp. 15–17.

60. Jim MacNeill, Pieter Winsemius, Taizo Yakushiji, *Beyond Interdependence: The Meshing of the World's Economy and the Earth's Ecology* (New York: Oxford University Press, 1991).

61. Maurice Strong in ibid., p. ix.

62. Ibid.

63. Ibid.

64. Ibid., p. x.

65. Ibid.

66. Ibid.

67. MacNeill, Winsemius, and Yakushiji, p. 128.

68. Ibid.

69. Ronald I. Spiers, "Keep the U.N. on a Roll," *New York Times*, March 13, 1992, p. A31.

70. George F. Kennan, "The Wall Falls: This is No Time for Talk of German Reunification," *Washington Post*, November 12, 1989.

71. Jessica Tuchman Mathews, "Two Views," *EPA Journal*, July/August 1990, p. 27.

72. Ibid.

73. "Global Commentary" "We must 'ecologize' our society before it's too late," *Birmingham* (Ala.) *News*, April 22, 1990.

74. Ibid.

75. "From Red to Green," *Audubon*, November-December 1994, quoted in Swanson, p. 272.

76. *Grassroots*, quoted in Swanson, p. 277.

77. "Man of the Decade: Mikhail Gorbachev" and "The Unlikely Patron of Change," *Time*, January 1, 1990, cover and pp. 42–72.

78. Mikhail S. Gorbachev, speech delivered November 2, 1987 at the Kremlin Palace of Congresses in Moscow before a gathering of party officials and foreign visitors. Translated into English by Tass, as reported by *Facts on File*, November 6, 1987, p. 820.

79. Mikhail Gorbachev, *Perestroika: New Thinking for Our Country and the World*, Hungarian edition (1st para.), quoted in *The New Republic*, December 21, 1987, p. 9.

80. Francis X. Clines, "Gorbachev: 'Enough' for Glasnost?" *New York Times* International, December 26, 1989, p. 11.

81. "Gorbachev Interview," *Time*, June 4, 1990, p. 31.

82. Mikhail Gorbachev, *Perestroika: New Thinking for Our Country and the World* (New York: Harper & Row, 1987), p. 51.

83. Ibid., pp. 32, 35.

84. Daniel Sitarz (ed.), *Agenda 21: The Earth Summit Strategy to Save the Planet* (Boulder, Colo.: EarthPress, 1993), pp. 69–70.

85. Ibid., p. 70.

86. Gail Sheehy, *The Man Who Changed the World: The Lives of Mikhail S. Gorbachev* (New York: HarperCollins Publishers, 1990), second page of section: "Quick Turn Artist."

87. See the following articles from *The New American*: John F. McManus, "A CFR Visit to Moscow," March 16, 1987, p. 21; William F. Jasper, "Global Gorby," October 30, 1995, p. 23. Also, State of the World Forum reports for 1995–2000, Gorbachev Foundation.

88. Richard N. Gardner, "The Hard Road to World Order," *Foreign Affairs*, April 1974, p. 558.

89. Ibid., p. 560.

90. See for example: Leslie H. Gelb, "Carter's Foreign Policies In Liberal Democratic Vein," *New York Times*, July 7, 1976, pp. 1, 12.

Chapter 7 • The UN's War on Private Property

1. Preamble to "The Vancouver Action Plan: 64 Recommendations for

National Action," conference report of "Habitat I," the United Nations Conference on Human Settlements, Vancouver, Canada, May 31 to June 11, 1976. For text, see www.undp.org/un/habitat/back/vp-intr.html.

2. Karl Marx and Frederick Engels, *The Communist Manifesto*, 1848. American Opinion edition with introduction by William P. Fall (Appleton, Wis.: 1974), p. 20.

3. Pierre Joseph Proudhon (1809–1865) quoted in John Bartlett, *Familiar Quotations* (15th and 125th anniv. edition) (Boston: Little, Brown, and Company, 1980), p. 527.

4. Abbé Augustin Barruel, *Memoirs Illustrating the History of Jacobinism* (Fraser, Michigan: American Council on Economics and Society, 1995), p. 410. This 1995 single-volume (846 pp.) edition is a reprint of a four-volume English translation published in 1798 by T. Burton, London.

5. Marx and Engels, p. 19.

6. Noah Webster, "Examination of the Leading Principles of the Federal Constitution, 1787," October 10, 1787, p. 48, quoted on the Potomac Institute web site: www.potomac-inc.org/2noahweb.html.

7. Joseph Story, *Wilkerson v. Leland*, (2 Peters, 657), quoted in Russell, *American Legal History, White vs. White*, 5 Barbour 474 (NY, 1849) at www.law.du.edu/russell/lh/alh/docs/whitevwhite.html.

8. "The Boston Gazette," April 4, 1768, quoted in Verna M. Hall (compiler), *The Christian History of the Constitution of the United States of America: Christian Self-Government With Union*, American Revolution Bicentennial Edition (San Francisco: Foundation for American Christian Education, 1985), p. 453.

9. Verna M. Hall (compiler), *Christian History of the Constitution of the United States of America* (San Francisco: The American Christian Constitution Press, 1960), p. 248A.

10. *Rerum Novarum: On Capital and Labor* (May 15, 1891), in *The Great Encyclical Letters of Pope Leo XIII* (New York: Benziger Brothers, 1903), pp. 237–238.

11. Friedrich A. Hayek, *The Road to Serfdom*, (Chicago: University of Chicago Press, 1969), pp. 103, 104.

12. Preamble to "The Vancouver Action Plan, op. cit., May 31 to June 11, 1976.

13. Ibid., "Recommendation D.1 Land resource management."

14. Daniel Sitarz (ed.), *Agenda 21: The Earth Summit Strategy to Save Our Planet* (Boulder, Colo.: EarthPress, 1993), p. 63.

15. Ibid., p. 65.

16. Ibid., p. 180.

17. Ibid.

18. V. H. Heywood (exec. ed.), *Global Biodiversity Assessment*, published for the United Nations Environment Programme (Cambridge, England: Cambridge University Press, 1995), p. 767.

19. Ibid., p. 787.

20. Ibid.

21. William Norman Grigg, "Sunset on the West?" *The New American*, February 5, 1996, p. 30.

22. *Sustainable America, A New Consensus*, President's Council on Sustainable Development report, 1995, p. 113.

23. William Reilly, *National Parks for a New Generation*, (Conservation Foundation, 1985), quoted in "Environmental Activist to Head EPA," *Human Events*, January 14, 1989, pp. 23–24.

24. Jeremy Rifkin, *Entropy: Into the Greenhouse World*, (New York: Bantam Books, 1989) p. 237.

25. Ibid., p. 245.

26. Turner Foundation website: www.turnerfoundation.org/turner/sprawl.html on March 15, 2001.

27. Ibid.

28. Marx and Engels, p. 19.

Chapter 8 • UN's International Court of Criminals

1. Charles Rice interviewed by William F. Jasper, "Courting Global Tyranny," *The*

New American, August 31, 1998, p. 17.

2. Robert S. McNamara and Benjamin B. Ferencz, "For Clinton's Last Act" [op-ed], *New York Times*, December 12, 2000, p. A3.

3. Statement of President Bill Clinton, quoted in "Clinton's Words: 'The Right Action,'" *New York Times*, January 1, 2001, p. 6.

4. Albert Ellery Bergh (ed.), *The Writings of Thomas Jefferson*, Vol. 15 (Washington, D.C.: The Thomas Jefferson Memorial Association, 1907), p. 331, quoted in *The American Freedom Library* (CD-rom) (Western Standard Publishing Co., 1997).

5. Anne Swardson, "Pinochet Case Tries Spanish Legal Establishment; Pinochet Case Tries Legal System," *Washington Post*, October 22, 1998, p. A27 f.

6. "A Litany of the Big Powers' 'Sins,'" *Terra Viva*, June 17, 1998, p. 4.

7. Barbara Crossette, "U.N. Monitor to Investigate U.S. Use of Death Penalty," *New York Times*, September 30, 1997, p. A-8.

8. Craig Turner, "U.S. death penalty called violation of international law," *Arizona Republic*, April 4, 1998, p. A16.

9. "Report of the Special Rapporteur on extrajudicial, summary or arbitrary executions, Mr. Bacre Waly Ndiaye," UN Economic and Social Council, Commission on Human Rights document E/CN.4/1998/68/Add.3, January 22, 1998, paragraphs 145, 156 (a) and (b).

10. "Report of the Independent Inquiry Into the Actions of the United Nations During the 1994 Genocide in Rwanda," December 15, 1999, paragraph 2 under II. Description of Key Events, Arusha Peace Agreement. Report posted at www.org/News/ossg/Rwanda_report.htm on 3/17/01.

11. William F. Jasper, "Courting Global Tyranny," *The New American*, August 31, 1998, p. 14.

12. "Police Brutality Deeply Rooted in US," *Terra Viva*, July 8, 1998, p. 7.

13. *Shielded From Justice: Police Brutality and Accountability in the United States*, (Human Rights Watch, 1998), as referenced in ibid.

14. The Ford Foundation website (www.fordfound.org/grants) lists grant information in the amount of $7,200,000 for Human Rights Watch for 1999.

15. Jessica T. Mathews, "Power Shift," *Foreign Affairs*, January/February 1997, p. 55.

16. For Emma Bonino (now Member of the European Parliament and Secretary of the Transnational Radical Party): "The 'Who's Who' of the Transnational Radical Party," www.radicalparty.org/member/emm.htm on 3/17/01. For Francesco Rutelli (Mayor of Rome): "The 'Who's Who' of the Transnational Radical Party," www.radicalparty.org/member/bio_r.htm on 3/17/01.

17. "Goldstone: US Stance Contradictory," *Terra Viva*, June 17, 1998, p. 7. Released report: "Making Justice Work."

18. CFR press release, "Morton Halperin Re-joins Council," January 25, 2001.

19. Coalition for the ICC web page (www.igc.org/icc/).

20. George C. Lodge, *Managing Globalization in the Age of Interdependence*, (San Diego, Calif.: Pfeiffer, 1995).

21. Thomas R. Dye, *Who's Running America?* (Englewood Cliffs, N.J.: Prentice Hall, Inc., 1976), pp. 193–94.

22. Charles Rice interviewed by author, William F. Jasper, "Courting Global Tyranny," *The New American*, August 31, 1998, p. 17.

23. Ibid.

24. For a more in-depth examination of the serious problems with the definitions of these "core crimes," see the following articles in *The New American*: "Court of International Criminals," May 30, 1994; "International Injustice," April 13, 1998; "The ICC: Courting Global Tyranny," August 31, 1998; and "International Court of Criminals," July 3, 2000 at www.thenewamerican.com/focus/ICC/.

25. S.J. Res. 32 (introduced by Senator Christopher Dodd on January 28, 1993

and referred to the Committee on Foreign Relations), Section 1., point (2).

26. William F. Jasper, "International Injustice," *The New American*, April 13, 1998, p. 23.

27. Betsy Pisik, "U.S. seeks changes to accept international criminal court," *Washington Times*, February 26, 1999, p. A17.

28. William F. Jasper, "Black-Robed Globalists," *The New American*, September 28, 1998, p. 23.

29. Jim Henderson, "Albright joins effort to spare Canadian's life," *Houston Chronicle*, December 2, 1998, pp. 1A, 16A.

30. Theodor Meron, "Answering for War Crimes," *Foreign Affairs*, January/February 1997, p. 8.

31. Robert Fox, "Balkans provide new riches for the Mafia," *The* (London) *Daily Telegraph*, December 15, 2000, p. 22.

32. Ibid.

33. James Blitz, "Mafia-buster charts course 'for UN of the future,'" *Financial Times*, December 12, 2000.

34. Ibid.

35. Mathews, op. cit., p. 58.

36. Robert Wright, "Pax Kapital," *Foreign Policy*, Summer 2000, p. 68.

37. Transcript of the October 12, 2000 CFR-sponsored meeting in New York, "Condoleezza Rice on Governor George W. Bush's Foreign Policy," posted on the CFR website: www.cfr.org/p/pubs/Rice_10-12-00_Transcript.html, page 12 of 17, on 3/22/01.

38. James Madison, quoted in Charles S. Hyneman and Donald S. Lutz, *American Political Writing during the Founding Era: 1760 – 1805*, Vol I. (Indianapolis: Liberty Press, 1983), p. 633.

Chapter 9 • Civilian Disarmament

1. Rudyard Kipling, "The Gods of the Copybook Headings," *Rudyard Kipling's Verse*, Inclusive Ed.: 1885–1932 (Garden City, N.Y.: Doubleday, Doran, and Co., Inc., 1934), p. 886.

2. "Combat Arms Survey," administered to several hundred Marines on May 10, 1994 at the Twentynine Palms, California Marine base. For more information, see note #94, below.

3. Walter Shapiro, "It's high time to gun down the 2nd Amendment," *USA Today*, September 17, 1999, p. 14A.

4. Roger Rosenblatt, "Get Rid of the Damned Things," *Time*, August 9, 1999, p. 38.

5. UN Backgrounder: "Millennium Forum Action Plan Adds People's Voice to Summit Debate" (Published by the United Nations Department of Public Information, DPI/2143 — August 2000, www.un.org/millennium/media/action_plan.htm viewed on 4/01/01.)

6. "High Noon," *Washington Post*, August 19, 1965, p. A20.

7. Jean Latz Griffin and William Recktenwald, "Warning: Health Risk — Guns Under Attack on New Front," *Chicago Tribune*, October 31, 1993, section "Perspective," p. 1f. See: www.archive.chicago.tribune.com.

8. Richard Harris, "A Reporter At Large," *The New Yorker*, July 26, 1976, pp. 57–58.

9. Editorial, "America's Gun Epidemic: What is the Best Medicine?," *Los Angeles Times*, November 8, 1993, p. 6f.

10. Editorial, "Gun Prohibition, Phase II," *Washington Times*, December 9, 1993, p. A20.

11. Rosie O'Donnell, TV show of April 21, 1999, quoted by Greg Pierce, *Washington Times*, April 26, 1999, section "Nation Inside Politics," p. A7.

12. Kofi Annan, *We the Peoples: The Role of the United Nations in the 21st Century* (New York: United Nations Department of Public Information, 2000), p. 52.

13. Ibid., pp. 52–53.

14. Ibid., p. 53.

15. Charles J. Hanley, "World gun control is U.N. body's aim," *Washington Times*, May 24, 1994, p. A1.

16. From combined dispatches, "U.S. OKS Study of U.N. Gun Control," *Washington Times*, May 24, 1994, p. A1.

17. Phone conversation with author.

18. *Freedom From War: The United States Program for General and Complete Disarmament in a Peaceful World* (Department of State Publication 7277) (Washington, D.C.: U.S. Government Printing Office, 1961), pp. 18–19.

19. Public Law 87-297 (H.R. 9118), "An Act: to establish a United States Arms Control and Disarmament Agency," Title I, Section 3. and 3.a.

20. ACDA "Second Annual Report to Congress: January 1, 1962 – December 31, 1962," U.S. Arms Control and Disarmament Agency Publication 14, released February 1963.

21. Kai Bird, *The Chairman: John J. McCloy, The Making of the American Establishment* (New York: Simon & Schuster, 1992), pp. 495–516. Also see: John F. Kennedy, "Address Before the General Assembly of the United Nations," New York City, September 25, 1961. Available at www.cs.umb.edu/jfklibrary/j092561. htm, the website of the John Fitzgerald Kennedy Library.

22. J. Anthony Lukas, "The Council on Foreign Relations: Is It a Club? Seminar? Presidium? 'Invisible Government'?" *New York Times Magazine*, November 21, 1971; Walter Isaacson and Evan Thomas, *The Wise Men* (New York: Simon & Schuster, 1986), pp. 19–20, 587–604; and John F. McManus, *Changing Commands: The Betrayal of America's Military* (Appleton, Wis.: The John Birch Society, 1995), p. 145.

23. Richard Rovere, "The American Establishment," *Esquire*, May 1962, p. 108.

24. Alan Brinkley, "Minister Without Portfolio," *Harper's*, February 1983.

25. Ibid.

26. Max Holland,"Citizen McCloy," *Wilson Quarterly*, Autumn, 1991, p. 37.

27. Bird, *The Chairman*, p. 505; William F. Jasper, "Gun Grabbers' Global Gestapo," *The New American*, November 22, 1999, p. 17; and The Arthur H. Dean Papers, Division of Rare and Manuscript Collections, Cornell University Library. (Library maintains extensive holdings of his records and correspondence regarding his activities as chairman of the U.S. delegation to several international disarmament conferences.)

28. Albin Krebs, "Arthur H. Dean, Envoy to Korea Talks, Dies at 89," *New York Times*, December 1, 1987, p. D28.

29. Joseph Keeley, *The China Lobby Man: The Story of Alfred Kohlberg* (New Rochelle, New York: Arlington House, 1969), p. 92.

30. Ibid., pp. 92–93.

31. "Institute of Pacific Relations," Report of the (Senate) Committee on the Judiciary, Eighty-Second Congress, Second Session, Hearings held July 25, 1951 – June 20, 1952 by the Internal Security Subcommittee (Washington, D.C.: U.S. Government Printing Office, 1952: ordered to be printed: July 2 [legislative day June 27]), p. 223.

32. Ibid., pp. 223–225.

33. Isaacson and Thomas, *The Wise Men*.

34. Bird, *The Chairman*, pp. 41–45. Also: "Grenville Clark, Lawyer, 84, Dies," *New York Times*, January 14, 1967.

35. *World Government Highlights: Facts, Opinions, & Personalities*, revised edition (New York: United World Federalists, May 1953), p.8. Also: "Announce Major Editorial Awards: Contest Honors Grenville Clark," *The Federalist*, vol. 9, no. 5, January 1963 (published by United World Federalists), p. 3.

36. "Grenville Clark, Lawyer, 84, Dies," *New York Times*, January 14, 1967. See also: William F. Jasper, "Hardselling the New World Order," *The New American*, September 7, 1992, p. 19; and: "Promoting World Government," *The Herald of Freedom*, Zarephath, N.J., Vol. XVIII, No. 13, October 25, 1974, pp. 3-4.

37. "Correction, Please!" *American Opinion* magazine, Vol. VI, No. 4, April 1963.

38. Grenville Clark and Louis B. Sohn, *World Peace Through World Law*,

Second Edition (revised) (Cambridge, Mass.: Harvard University Press, 1962).

39. Ibid., p. xxix.

40. Ibid.

41. Ibid.

42. Ibid., p. 247.

43. Ibid., pp. 247–248.

44. Ibid., p. 248.

45. Ibid., p. 256.

46. Ibid., p. 225.

47. Ibid., p. 212

48. Ibid.

49. Ibid., p. xxxi.

50. Ibid., p. 330.

51. UN "Report of the Group of Governmental Experts on Small Arms," August 19, 1999. Document A/54/258, p. 24, note #5.

52. Ibid., cover page lists this document as "Item 76(f) of the provisional agenda [A/54/150] General and complete disarmament."

53. Clark and Sohn, p. xxxv

54. *Our Global Neighborhood: The Report of the Commission on Global Governance* (New York, Oxford: Oxford University Press, 1995.)

55. Ibid., pp. 16, 131.

56. Ibid., p. 131.

57. Ibid.

58. "Experts on Small Arms," p. 17.

59. Ibid., pp. 17, 22.

60. UN Charter, Article 2, Item number 7, (see UN website: www.un.org/about un/charter/).

61. "Secretary-General Presents His Annual Report to General Assembly," UN Press Release SG/SM/7136 GA/9596, September 20, 1999.

62. Kofi Annan statement in "Security Council Meets at Ministerial Level to Consider Issue of Small Arms," UN Press Release SC/6732, September 24, 1999.

63. Kofi Annan, foreword, "Report of the Group of Governmental Experts on Small Arms," document A/54/258, August 19, 1999, p. 2.

64. Madeleine K. Albright, Remarks at UN Security Council Small Arms Ministerial, September 24, 1999, as released by the Office of the Spokesman U.S. Department of State. See: http://secretary.state.gov/www/ statements/ 1999/990924a.html.

65. Amy Otchet, "Small Arms, Many Hands," *UNESCO Courier*, November 1998. See: www.unesco.org/courier/ 1998_11/uk/ethique/txt1.html.

66. Kofi Annan, remarks to Security Council meeting, September 24, 1999 in Press Release SG/SM/7145 SC/6733, "Addressing the Security Council, Secretary-General Says International Community Must Reverse Global Proliferation of Small Arms," p. 3.

67. IANSA website (www.iansa.org/action/ index.html), "IANSA Action Framework."

68. "Founding Document of IANSA." Section III. Program of Action, items 1,3,4,&5. See: www.iansa.org/mission/ m1/html.

69. *Armed to the Teeth* (UN video), (New York: UN Department of Public Information, 2000).

70. Jay Simkin, Aaron Zelman, and Alan M. Rice, *Rwanda's Genocide, 1994*, (Milwaukee: Jews for the Preservation of Firearms Ownership, 1997), p. 12.

71. Ibid., p. 10.

72. Ibid., p. 25.

73. Ibid.

74. *Lethal Laws: "Gun Control" is the Key to Genocide* (Milwaukee: Jews for the Preservation of Firearms Ownership, 1994).

75. *The Blue Helmets: A Review of United Nations Peace-keeping* (New York: United Nations Department of Public Information, 1990), p. 215.

76. G. Edward Griffin, *The Fearful Master: A Second Look at the United Nations* (Appleton, Wis.: Western Islands, 1964), pp. 18–20.

77. Ibid., p. 20.

78. Ibid.

79. *The Blue Helmets*, p. 248.

80. Griffin, *The Fearful Master*, p. 49.

81. Ibid.

82. Philippa Schuyler, *Who Killed the Congo?* (New York: Devin-Adair, 1962).

83. Smith Hempstone, *Rebels, Mercen-*

aries, and Dividends: The Katanga Story (New York: Frederick A. Praeger, 1962).

84. The 46 Civilian Doctors of Elisabethville, *46 Angry Men* (Belmont, Mass.: *American Opinion*, 1962; originally published by Dr. T. Vleurinck, 96 Avenue de Broqueville, Bruxelles 15, 1962).

85. Congressman Donald L. Jackson (narrator), *Katanga: The Untold Story*, available on video (VHS, 59 minutes) from American Media, Westlake Village, Calif.

86. "Visa Procedures of Department of State: The Struelens Case," Report of the Senate Internal Security Subcommittee (Washington, D.C.: U.S Government Printing Office, 1962), p. 28.

87. Tom Farer, *The Report of an Inquiry, Conducted Pursuant to Security Council Resolution 837, Into the 5 June 1993 Attack on UN Forces in Somalia*, August 23, 1993.

88. Ibid., pp. 21–31.

89. Ibid., pp. 96–98.

90. William F. Jasper, "Behind Our Defeat in Somalia," *The New American*, September 5, 1994, p. 4.

91. Julia Preston, "U.N., U.S. Clash on Disarming Haitians," *Washington Post*, October 20, 1994, p. A31.

92. Jerry Seper, "KLA finances fight with heroin sales," *Washington Times*, May 3, 1999, pp. A1, A11.

93. "The Kosovo Liberation Army: Does Clinton Policy Support Group with Terror, Drug Ties?," press release of United States Senate, Republican Policy Committee, March 31, 1999, quoted on www.senate.gov/~rpc/releases/1999/fr033199.htm viewed on April 19, 1999.

94. "Combat Arms Survey" administered to several hundred Marines at the Twentynine Palms, California Marine base on May 10, 1994. According to Marine spokesmen at Twentynine Palms, the survey was conducted as part of a Master's Degree thesis of a Navy Commander studying at the Naval Postgraduate School in Monterey, California. John Sanders, public affairs officer at the school, told *The New American* that the survey was designed by the student "to determine if non-traditional missions are undermining unit morale and cohesiveness" and was supervised by two civilian faculty members, one of whom is a former Assistant Secretary of Defense. Copy of full Survey on file. Interestingly, the Twentynine Palms base weekly newspaper for March of that year carried a report by Cpl. M.T. Mink, "Council on Foreign Relations Visits Combat Center," describing a tour by 40 members of the CFR.

95. Ibid., p. 6.

96. "Insider Report," *The New American*, July 11, 1994, p. 10.

97. "Survey of Marines On the Use of Military Forces in Non-Traditional Missions," news release of Naval Postgraduate School, Monterey, Calif., Dept. of the Navy, undated circa July-Sept. 1994. See also: William F. Jasper, "I Am a United Nations Fighting Person," *The New American*, September 19, 1994, sidebar, p. 6.

98. Robert W. Lee, "Gun Report," *The New American*, July 13, 1992, p. 38.

99. See respectively: "Bush triggers petition to oust him from NRA," *USA Today*, July 12, 1989, p. 4A; and *Weekly Compilation of Presidential Documents*, March 18, 1991, pp. 289–290.

100. Interviewed on *The Joe Redburn Show*, radio station KTKK in Salt Lake City, on April 26, 1991.

101. Armando Villafranca, "Former President Bush angrily resigns from NRA," *Houston Chronicle*, May 11, 1995, pp. 1A, 21A.

102. Steve Bonta, "The Power Elite & George W.," *The New American*, July 17, 2000, pp. 18–19.

103. Steve Mufson, "Secretary of State Gets Hero's Welcome to Work," *Washington Post*, January 23, 2001, p. A.3. Also see: "Reviving the State Department," *Washington Post*, January 31, 2001, p. A20.

104. Barbara Crossette, "Powell Vows Strong Support for Many U.N. Activities: Reassures Annan on Bush Administration," *New York Times*, February 15, 2001, p. A10.
105. James M. Lindsay, "The New Apathy: How an Uninterested Public Is Reshaping Foreign Policy," *Foreign Affairs*, Vol. 79, Number 5, September/October 2000, p. 8.

Chapter 10 • Regionalism

1. Zbigniew Brzezinski, Gorbachev State of the World Forum, Fairmont Hotel, San Francisco, September 28, 1995, as audiotaped by author.
2. John Logue, "The Proper Goal" in Barbara Walker (compiler), *Uniting the Peoples and Nations: Readings in World Federalism* (World Federalist Movement & World Federalist Association, 1993), p. 347.
3. *The Millennium Year and the Reform Process* (London: Commission on Global Governance, 1999), p. 55.
4. Merry and Serge Bromberger, *Jean Monnet and the United States of Europe* (New York: Coward-McCann Publishers, 1969), p. 123.
5. Joseph Stalin, "Marxism and the National Question," in *Marxism and the National and Colonial Question* (New York: International Publishers, 1942), p. 58.
6. *Program of the Communist International* (New York: Workers Library Publishers, 1936), p.36.
7. Richard N. Gardner, "The Hard Road To World Order," *Foreign Affairs*, April 1974, p. 558.
8. Mark D. Isaacs, "Forcing a United Europe," *The New American*, November 16, 1992, p. 10.
9. M. Delal Baer, "North American Free Trade," *Foreign Affairs*, Fall 1991, p.148.
10. Ibid.
11. Ibid.
12. William F. Jasper, *Global Tyranny... Step By Step* (Appleton, Wis.: Western Islands, 1992), Chapter 13, "UN Regionalism – The European Community."
13. "The Story of the Common Market – Part Six (The End)," *HduB Reports*, January 1973, p. 2.
14. "European Community Leaders Agree at Maastricht Summit to Treaties on Monetary and Political Union," *Facts on File*, December 12, 1991, pp. 940–941.
15. Carroll Quigley, *Tragedy and Hope: A History of the World in Our Time* (New York: Macmillan, 1966), p. 1284.
16. Ibid.
17. Michael J. Hogan, *The Marshall Plan: America, Britain, and the reconstruction of Western Europe, 1947–1952* (Cambridge: Cambridge University Press, 1987), p. 367.
18. Ibid.
19. "The Men Behind the Common Market," *HduB Reports*, May 1972, p. 1.
20. Ibid., p. 6.
21. Bromberger, op. cit., p. 123.
22. Ibid.
23. Ernst H. van der Beugel, *From Marshall Aid to Atlantic Partnership* (Amsterdam, N.Y.: Elsevier Publishing Co., 1966), p. 323.
24. *HduB Reports*, November-December 1972, p. 6.
25. Hogan, p. 98.
26. Ibid, p. 97.
27. Ambrose Evans-Pritchard, "Euro-federalists financed by US spy chiefs," *The* (London) *Telegraph*, issue 1943, September 19, 2000 quoted on *Telegraph* website.
28. Ibid.
29. Ibid.
30. Lord Bruce of Donington, *International Currency Review*, Vol. 23, No. 3, Summer 1996, p. 21.
31. Sir Peregrine Worsthorne, "When Democracy Betrays the People," London *Sunday Telegraph*, August 4, 1991. (Quoted in *HduB Reports*, September 1991, p. 3.)
32. Lord Bruce of Donington, p. 21.
33. Ibid., p. 8.
34. For more a more detailed examination of NAFTA, see the following articles

from *The New American* magazine: Thomas R. Eddlem, "NAFTA: The Misnamed Treaty," December 28, 1992; Eddlem, "NAFTA: Bureacracy Unlimited," October 18, 1993; William P. Hoar, "The Great Sovereignty Sellout," December 13, 1993; Hoar, "NAFTA and Beyond," December 27, 1993. Also see the following articles from *The John Birch Society Bulletin*: John F. McManus, "It All Fits!" November 1993; Eddlem, "Nix NAFTA Now!" November 1993; McManus, "An Open Letter to Members of Congress," May 1995; William F. Jasper, "The 'Dollarization' of the Americas," August 1999.

35. Gardner, p. 558.

36. Richard N. Cooper, "A Monetary System for the Future," *Foreign Affairs*, Fall 1984, p. 166.

37. Ibid., p. 177.

38. Zanny Minton Beddoes, "From EMU to AMU?: The Case for Regional Currencies," *Foreign Affairs*, July/August 1999, p. 8.

39. Ibid., p. 12.

40. Joshua Cooper Ramo, "The Committee to Save the World," *Time*, February 15, 1999.

41. Ibid., pp. 34–42.

42. Judy Shelton, "The Dollarization Debate" (op-ed), *Wall Street Journal*, April 29, 1999, p. A26 f.

43. Martin Walker, *London Observer*, quoted on "Praise for the Institute" webpage of the International Institute for Economics (IIE) website.

44. Gary Clyde Hufbauer and Jeffrey J. Schott, *Western Hemisphere Economic Integration* (Washington, D.C.: Institute for International Economics, 1994).

45. Ibid., pp. 1–2.

46. Ibid., p. 5.

47. Ibid., p. 182.

48. The Council of the Americas' website: counciloftheamericas.org/about/history.html.

49. Ibid., www.counciloftheamericas.org/membersnetwork/coacr.html.

50. C. Fred Bergsten in Hufbauer and Schott, *Western Hemisphere Economic*

Integration, preface, p. xii.

Chapter 11 • World Money System

1. Barry Goldwater, *With No Apologies* (New York: William Morrow and Co., Inc., 1979), p. 285.

2. C. Fred Bergsten (co-author), "Future of the International Economic Order," (paper distributed at April 1989 TC meeting in Tokyo), quoted in *Financial Terrorism* (Appleton, Wis.: The John Birch Society, 1993), p. 82.

3. David Rockefeller, "Why We Need the IMF," *Wall Street Journal*, May 1, 1998, p. A14.

4. Hilary Marquand, "The Theory and Practice of Planning," *Economic Development and Social Change* (London: Socialist International Publications, undated circa 1962–63), p. 28, as quoted in Rose L. Martin, *Fabian Freeway* (Belmont, Mass.: Western Islands, 1966), p. 109.

5. Richard N. Cooper, "A Monetary System for the Future," *Foreign Affairs*, Fall 1984, pp. 177, 179.

6. Robert A. Mundell, "Mundell on Supply-Side Economics," *Wall Street Journal*, October 14, 1999, p. A26.

7. Lead editorial, "A Supply-Side Nobel," *Wall Street Journal*, October 14, 1999, p. A26.

8. Karl Marx, *The Communist Manifesto* (Appleton, Wis.: American Opinion Book Services, 1974), p. 25.

9. Frank Vanderlip, "From Farm Boy to Financier," *Saturday Evening Post*, February 9, 1935, p. 25.

10. William H. McIlhany II, *The Tax-Exempt Foundations* (Westport, Conn.: Arlington House, 1980), p. 63. As recorded in note number 30 (p. 235) to Chapter 3, McIlhany interviewed Norman Dodd in 1976 and recorded that conversation as the "Dodd Interview Transcript." McIlhany also compared Mr. Dodd's memory of the conversation in 1976 "with his description of it years earlier in a letter he wrote to Howard E. Kershner on December 29, 1962." "Where there are

any slight discrepancies between the two accounts [Mr. McIlhany] used the 1962 version." In later years, Mr. Dodd gave similar statements in other interviews.

11. Robert Lenzner, "A Wealth of Names," *Forbes* magazine, January 10, 2000.

12. *Collective Speeches of Congressman Louis T. McFadden: As Compiled from the Congressional Record* (Hawthorne, Calif.: Omni Publications, 1970), p. 398.

13. Gary Allen, *The Rockefeller File* (Seal Beach, Calif.: '76 Press, 1976), p. 119.

14. See collection of articles on the World Bank and the IMF at: www.thenewamerican.com/focus/world_bank/.

15. Zygmund Dobbs, *Keynes At Harvard: Economic Deception as a Political Credo* (West Sayville, N.Y.: Probe Research, Inc., 1969 edition), pp. 90, 138. Dobbs also references: Bruce Page, David Leitch, Phillip Knightley, *The Philby Conspiracy* (New York: New American Library, 1969), pp. 80, 174.

16. Richard L. Strout, "White Case Stuns Washington," *The Christian Science Monitor*, November 12, 1953.

17. William P. Hoar, "Harry Truman," *American Opinion*, Vol. XXII, No. 4, April 1979, p. 54.

18. Strout.

19. Whittaker Chambers, "The Herring and ...," *Look*, December 29, 1953, Vol. 17, No. 26, p. 14.

20. Allen Weinstein, *Perjury: The Hiss-Chambers Case* (New York: Alfred A. Knopf, 1978), p. 230.

21. Dobbs, *Keynes At Harvard*, pp. 117–122,133; Yuri Modin, *My Five Cambridge Friends: Burgess, Mac-Lean, Philby, Blunt, and Cairncross by their KGB controller* (New York: Farrar Straus Giroux, 1994), pp. 49, 67; Michael Straight, *After Long Silence* (New York: W.W. Norton, 1983), p. 80; Page, Leitch, Knightley, *The Philby Conspiracy*, pp. 43–47.

22. Michael Holroyd, *Lytton Strachey: A Critical Biography* (London: Heinemann, 1967).

23. Dobbs.

24. *U.S. News and World Report*, June 29,

1959, p. 73, quoted in Anthony Kubek, *How the Far East Was Lost: American Policy and the Creation of Communist China, 1941–1949* (Chicago: Henry Regnery Company, 1963), pp. 201–202.

25. James Burnham, *The Web of Subversion*, Americanist Library Edition (Boston: Western Islands, 1965), pp. 113–115, 128–129.

26. Doug Bandow, "The IMF: A Record of Addition and Failure" in Doug Bandow and Ian Vásquez (eds.), *Perpetuating Poverty: The World Bank, the IMF, and the Developing World* (Washington, D.C.: Cato Institute, 1994), p. 19.

27. Richard C. Paddock (*Los Angeles Times*), "Yeltsin crony says Russia 'conned' lenders in West," *Seattle Times*, (On-line edition), September 9, 1998; Christopher Story, "Folly of Lending to the Russians is Exposed as Scandals Multiply," *Soviet Analyst*, Vol. 25, No. 2, April 1999.

28. Marquand, p. 28.

29. Henry Hazlitt, *From Bretton Woods to World Inflation* (Chicago: Regnery Gateway, 1984), pp. 26–27.

30. Bovard, "The World Bank and the Impoverishment of Nations," in *Perpetuating Poverty*, op. cit., p. 59.

31. Ibid.

32. Edith Kermit Roosevelt, "The United Nations' Spiritual Companion," *Long Island Press*, March 31, 1962. Also: Edith Kermit Roosevelt, "A Temple of Propaganda," *The Wanderer*, July 14, 1966.

33. Peter G. Peterson, *1996 Annual Report* (New York: Council on Foreign Relations, 1996), p. 7.

34. Goldwater, p. 278.

35. David Rockefeller, "From a China Traveler," *New York Times*, August 10, 1973.

36. "The Human Cost of Communism in China," report of the U.S. Senate Subcommittee on Internal Security (Washington, D.C.: U.S. Government Printing Office, 1971), pp. iv, 16.

37. Joseph Finder, *Red Carpet* (New York: Holt, Rinehart and Winston, 1983), p. 297.

38. Jay Ross, "Rockefeller: US business unhampered in Angola," *Boston Globe*, March 3, 1982, p. 36.
39. Ibid.
40. Daniel Wood, "The Wizard of Baca Grande," *West*, May 1990, p. 35.
41. Ibid.
42. Ibid., p. 33.
43. Paul Raeburn, "Ecology Remedy Costly," *Sacramento* [Calif.] *Bee*, March 12, 1992.
44. Maurice F. Strong, "The relationship between demographics trends, economic growth, unsustainable consumption patterns and environmental degradation," an UNCED PrepCom report, August 1991, quoted by GreenTrack International, Report 26, August 15, 1991, Libertytown, Md., p. 3.
45. Maurice F. Strong, Introduction to Jim MacNeil, Pieter Winsemius, and Taizo Yakushiji, *Beyond Interdependence: The Meshing of the World's Economy and the Earth's Ecology* (New York: Oxford University Press, 1991), pp. ix-x.
46. Ibid., p. 128.
47. The Earth Charter, Principle No. 10. See: http://www.earthcharter.org/draft/charter.htm.
48. Cooper, "A Monetary System for the Future," p. 166.
49. Ibid., p. 179.
50. Ibid., p. 177.
51. Editorial, "Mr. Kohl's Common Currency," *Washington Post*, February 8, 1990, p. A24.
52. Cooper, pp. 181–82.
53. Ibid., p. 184

Chapter 12 • One-World Religion

1. H. G. Wells, *The Open Conspiracy: Blue Prints For a World Revolution* (London: Victor Gollancz Ltd., 1928), pp. 24, 33.
2. See Chinmoy quote in speech by Donald Keys, President of Planetary Citizens (consultative status at UN), November 11, 1984, cited in Dennis L. Cuddy, Ph.D., *Now is the Dawning of the New Age New World Order* (Oklahoma City, Okla.: Hearthstone Publishing Ltd., 1991), p. 269.
3. "The Declaration of the Sacred Earth Gathering, Rio 92," *Earth Summit Times*, June 3, 1992; William F. Jasper, "ECO '92: Launching Pad for International Global Governance" (a report from the Rio Earth Summit), *The New American*, July 13, 1992, p. 5.
4. *In Our Hands: Earth Summit '92: A Reference Booklet About the United Nations Conference on Environment and Development* [UNCED]," (UNCED Publications), p. 23.
5. Mary Daly, *Beyond God the Father: Toward a Philosophy of Women's Liberation* (Boston: Beacon Press, 1973), p. 96.
6. Gloria Steinem, "Words and Change," *Ms.*, September/October 1995, p. 94.
7. H.G. Wells, *The Open Conspiracy: Blue Prints For a World Revolution* (Garden City, N.Y.: Doubleday, Doran, and Company, Inc., 1928), p. 33.
8. Ibid., pp. 18, 19.
9. Ibid., p. ix.
10. Ibid., p. 163.
11. Steve Bonta, "Creating the New World Religions," *The New American*, July 3, 2000, p. 40. (Includes photo of Lucis Trust Library plaque by William Norman Grigg.)
12. "The Lucis Trust," a pamphlet distributed by the Lucis Trust.
13. *The New Group of World Servers*, a pamphlet distributed by World Goodwill, an activity of the Lucis Trust, p. 3. For current information see the Radio For Peace International website: www.rfpi.org.
14. Claire Chambers, *The SIECUS Circle: A Humanist Revolution* (Appleton, Wis.: Western Islands, 1977), p. 34.
15. Don Shannon, " 'Silent' Room: Tranquil Center at U.N.'s Heart," *Los Angeles Times*, May 15, 1974, p.1.
16. Eunice S. Layton and Felix Layton, *Theosophy: Key to Understanding* (Wheaton, Ill.: The Theosophical Publishing House, 1967), pp. 12,13.
17. Facsimile reproduction of *The Last Will and Testament of Cecil John Rhodes*, with additional chapters by W. T. Stead (1902 edition), in Herbert

Baker and W. T. Stead, *Cecil Rhodes: The Man and His Dream*, Rhodesiana Reprint Library – Silver Series, Vol. 14 (Bulawayo, Rhodesia: Books of Rhodesia, 1977), p. 74.

18. Frank Aydelotte (American Secretary to the Rhodes Trustees), *The American Rhodes Scholarships: A review of the First Forty Years* (Princeton, N.J.: Princeton University Press, 1946), p. 5.

19. See: Edith Kermit Roosevelt, "Temple of Understanding," *The Freedom Press*, November 5, 1962, pp. 1–2; Claire Chambers, *The SIECUS Circle: A Humanist Revolution* (Belmont, Mass.: Western Islands, 1977), pp. 32–35.

20. H. G. Wells, "How a Federal World Government May Come About," reprinted from his *The Outline of History* in Barbara Walker (compiler), *Uniting the Peoples and Nations: Readings in World Federalism* (World Federalist Movement & World Federalist Association, 1993), p. 106.

21. Ibid.

22. Ibid.

23. Wells, p. 29.

24. "American Malvern," *Time* magazine, March 16, 1942, p. 44 f., quoted on www.jps.net/landmark/TIME.htm on 3/22/01.

25. Ibid.

26. Ibid.

27. Benjamin J. Hubbard, *The Los Angeles Times* (On-line Record Edition) September 10, 2000, Start Page: 13.

28. "John Paul canonizes 87 Chinese...," (Minneapolis) *Star Tribune* (On-line Metro Edition) October 2, 2000, Start Page: 05A

29. "Cardinal Ignatius Kung, 98, Long Jailed by China, Dies," *New York Times*, (On-line Late Edition) March 14, 2000, p. C.30 f.

30. Associated Press, "Archbishop Arrested," ABCNEWS.com February 14, 2000.

31. "Chinese authorities arrest two bishops, priests," New Briefs by Catholic News Services, September 19, 2000. Also: "Catholic 'Criminals' in China," *Washington Post* (On-line Final

Edition) September 19, 2000, p. A.22 f.

32. Hannah Beech, "When the Smugglers Are Working for Jesus," *Time Asia*.com, September 18, 2000.

33. "Our Sorrowful Confession," DC Office of Free China Movement, www.freechina.net/bbs/messages/882.html, posted October 29, 1999.

34. Erik Eckholm, "Psychiatric Abuse by China Reported in Repressing [Falun Gong] Sect," *New York Times*, February 18, 2001, p. 1. Also see: "China Executes 11 Muslims on Eve of UNHRC Meeting," Lexington Area Muslim Network, April 4, 2000, www.muslimedia.com/chinamuslim. htm.

35. "Chinese Bishop Calls for Purity of Religion," *People's Daily*, (People's Daily Online), August 30, 2000.

36. Ibid.

37. "Turner remarks on tolerance, religion, bears," *The Atlanta Journal-Constitution*, (On-line edition), August 30, 2000.

38. Larry Witham, "Religions asked to come together for world peace," *Washington Times*, November 9, 1991, p. B1.

39. Hans Kung, *Global Responsibility: In Search of a New World Ethic* (New York: Crossroad, 1991), p. 23.

40. Ibid., p. 35.

41. Robert Muller, *New Genesis: Shaping a Global Spirituality* (Garden City, N.Y.: Image Books, 1984), p. 19.

42. Ibid., p. 30.

43. See note 2, above.

44. "Insider Report," *The New American*, July 8, 1996, pp. 11–12.

45. "Lenin Aims Like U.N.'s, Thant Says," *Los Angeles Times*, April 2, 1970.

46. Matthew Fox, *The Coming of the Cosmic Christ: The Healing of Mother Earth and the Birth of a Global Renaissance* (San Francisco: Harper & Row, 1988), pp. 145,149.

47. Gerald O. Barney, *Global 2000 Revisited: What Shall We Do?* (Arlington, Va.: Millennium Institute, 1993), p. 2.

48. Gerald O. Barney, keynote address to Parliament of World Religions, pp. 31,

34.

49. Barney, *Global 2000* Revisited, p. 13.

50. Cuddy, *Now is the Dawning of the New Age New World Order*, op. cit., p. 312.

51. Mikhail Gorbachev, interview in *Los Angeles Times*, May 8, 1997.

52. The Earth Charter, March 2000 – English at www.earthcharter.org/draft/charter.htm.

53. "Major gay law reform in Tasmania, Australia," IGLHRC (International Gay & Lesbian Human Rights Commission) News & Events (On-line), May 2, 1997.

54. Brice Wallace, "Gorbachev laments delays in creating new world order," *Deseret News*, September 28, 2000.

55. "Gorbachev Takes Southland Stage...," *Los Angeles Times* (On-line Record Edition), October 8, 2000, Start Page: B.1.

56. Jeremy Bransten, "USSR: The Year 1989 Foreshadowed The Fall," Radio Free Europe/Radio Liberty report, October 6, 1999.

57. Gail Sheehy, *The Man Who Changed the World: The Lives of Mikhail S. Gorbachev* (New York: Harper Collins, 1990), pp. 76–77.

58. "Gorbachev Takes Southland Stage...," op. cit.

59. Vatican Information Service, June 20, 2000.

60. Sheehy, p. 77.

61. Li Wei Han, *The Catholic Church and Cuba: A Program of Action* (Peking, Foreign Language Press, 1959), cited by Fatima Network: Our Lady's Library Online: www.fatima.org/library/cr19pg06.html on March 23, 2001.

62. Raimundo Garcia Franco, *Christian-Marxist Unity: A Miraculous, Explosive Prescription* (New York: Circus Publications, Inc., 1989), p.58.

63. "New World Order Revisited," *San Francisco Chronicle* (Online Sunday Edition), September 24, 1995, Start Page: 6.

64. "State of the Hidden Arts: An Overview of Esotericism Today," *Gnosis*, Fall 1995 pp. 14–21.

65. Christopher Bamford, "Esoteric Christianity: The Recovery of a Lost Tradition?," *Gnosis*, p. 15.

66. Diane Conn Darling, "Neopaganism: In Diversity There is Unity," *Gnosis*, p. 18.

67. Ibid.

68. Maurice F. Strong, "Statement at Opening of United Nations Conference on Environment and Development," Rio de Janeiro, Brazil, 3 June 1992, pp. 11–12.

69. "The Declaration of the Sacred Earth Gathering, Rio 92," *Earth Summit Times*, June 3, 1992.

70. Author's notes: The outdoor exhibit featuring life-size photographs of fully nude men engaged in various homosexual acts was sponsored by Atoba, a Brazilian homosexual organization. An informational plaque at the exhibit explained that this "art" was supported by a grant from the Ford Foundation.

Chapter 13 • War On Family

1. Karl Marx and Frederick Engels, *The Communist Manifesto*, 1848. American Opinion edition with introduction by William P. Fall (Appleton, Wis.: 1974), p. 22.

2. "Towards World Understanding: In the Classroom With Children Under Thirteen Years of Age," Part V, UNESCO Publication 356 (Paris: Georges Lang, 1949), pp. 9, 58.

3. *Brock Chisholm on Education*, speeches by Dr. Chisholm at the Asilomar Conference on Education, September 10–12, 1954, published by Asilomar Conference of the Mental Health Society of Northern California, p. 20.

4. Dolores Barclay, "It's Surviving and Healthy...," *Tulsa World*, Sunday, August 21, 1977.

5. Motto in letterhead of United States Committee for UNICEF, 333 East 38th St., New York, NY 10016 (undated [circa 1993–94] letter from Chair Hugh Downs in file).

6. Matt Cvetic, *The Big Decision* (USA, 1959), p. 143.

7. Jasper, "U.S.-Soviet Educational Exchanges," *The New American*, March 13, 1989, p. 12.
8. Edward Crankshaw, *Khrushchev Remembers* (Boston: Little Brown, 1970), p. 22.
9. "The Crimes of Khrushchev," Parts 1–7, Committee on Un-American Activities, House of Representatives (Washington, D.C.: U.S. Government Printing Office, 1959-60).
10. Ibid., Part 1, "Consultation with Mr. Eugene Lyons," p. 7.
11. Ibid.
12. "'Butcher of Budapest,'" *Honolulu Star-Bulletin*, September 15, 1971, p. A-23.
13. *Congressional Record*, "Extension of Remarks of Hon. John H. Rousselot of California," September 20, 1961.
14. Bernard Moran, "Race Relations, Churches, Peace Movement," in Dennis L. Bark and Owen Harries (eds.), *The Red Orchestra*, Volume 3: "The Case of the Southwest Pacific" (Stanford University, Stanford, Calif.: Hoover Institution Press, 1989), p. 181.
15. Ibid.
16. *A Nation at Risk* (The National Commission on Excellence in Education, 1983), p. 5. Report posted on U. S. Department of Education website: www.ed.gov/pubs/NatAtRisk/risk.html on 3/29/01. See p.1 of web page.
17. Ibid.
18. "Towards World Understanding: In the Classroom With Children Under Thirteen Years of Age," Part V, UNESCO Publication 356 (Paris: Georges Lang, 1949), pp. 7, 53.
19. Ibid., pp. 54–55.
20. Samuel L. Blumenfeld, *NEA: Trojan Horse in American Education* (Boise, Idaho: The Paradigm Company, 1984), pp. 193–197.
21. Joy Elmer Morgan, "The Teacher and World Government," [NEA] *Journal*, January 1946, quoted in Blumenfeld, op. cit., p. 194.
22. See Education International website, "A few words about EI,": www.ei-ie.org/ei/english/eeiabout.htm viewed on 03/27/2001.
23. "Executive Board of EI," Education International website: www.ei-ie.org/ei/eiexbo.htm viewed on 03/27/01.
24. For EI status with UNESCO, see: "EI/UNESCO Partnership," www.ei-ie.org/ei/english/eeipartnership_unesco.html viewed on 3/27/2001.
25. "NEA 2000-2001 Resolutions": I-1. Peace and International Relations.
26. Ibid. For Education International see its website: www.ei-ie.org, viewed on 04/01/01.
27. "A few words about EI," Education International website: www.ei-ie.org/english/eeiabout.htm, viewed on 04/01/01.
28. William F. Jasper, "Outcome-Based Education: Skinnerian Conditioning in the Classroom," *The New American*, August 23, 1993, p. 8.
29. Ibid.
30. Jasper, "Communist 'Scholars'; Teacher Training; and a 'New Age' Hero," *The New American*, January 13, 1986, p. 36.
31. Ibid.
32. Robert Muller, *World Core Curriculum Manual* (Arlington, Texas: Robert Muller School, 1986), Preface.
33. Douglas R. Groothuis, *Unmasking the New Age* (Downers Grove, Ill.: InterVarsity Press, 1986), p. 119; Alice A. Bailey, *The Externalisation of the Hiercharchy* (New York: Lucis Publishing Company, 1989). *Lucifer* is on file at the Harvard University Library.
34. *Congressional Record*, March 20, 1953.
35. "The Climate of Freedom," Editorial, *Saturday Review*, July 19, 1952.
36. Julian Huxley, *UNESCO: Its Purpose and Its Philosophy* (Washington, D.C.: Public Affairs Press, 1947), p. 33.
37. Ibid.
38. Samuel L. Blumenfeld, "It Takes a Global Village," *The New American*, July 3, 2000, p. 31.
39. "World Conference on Education for all (EFA) Jomtien, Thailand, 5-9 March 1990." See: www.un.org.lb/undbase/conf/EFA/brief.htm on 3/27/01.
40. Ibid.
41. Six goal areas arrived at in Jomtien,

Thailand reported in "Learning for All: Bridging Domestic and International Education," Conference Report, October 30, 31, November 1, 1991, Alexandria, Virginia (United States Coalition for Education for All), p. 1. Compare to Bush program in: Carol Innerst, "By any other name: America 2000 isn't dead yet," *Washington Times*, February 8, 1993, p. A3.

42. "Learning for All:..." Conference Report, op. cit., p. 1.

43. Jasper, "Outcome-Based Education: Skinnerian Conditioning in the Classroom," p. 11.

44. Ibid.

45. Jack C. Westman, M.D., *Licensing Parents: Can We Prevent Child Abuse and Neglect?* (New York: Plenum Press, 1994), p. 153.

46. Charles D. Gill, "Essay on the Status of the American Child, 2000 A.D.: Chattel or Constitutionally Protected Child-Citizen?," *Ohio Northern University Law Review*, Vol. XVII, No. 3, 1991, p. 578.

47. See, for example, the following articles in *The New American*: William F. Jasper, "Death March to Cairo," June 27, 1994, p. 5; Julie Makimaa,"Wolf in 'Humanitarian' Clothing," July 3, 2000, pp. 35–37.

48. See, for example, the following articles in *The New American*: Makimaa,"Wolf in 'Humanitarian' Clothing," July 3, 2000, pp. 35–37; Jasper, "Unleashing the Killer Pill," November 6, 2000, pp. 12-17; Steve Bonta, "Exporting Infanticide," December 4, 2000, p. 19.

49. See, for example, the following articles in *The New American*: William Norman Grigg, "Anti-Natalist Assault," April 3, 1995, pp. 35–36; Grigg, "Gender Politics in Beijing," October 30, 1995, p. 5; Jasper, "Unleashing the Killer Pill," November 6, 2000, pp. 12–17.

Chapter 14 • What Must Be Done

1. John Bartlett, *Familiar Quotations* (16th ed.) (Boston: Little, Brown, and Company, 1992), p. 330.

2. Tom Rose, "The American That Once Was, And Could Be Again," July 4, 2000 column, Chalcedon, Inc. (Note: different source used by author.)

3. Norine Dickson Campbell, *Patrick Henry: Patriot and Statesman* (Old Greenwich, Conn.: Devin-Adair, 1975), pp. 129–130.

4. James Madison, quoted in Charles S. Hyneman and Donald S. Lutz, *American Political Writing During the Founding Era: 1760–1805*, Vol I., (Indianapolis: Liberty Press, 1983), p. 633.

5. Campbell, *Patrick Henry*, p. 128.

6. Ibid., p. 130.

7. John Emerich Edward Dalberg-Acton (Lord Acton) (1834–1902), quoted in John Bartlett, *Familiar Quotations* (16th ed.) (Boston: Little, Brown, and Company, 1992), p. 521.

8. Thomas Jefferson, *The Kentucky Resolutions* (1798), Bergh 17:388, in *The Real Thomas Jefferson*, p. 382, quoted in *The American Freedom Library* (on CD) (Western Standard Publishing Company, 1997).

9. John Locke, *The Second Treatise on Government: An Essay Concerning the True Original, Extent, and End of Civil Government*, Section 92, in *The American Freedom Library* (on CD) (Western Standard Publishing Company, 1997).

10. R.J. Rummel, *Death by Government*, (New Brunswick, N.J.: Transaction Publishers, 1994).

11. Ibid., pp. 25, 9.

12. Ibid., pp. 26, 69, 27.

13. Ibid., p. 13.

14. Ibid., p. 3.

15. David Rockefeller, "From a China Traveler," *New York Times*, August 10, 1973.

16. Campbell, *Patrick Henry*, p. 129.

17. Bestsellers by John Douglas and Mark Olshaker: *Mindhunter: Inside the FBI's Elite Serial Crime Unit* (1995); *Unabomber: On the Trail of America's Most-Wanted Serial Killer, Journey Into Darkness* (1997), *Obsession* (1998),

The Anatomy of Motive (1999). Professional works by John Douglas: *Crime Classification Manual* (with Ann W. Burgess, Allen G. Burgess, and Robert K. Ressler); *Sexual Homicide: Patterns and Motives* (with Robert K. Ressler and Ann W. Burgess).

18. Douglas, *Mindhunter*, p. 350; Douglas, *Journey Into Darkness*, p. 19.

19. Paul Hollander, *Political Pilgrims* (New York: Oxford University Press, 1981), pp. 57–59, 169; Erik von Kuehnelt-Leddihn, *Leftism: From de Sade and Marx to Hitler and Marcuse* (New Rochelle, N.Y.: Arlington House, 1974), chapters 14, 16; Eugene Lyons, *The Red Decade* (New Rochelle, N.Y.: Arlington House, 1970), chapter 29; James J. Martin, *Revisionist Viewpoints: Essays in a Dissident Historical Tradition* (Colorado Springs, Colo.: Ralph Myles Publisher, 1971), pp. 60–61; George T. Eggleston, *Roosevelt, Churchill, and the World War II Opposition* (Old Greenwich, Conn.: Devin-Adair, 1979), p. 70; Friedrich A. Hayek, *The Road to Serfdom* (Chicago: University of Chicago Press, 1944), pp. 186–189.

20. Jay Robert Nash, *World Encyclopedia of Organized Crime* (New York: Da Capo Press, 1993), p. 78.

21. Ibid.

22. Ibid., pp. 81–82, 93.

23. Ibid. pp. 154–155

24. Antony C. Sutton, *The Best Enemy Money Can Buy* (Billings, Mont.: Liberty House Press, 1986); Senator William Armstrong (R-Colo.), *Technology Transfer: Selling the Soviets the Rope*, Speech to U.S. Senate, Congressional Record, April 13, 1982, pp. S3386-89; Graham Hancock, *Lords of Poverty: The Power, Prestige and Corruption of International Aid* (New York: Atlantic Monthly, 1989); Staff, *Perpetuating Poverty: The World Bank, the IMF and the Developing World* (Washington, D.C.: Heritage Foundation, 1994).

25. John Stormer, *None Dare Call It Treason* (Florissant, Mo.: Liberty Bell Press, 1964); Hilaire du Berrier, *Background to Betrayal: The Tragedy of Vietnam* (Belmont, Mass., Western Islands, 1965); John F. McManus, *Changing Commands: The Betrayal of America's Military* (Appleton, Wis.: The John Birch Society, 1995).

26. George B.N. Ayittey, *Africa Betrayed* (New York: St. Martin's Press, 1992); Lt. Gen. William P. Yarborough, USA (Ret.), *Trial in Africa: The Failure of U.S. Policy* (Washington, D.C.: Heritage Foundation, 1976); Robert H.W. Welch, *May God Forgive Us* (Chicago: Regnery, 1952); Arthur Bliss Lane, *I Saw Poland Betrayed* (Indianapolis: Bobbs-Merrill, 1948); Anastasio Somoza, *Nicaragua Betrayed* (Belmont. Mass.: Western Islands, 1980); Anthony Kubek, *How the Far East Was Lost* (Chicago: Regnery, 1963).

27. Candlin, A.H. Stanton, *Psycho-Chemical Warfare* (New Rochelle, N.Y.: Arlington House, 1973); Douglass, Joseph D., *Red Cocaine* (Atlanta, Ga.: Clarion House, 1990); Michael Levine, *Deep Cover: DEA Incompetence and the Lost Battle of the Drug War* (New York: Delacorte Press, 1990).

28. George Orwell, *1984* (New York, A Signet Classic, New American Library, 1983), p. 220.

29. Ibid.

30. Chester Ward, *Kissinger on the Couch*, (New Rochelle, N.Y.: Arlington House Publishers,1975), p. 151.

31. *Public Papers of the Presidents, L. B. Johnson*, 1966, p. 298, quoted in *The American Freedom Library* (on CD) (Western Standard Publishing Company, 1997).

32. Amendment to H.R. 1757, the 1998-99 State Department Authorization Act, introduced by Rep. Ron Paul (R-Texas). Rejected June 4, 1997 by a vote of 54 to 369. (*Congressional Record*, page H3343, roll call 163.)

33. Amendment to H.R. 2415, State Department Reauthorization Bill, introduced by Rep. Ron Paul. Rejected July 20, 1999 by a vote of 74-342 (Roll Call 314.)

34. For information about The John Birch Society's drive to get the United States out of the United Nations, contact: The John Birch Society, P.O. Box 8040, Appleton, WI 54912. Phone: (800) JBS-USA1 [(800) 527-8721]. Or contact us through our website: www.jbs.org. For information specific to the Society's campaign to *Get US out!* of the United Nations, also see: www.getusout.org.

35. Campbell, *Patrick Henry*, pp. 129–130.

Index

"Declaration of a Global Ethic,"
247, 256
Declaration of Independence, 82,
129, 145
Declaration of the Sacred Earth
Gathering, 256
Defense Department (see Department of Defense)
deforestation, 93-94, 100-101, 114
Delors, Jacques, 194
democide, 7, 284-285, 291
Democratic Party, 8, 165
Denmark, 34, 198
Department of Defense (DOD),
140, 186
Department of Health and Human
Services, 17, 262
Devil, 155
dialectical materialism, 253
Dicker, Richard, 138-139, 142
dictatorship, 8, 15, 55, 79, 104,
179-180, 182, 193, 216, 290
dictatorship of the proletariat, 216
Dillon, C. Douglas, 202
disarmament, 26-27, 29-35, 37, 39,
52, 81-83, 85-90, 102, 131, 138,
143, 155-167, 169-171, 173-177,
179, 181-185, 187, 196, 237,
253, 268, 270, 281-282
disaster relief, 185
disinformation, 108, 157, 180, 208,
265
Dobbs, Zygmund, 221
Dobson, Dr. James, 258
DOD (see Department of Defense)
Dodd, Bella, 55, 60
Dodd, Christopher, 146
Dodd, Norman, 64
Dole, Bob, 184, 196, 223
dollarization, 207-210
Dome Petroleum of Canada, 229
Donovan, Hedley, 51

Donovan, William J., 204-205
Douglas, John, 202, 286
Douglass, Joseph, 151
drug enforcement, 185
drugs, 146, 150-151, 184-185, 221,
288-290
du Berrier, Hilaire, 46, 191, 197-
198, 202-203
Dublin, New Hampshire, 167
DuBois Club, 85
Dubos, Rene, 110
Duggan, Lawrence, 57
Dulles, Allen, 204, 243
Dulles, John Foster, 43, 165, 200,
202-203, 243
Dumbarton Oaks Conference, 56-
58
Dye, Thomas R., 144

Eakman, Beverly K., 267
Earth Charter, 72, 115, 230, 251
Earth Council, 113, 124, 229
Earth Day, 94, 105, 108
*Earth In The Balance: Ecology
and the Human Spirit*, 112
Earth Summit, 95, 97, 99-101,
108-109, 111-115, 117, 122-125,
139, 228-230, 235, 249, 251,
256-258
Earthwatch, 2
East Timor, 24, 40, 136
Eastland, James O., 61
Eduardo, Evaristo, 100, 135
Education Development Center,
Inc., 276
Education For All, 26, 275
education, 17, 20, 26, 51, 64, 80,
133, 192, 195, 216, 241-242,
261-263, 265-271, 274-276, 283,
297-298
Egypt, 222-223
Eisenhower, Dwight D. ???, 44,

POWs, 82
PrepComs (Preparatory Committee meetings), 142
President's Council on Sustainable Development (PCSD), 124
pressure from above and below, 79, 87, 158
pressure from below, 79-80, 84-85, 90, 126, 142, 173
prison, 132, 147, 159, 162, 185, 245, 286
private property, 95, 102, 119-121, 123, 125-127, 290
private schools, 277
Prodi, Romano, 140
promiscuity, 267
propaganda campaign, 18, 106, 174
property rights, 17, 95, 123, 126-127, 194, 282
Proudhon, Joseph Pierre, 119
Provenzano, Bernardo, 150
pro-Vietcong, 82
Putin, Vladimir, 110, 134-135

Qaddafi, Muammar, 2, 7
Quigley, Carroll, 41, 48-51, 62-63, 191, 199

Radio For Peace International, 239
Radio Mogadishu, 183
Radio Radicale, 140
Ramadan, Mohammed, 249
Ramo, Joshua Cooper, 209
Rand Corporation, 35
Rangel, Charles, 108
Rather, Dan, 45
Ray, Dixy Lee, 95-96
Rebels, Mercenaries, and Dividends, 181
Red Cross, 180-181

Red Guard, 262, 277
red herring, 153
Red Orchestra, 72
redistribution of wealth, 127, 230
Reece Committee, 64
regional autonomy, 192
regionalism, 118, 170-172, 189, 191-195, 197-199, 201, 203, 205-209, 211, 213, 219-220
regulation, 14, 65, 96, 102, 105, 160, 168-170, 194, 282
rehabilitation, 35, 59, 286
Reich, Robert, 51
Reichsbank, 49
Reifsnyder, William, 99
Reilly, William, 125-126
Reisman, Judith A., 268
religious freedom, 246
religious persecution, 146, 237, 245
religious schools, 277
religious syncretism, 237, 240
religious upbringing, 263
reloading equipment, 170
relocation, 277, 283
Report From Iron Mountain, 104
Reporter's Life, A, 20
Republican Party, 8, 165, 187
Rerum Novarum, 120
resource exhaustion, 94
Retinger, Joseph, 202-205
revolutionary parliamentarianism, 79
Rhodes Scholar, 51
Rhodes Scholarships, 50-51
Rhodes, Cecil, 49-51, 191, 218, 239-240
Rhodes-Milner network, 50
Rice, Charles, 129, 145
Rice, Condoleezza, 153, 187
Rifkin, Jeremy, 106, 108, 111, 126-127

Personal Acknowledgments

This book would not have been possible without the dedicated assistance of many able minds and willing hands. Tom Gow, in addition to his many other duties, heroically shepherded this project from start to finish, serving as editor, adviser, critic, researcher, fact checker, footnoter, and indexer. For his support and understanding during my time of personal loss, and his tireless efforts, especially during the final hectic race to make our printing deadline, I will always be grateful.

Warren Mass and Larry Greenley also deserve special thanks for seeing this project through and joining Tom Gow in many late-night sessions. John F. McManus offered many valuable editorial suggestions and greatly assisted my research efforts. Gary Benoit took time away from his responsibilities with the magazine to read the manuscript and offer suggestions. Also providing invaluable assistance in research and footnoting efforts were Heather Brick, John Burns, Thomas Burzynski, Dennis Cuddy, Tom Eddlem, Brian Farmer, Larry Greenley, William Norman Grigg, Jennifer Gritt, Robert W. Lee, Warren Mass, John McManus, Lynn Raether, Alan Scholl, Paul Smith, and Jim Toft. Warren Mass did a magnificent job of desktop publishing, providing editorial assistance, assembling and compiling documentation, indexing, and managing quality control, under trying circumstances. Thanks are due to Gary Benoit and Dennis Behreandt for final proof-reading.

For technical assistance during my many troubles with computer insubordination, I am especially indebted to Paul Smith, Dennis Behreandt, and Steve DuBord. I commend Joe Kelly for coming up with several creative book cover options, under severe time constraints and pressure. To Vance Smith I owe tremendous thanks for great patience, understanding, and support, as this project grew from what was originally intended to be a "booklet," into its present full-length book form.

Finally, to my wife, Carmen, and my sons Jonathan and Christopher, who put up with months of disruption and turmoil — not to mention the covering of floors, tables, and every horizontal surface with papers, books, and manuscripts — I am forever indebted for love, patience, encouragement, and prayers.

About the Author

For the past decade, William F. Jasper has served as a senior editor of *The New American* magazine, published by an affiliate of The John Birch Society.

Mr. Jasper has covered firsthand many of the major UN conferences, including the 1992 "Earth Summit" in Rio de Janeiro, the 1998 Rome summit for an International Criminal Court, and the September 2000 UN Millennium Summit in New York. His previous book, *Global Tyranny — Step by Step: The United Nations and the Emerging New World Order* (1992), has been praised as the most authoritative and detailed exposé of the UN ever written.

As a student, William Jasper was an early victim of the radical Marxist indoctrination so prevalent on our nation's campuses. However, following a thorough investigation into the authenticity of what he had been taught, Mr. Jasper went through a conversion. That conversion led to his joining The John Birch Society staff in 1976 as Director of Research for the Society's West Coast office. He soon began contributing to the Society's magazines, *American Opinion* and *The Review of the News*, which were superseded in 1985 by *The New American*.

During the late 1970s and early 1980s, Mr. Jasper attended, as an undercover reporter, numerous meetings of revolutionary, terrorist, and/or subversive groups. He also worked as a research adviser for the video documentary *No Place to Hide: The Strategy and Tactics of Terrorism*, produced by Congressman Larry McDonald's Western Goals Foundation.

In 1988, Mr. Jasper scripted and produced his own video documentary, *Out of Control: The Immigration Invasion*, based on a decade of research, which included numerous trips to our southern border riding alongside members of our border patrol. That documentary was perhaps the first effort to thoroughly expose the revolutionary agendas at work in creating the immigration crisis — a crisis that didn't gain widespread public recognition until several years later.

In the months following the 1995 Oklahoma City bombing tragedy, Mr. Jasper interviewed literally hundreds of witnesses. His series of articles in *The New American* provided devastating evidence contradicting the official "lone-bomber" scenario so tenaciously promoted by the Janet Reno Justice Department.